**Constructing Risk**

**Catastrophes in Context**

General Editors:
Gregory V. Button, University of Michigan at Ann Arbor
Anthony Oliver-Smith, University of Florida
Mark Schuller, Northern Illinois University

*Catastrophes in Context* aims to bring critical attention to the social, political, economic, and cultural structures that create disasters out of natural hazards or political events and that shape the responses. Combining long-term ethnographic fieldwork typical of anthropology and increasingly adopted in similar social science disciplines such as geography and sociology with a comparative frame that enlightens global structures and policy frameworks, *Catastrophes in Context* includes monographs and edited volumes that bring critical scrutiny to the multiple dimensions of specific disasters and important policy/practice questions for the field of disaster research and management. Theoretically innovative, our goal is to publish readable, lucid texts to be accessible to a wide range of audiences across academic disciplines and specifically practitioners and policymakers.

**Volume 4**
*Constructing Risk: Disaster, Development, and the Built Environment*
Stephen O. Bender

**Volume 3**
*Going Forward by Looking Back: Archaeological Perspectives on Socio-ecological Crisis, Response, and Collapse*
Edited by Felix Riede and Payson Sheets

**Volume 2**
*Disaster Upon Disaster: Exploring the Gap Between Knowledge, Policy and Practice*
Edited by Susanna M. Hoffman and Roberto E. Barrios

**Volume 1**
*Contextualizing Disaster*
Edited by Gregory V. Button and Mark Schuller

# Constructing Risk
*Disaster, Development, and the Built Environment*

Stephen O. Bender

berghahn
NEW YORK • OXFORD
www.berghahnbooks.com

First published in 2021 by
Berghahn Books
www.berghahnbooks.com

© 2021, 2024 Stephen O. Bender
First paperback edition published in 2024

All rights reserved. Except for the quotation of short passages
for the purposes of criticism and review, no part of this book
may be reproduced in any form or by any means, electronic or
mechanical, including photocopying, recording, or any information
storage and retrieval system now known or to be invented,
without written permission of the publisher.

**Library of Congress Cataloging-in-Publication Data**

A C.I.P. cataloging record is available from the Library of Congress
Library of Congress Cataloging in Publication Control Number: 2021031575

**British Library Cataloguing in Publication Data**

A catalogue record for this book is available from the British Library

ISBN 978-1-80073-162-2 hardback
ISBN 978-1-80539-309-2 paperback
ISBN 978-1-80539-423-5 epub
ISBN 978-1-80073-163-9 web pdf

https://doi.org/10.3167/9781800731622

To my children, Clare, Eddie, Ellen, Mary, and Sara,
their spouses—Ben, Katy, Steve, Mark, and Frank, respectively,
and my grandchildren—Clare Jane, Emma, Henry, Jack, Jackson,
Janie, Mathew, Stanley, and Winnie

# Contents

| | |
|---|---|
| Foreword<br>  *Allan Lavell* | ix |
| Acknowledgments | xiii |
| List of Abbreviations | xv |
| Chronology. Stakeholder Statements on Disaster, Development, and the Built Environment | xviii |
| Introduction | 1 |

### Part I. We Got Here for a Reason

| | |
|---|---|
| **Chapter 1.** Linkage between Disaster and Development | 13 |
| **Chapter 2.** Deliberate Actions and Debilitating Outcomes—Gaps Appear | 25 |
| **Chapter 3.** What Development Has Brought and Disaster Wrought | 38 |
| **Chapter 4.** Understanding Where the Disaster-Development Link Leads | 52 |
| **Chapter 5.** Disaster-Development Linkage through the Lens of Disaster Recovery | 64 |
| **Chapter 6.** Continuity in the Name of Constituents | 78 |

### Part II. Once and Future Disaster Risk Reduction

| | |
|---|---|
| **Chapter 7.** Redefining Disaster Risk Reduction in Development of the Built Environment | 91 |

**Chapter 8.** Making Risk Information Visible — 107

**Chapter 9.** Risk within Present and Emerging Economic Development Forces — 118

## Part III. Disaster Risk Reduction Will Be What It Is Conceived to Be

**Chapter 10.** Sustaining Nature of Disaster-Development Linkage — 135

**Chapter 11.** Climate Change Adaptation and Disaster Risk Reduction in Development — 149

## Part IV. They Who Call the Tune

**Chapter 12.** Built Environment Vulnerability and Development Processes — 165

**Chapter 13.** Monitoring, Evaluation, Reporting, Regulation, and Enforcement — 178

**Chapter 14.** Policy Guidance on Disaster Risk Reduction Taken to Development — 195

**Chapter 15.** What Has Been Found about the Future: Changes That Change Positions — 207

Conclusion — 222

Glossary — 235

References — 241

Index — 249

# Foreword

## ALLAN LAVELL

Increasingly, the bases for and mode of operation of disaster risk management (DRM), the methods and instruments it uses, and their application in practice are under fire. The increasing acceptance of the systemic nature of risk has made the inadequacy of many DRM national and local structures to deal with such risk clear.

The biannual *Global Assessment Report on Disaster Risk Reduction*, elaborated by the United Nations Office for Disaster Risk Reduction since 2009, has continuously analyzed the ever-growing disaster risk, loss, and damage society suffers. The continuous emergence of new risk drivers and the systemic risk this signifies requires important transformations in management practice if risk is to be contained and disaster losses not increasingly unsustainable. Transnational, globalized world economic development, rapid urban growth in small- and intermediate-sized cities, climate change, zoonosis, and migration of human populations in and between countries are to be counted among these drivers.

If societies in general have not been able to contain losses under historically known and dimensioned hazard and vulnerability patterns, what chance is there that this can be done with so many new and imposing risk drivers present or on the horizon? This is especially true in societies where inequality and poverty grow day by day, fueled by every new crisis, whether financial, sanitary, or physical hazard based.

Faced with this, it seems that despair and convenience lead to financial risk management, risk transfer, and budgetary concerns dominating the risk reduction scene instead of more direct and effective risk reduction and control mechanisms. Financial protection is more "convenient" than reduction of possibilities of real death, loss, and damage, as well as being more profitable. The logic is palpable and the actors apparent. How to overcome this is the principal question to be asked of DRM today.

Stephen Bender's comprehensive treatise is based on decades of direct experience with the disaster risk and hazard problem, particularly as it relates to infrastructure, urban development, and planning in the frame of international organizations and national and local governments. As he is an architect and planner, his concern for the specific, whether sites, types of economic and social infrastructure, or social actors, comes over clearly and convincingly in his analysis. It helps us see the importance today not only of the systemic nature of risk and the complexities it involves analytically and intervention wise, but also the simple, ignored, or forgotten practical intervention principles that indicate the need for thorough risk analysis and application of land use and building norms with new investment and in recovery post-disaster and the retrofitting of existing vulnerable infrastructure. Bender's unique mix of critical, fact-based analysis and to-the-point questioning, combined with an acute sense of realism and need for equity and social justice, provides a backdrop for both a very pertinent and very "entertaining" read.

The collapse of some thirty medium-sized apartment buildings during the recent Ismir earthquake in Turkey was due to the lack of adherence to simple textbook dictates on seismic building security. The collapse of roads and routes and bridges during the Eta and Iota hurricanes in Central America in November this year also reflect lack of consideration of environmental conditions in design, lack of time and resource investment, and prevalence of the overriding objective of providing a service but not necessarily the security needed to guarantee service continuity. The costs of such decision-making and implementation processes are exorbitant and growing, socially and economically.

The detailed and suggestive analysis Bender provides in multiple circumstances and conditions, the evocative use of subtle and poignant summary phrases, the vast range of contexts dealt with, and the simplicity of the explanation and veracity of its content provide an easily read and understood message that is critical for decision makers to listen to and heed. In a world of climate change and globalization, new risk drivers, increasing risk and complexity, the singular failings associated with the past, under ongoing routine climate and geological, geomorphic, and oceanic normality, does not bode well for disaster risk reduction in a future where dynamic change and uncertainty as to the risks involved will prevail.

In essence what is in play, beyond the obvious need for action and change, is how we can convert updated and increasingly consensual thought on risk construction processes into a tool for action and response in a framework guided not by disaster as such, but by risk management. Rather than a disaster cycle approach, we need a risk continuum or cycle approach and understanding that risk is socially constructed through the different ways society and its members interact and deal with the environment and search to provide conditions for both work, living, pleasure, and movement. Recognizing risk construction automatically leads to the conclusion that what is constructed or created as built environment through human action, choice, and decision can also in theory be reduced or controlled and prevented, deconstructed. This in itself assumes that risk has different states of being—it exists now, it can exist in the future in new forms and expressions, it has been dealt with or ignored, and response to it can be reactive, corrective, or prospective.

This latter form of analyzing and considering risk intervention has led to the notions of corrective, prospective, reactive, and compensatory disaster risk management focuses, particularly in Latin America, where these notions were developed first, but also in the Sendai Framework and the Hyogo Action Framework before it and in each successive *Global Assessment Report* between 2007 and 2019.

Correction means dealing ex post facto with the risk conditions of infrastructure, livelihoods, and production, born and bred in the series of errors and processes Bender so thoroughly analyzes in this book. This is expensive and few governments face up to the wide-scale need for retrofitting infrastructure and reducing existing risk in production and livelihoods. When the impact of climate change and the increased risk associated with previously safe structures and processes are considered, the whole notion of correction becomes almost inaccessible for many global south countries and even many in the north. Given other decision domains, it is simply not cost-effective and viable. The consequences are that new disasters will occur, and preparedness and response, reconstruction and resilience compensatory methods will be required. But with reconstruction and recovery, despite calls for building back better with less risk in the future, there is no guarantee this can and will happen, given time imperatives, financial restrictions, and the demand for celerity in recovery. As Bender points out, there is no guarantee and in fact there are many factors that suggest that the processes and decision criteria used pre-impact will continue post-impact unless major transformational motives are involved that reduce the process of social construction of risk still now so common.

Considering risk avoidance in reconstruction and recovery places the prospective mode firmly at the center of analysis where the questions are as follows: what do we know about risk and its construction, how much new risk do we want or are we willing to put up with, and do we have the resources and will to avoid unacceptable risk? These are the questions asked today as attempts are made to introduce prospective disaster risk management criteria and practice alongside more traditional approaches through corrective and reactive management.

But as the push for prospective approaches to avoid future risk increases in rapidly growing national and urban economies worldwide (post-recession and post-crisis of course!), we also face the fact that development actors, those who need to change practices and incorporate disaster risk reduction and control into their institutional DNA, are little interested in complicating their lives with one more mainstreaming argument, need, or demand. Disaster management as opposed to risk is still seen predominantly as a sector affair where others are responsible for its use and implementation. Disasters are still seen as something that affects development but are not caused by skewed development processes. Forgetting the challenge is a best option, as not doing so involves accepting responsibility, a responsibility few private or public sector risk constructers are willing to entertain. The status quo of disaster risk correction and reaction is the best option and, also, a good investment for many.

Bender's analysis and coverage most adequately and critically pose the problems and introduce the imperative of a more development-based approach to DRM with emphasis on improved professional practice and concern, such that DRM is essentially the application of good building and development principles. It is in fact prospectively not DRM, but rather sustainable development practice and management.

**Allan Lavell** received the United Nations Sasakawa Award for Disaster Risk Reduction in 2015 and is a member of the ICSU Science Committee and Regional Office for Latin America and the Caribbean (ICSU ROLAC). He has lived and worked in academic institutions in the UK, Mexico, and Costa Rica over the last fifty years. He is a specialist in urban and regional development, disaster risk reduction, and climate change adaptation and has undertaken more than seventy international consultancies in thirty-five countries worldwide.

# Acknowledgments

I am ever indebted to Tony Oliver-Smith, coeditor of the *Catastrophes in Context* series of Berghahn Books, for the invitation to write this book and for his encouragement and guidance. Through many encounters since Peru in the early 1970s, I have admired Tony's work as a researcher, lecturer, and writer with an inspiring and deft ability to explain disasters to those of other disciplines than anthropology. In addition, he, Susanna Hoffman, Mark Schuller, and Roberto Barrios, together with other members of the Society for Applied Anthropology, have encouraged me over the past nine years to partake in discussions on development, disasters, and environment in a way that only learned academics and researchers can do. It has been very rewarding, and I am very grateful for the encounters.

Going back many years in some cases, the following persons have given advice and criticism, both solicited and unsolicited, and for which I am extremely grateful. These include Laura Aquaviva, Margaret Arnold, Charlotte Benson, Neil Briton, Carmen Paz Castro, Nelly Gray de Cerdan, Oliver Davidson, Claude de Ville de Goyet, William Hooke, John Horberry, Gulam Juma, Alcira Kreimer, Frederick Krimgold, Larry Larson, Allan Lavell, Elizabeth Manzilla, and Richard Saunier. I also want to acknowledge the insights and candid comments of those who gave freely of their time and talent to me in times past. These individuals who have passed away but are not forgotten include William Anderson, Fr. Ernest Bartell, C.S.C., Newton Cordeiro, Margaret Davidson, Edward Echevarria, Alberto Gieseke, Arthur Heyman, Gudrun Huden, Terry Jeggle, William Kockleman, Lacy Suiter, and Julia Taft. All these friends and professional acquaintances have enriched my efforts, but any errors or omissions present in this work are mine alone.

I wish to thank the Rockefeller Foundation and its Bellagio Center for the Practitioner Residency invitation extended to me in the autumn of 2015 to work on my book and participate for four weeks in lively exchanges with policy makers, nonprofit leaders, social entrepreneurs, individuals from social investment projects, and journalists from around the world. Much insight was gained in exploring the Bellagio Center's themes with the other residency invitees during my stay. Thank you again.

To Marion Berghahn, publisher and editor-in-chief of Berghahn Books; to Tony Mason, senior editor; to Tom Bonnington, assistant editor; to Lizzie Martinez, production editor; and to Peggy Ann Shaffer, marketing assistant, and Alina Zihharev, assistant marketing manager: your encouragement and guidance during preparation of the manuscript through to completion were not only essential but a gratifying experience.

To Jane Traver Phelan, my wife, I cannot thank her enough for her support, nor can I grasp the enormity of the gift given me—with direction and clarity of purpose—during the editing of the manuscript. Thank you once again.

I want to thank my family for their support, and in particular my gratitude to my dear departed wife, Jane O'Rourke Bender, who for forty years together went about observing and writing on the world around her much more insightfully than I. She always found ways to help me through rough spots with humor and common sense, which were sometimes lacking on my part. I am in awe of the burdens she bore, and the support and love she showered on me and on our children and grandchildren.

Stephen O. Bender<br>
April 2021<br>
Tilghman's Island, Maryland

# Abbreviations

| | |
|---|---|
| APF | Adaptation Policy Framework |
| BRS | building regulatory system (also includes building regulation and enforcement) |
| CABEI | Central American Bank for Economic Integration |
| CAT bonds | catastrophic bond |
| CCA | climate change adaptation |
| CIDIE | Committee of International Development Institutions on the Environment |
| CODATA | Committee on Data for Science and Technology |
| COMEST | World Commission on the Ethics of Scientific Knowledge and Technology |
| DICAN | Disaster and Crisis Anthropology Network |
| DM | disaster management |
| DMDA | disaster management and development agency |
| DRM | disaster risk management |
| DRR | disaster risk reduction |
| EDUPLANHemisferico | Hemispheric Action Plan for the Vulnerability Reduction of the Education Sector to Natural Hazards |
| EIA | environmental impact assessment |
| EIS | environmental impact statement |
| EM | emergency management |
| ERM | enterprise risk management |
| FORIN | Forensic Investigations of Disasters |
| GAD3RES | Global Alliance for Disaster Risk Reduction and Resilience in the Education Sector |

| | |
|---|---|
| GAR | *Global Assessment Report on Disaster Risk Reduction* |
| GDP | gross domestic product |
| GHG | greenhouse gas |
| GPI | genuine progress indicator |
| GRAF | Global Risk Assessment Framework |
| HEVRL | hazard, exposure, vulnerability, risk, and loss |
| HFA | Hyogo Framework for Action |
| IACNDR | Inter-American Committee on Natural Disaster Reduction |
| IADB, IDB | Inter-American Development Bank |
| IASP | *Inter-American Strategic Plan for Policy on Vulnerability Reduction, Risk Management and Disaster Response* |
| IDC | international development community |
| IDNDR | International Decade for Natural Disaster Reduction |
| IEG | Independent Evaluation Group |
| IPCC | Intergovernmental Panel on Climate Change |
| IRF | International Road Federation |
| IWRM | integrated water resource management |
| LDC | least developed country |
| LODGD | Linked Open Data for Global Disaster Risk Research |
| MDB | multilateral development bank |
| MERRE | monitoring, evaluation, reporting, regulation, and enforcement |
| NAPA | national adaptation program of action |
| NAS | National Academy of Sciences |
| NGO | nongovernmental organization |
| NRCS | Natural Resource Conservation Service |
| OAS | Organization of American States |
| OAS-DSD | Organization of American States–Department of Sustainable Development |
| PAHO | Pan American Health Organization |
| PVO | private voluntary organization |

| | |
|---|---|
| SDGs | Sustainable Development Goals |
| SFDRR | Sendai Framework for Disaster Risk Reduction; also Sendai Framework |
| SFM | Sendai Framework Monitor |
| SIA | sustainability impact assessment |
| SocIA | social impact assessment |
| UN | United Nations |
| UNDP | United Nations Development Programme |
| UNDRR | United Nations Office for Disaster Risk Reduction |
| UNEP | United Nations Environment Programme |
| UNESCO | United Nations Educational, Scientific and Cultural Organization |
| UNFCCC | United Nations Framework Convention on Climate Change |
| UNISDR | United Nations International Strategy for Disaster Reduction |
| WCNDR | World Conference on Natural Disaster Reduction |

# Chronology
## Stakeholder Statements on Disaster, Development, and the Built Environment

*Note:* "Other" stakeholders refer to academicians, researchers, and practitioners publishing under their own name.

1972 **Sovereign States and Their Organizations**
"Principle 9: Environmental deficiencies generated by the conditions of underdevelopment and natural disasters pose grave problems and can best be remedied by accelerated development through the transfer of financial and technological assistance as a supplement to the domestic effort of the developing countries" (UN Stockholm Declaration 1972).

1976 **Other**
"In the long run, however, precautionary planning would be more beneficial than relief work since it would aim to consider and alleviate the causes and not merely the symptoms of disaster. Successful precautionary planning, then in focusing on the population's vulnerability, depends upon the identification of cultural attitudes towards the use of indigenous resources at local and regional levels, and the incorporation into development planning of strategies to mitigate disasters; precautionary planning should be seen as the insurance chapter in any development plan. The aim would be to raise the standards of life of people currently ill-placed to resist disasters because those standards are too low" (O'Keefe, Westgate, and Wisner 1976: 567).

1984 **Sovereign States and Their Organizations**
"7. Defenses against natural disasters should be built into regional development plans. The keys here are incorporating better risk-assessment information and designing development projects

to minimize damage to investments in the event of flood, earthquakes, hurricanes, and other disasters" (OAS 1984).

1984    **Other**
"When a disaster has occurred, development agencies have regarded it as a nuisance and tried to avoid becoming involved; or even worse, the risk of existing or new potential hazards has been over-looked in the planning and implementation of some development activities. It is now being observed that intensive development may be the cause of many new disasters in poor countries" (Hagman 1984).

1984    **Other**
"The book's conclusion is not that we might someday find a way to end tornadoes or earthquakes, but rather, that most disaster problems, especially in the Third World, are unsolved development problems. Disaster prevention and mitigation is thus primarily an aspect of development" (Wijkman and Timberlake 1984).

1986    **Other**
"In contrast to all earlier epochs (including industrial society), the risk society is characterized essentially by a lack: the impossibility of an external attribution of hazards. In other words, risks depend on decisions, they are industrially produced and in this sense politically reflexive" (Beck 1992b: 183; originally published in 1986).

1987    **Sovereign States and Their Organizations**
"Sustainable development is development that meets the needs of the present without compromising the ability of future generations to meet their own needs" (Brundtland 1987: 37).

1988    **Sovereign States and Their Organizations**
"The OAS has initiated programs . . . through direct technical cooperation, training, applied research, and participation in international conferences and workshops. But the need for such activities to be carried forward by the OAS and other technical cooperation agencies is much greater than present resources allow. Moreover, a strategy to promote natural hazards assessment and mitigation must also find means of inducing the cooperation of the agencies that actually fund the investment projects. There are three elements that may offer this inducement: (1) a change in the context in which the donors perceive the governments and collaborating

technical cooperation agencies to be addressing natural hazard assessment and mitigation issues; (2) incentives for analysis; and (3) the assignment of accountability for losses" (CIDIE 1988).

**1989** **Other**
"[We] must avoid a situation where disaster relief becomes synonymous with development assistance, and where post-disaster reconstruction depletes scarce resources otherwise destined for new investments. We must be vigilant over institutional divisions between disaster management and development assistance so as not to create a void in policies, programs and projects which address the utilization of resources in the face of ever-increasing demands and vulnerability, particularly of the poor" (Bender 1989).

**1990–** **United Nations International Decade for Natural Disaster**
**1999** **Reduction (UN IDNDR)**

**1991** **Sovereign States and Their Organizations**
"The critical factor for the successful incorporation of natural hazard considerations into the project formulation phase is the ability of project planners to use hazard information in the design" (OAS-DRD 1991).

**1994** **Sovereign States and Their Organizations**
"(j) Consider the possibility of incorporating in their developmental plans the conducting of Environmental Impact Assessments with a view to disaster reduction" (UN-WCNDR 1994).

**1994** **Other**
"However, I believe that much remains to be done: evaluation of natural risks (estimations of severity, frequence and location of natural phenomena that could cause disaster); studies of community vulnerability, be it structural, social, economic or cultural; estimation of losses; research that leads to a better understanding of the factors that contribute to natural phenomena prediction methods . . . and social studies to identify human activities that exacerbates the impact of natural phenomena" (Giesecke 1994, punctuation added for clarity).

**1994** **Sovereign States and Their Organizations**
"2. Understanding vulnerability as a weakness in development and a negative charge for the environment, needed is to stimu-

late the political will that recognizes vulnerability reduction as an explicit objective of sustainable development planning and as an indicator in the accounting of environmental assets. The development of monitoring and follow-up techniques for the accumulation of territorial and social vulnerabilities should be promoted as a fundamental tool for disaster prevention and mitigation. . . . 11. Global and regional financing institutions must establish and apply financing policies that support disaster prevention and mitigation initiatives and encourage the incorporation of these policies in regional and national development programs" (DIRDN 1994).

1998 **Other**
"A few innovated jurisdictions—those with extraordinary local leadership and those who have suffered severe losses in the past—will plan for managing land use in hazardous areas. Most, however, will not, either because they lack the adequate information about hazards and planning, or, more importantly, because there is no local constituency pushing in this direction. Thus, hazard mitigation requires partnership. Impetus for land use planning and management must come from above, but the actual planning and conduct of programs must occur at the local level" (Burby 1998).

1999 **Multilateral Development Banks**
"Reconstruction must not be at the expense of transformation" (IADB 1999).

1999 **Others**
"Until people are ready to address the interdependent root causes of disasters and to do the difficult work of coming to negotiated consensus about which losses are acceptable, which are unacceptable, and what type of action to take, our nations will continue on a path toward ever-larger natural catastrophes" (Mileti 1999).

2000 **Sovereign States and Their Organizations**
"Once a facility's weaknesses are identified, a mitigation plan can be developed. . . . All parties concerned (the clients or owner of the institution, financial officers, and technical personnel) should discuss the decision to undertake a mitigation program at the national or local level. Where there are limited economic and technical resources, the mitigation plan should be programmed for completion over a period of several years" (PAHO 2000).

**2000** **Multilateral Development Banks**
"The document [*Facing the Challenge of Natural Disasters in Latin America and the Caribbean: An IDB Action Plan*] explores why Latin America and the Caribbean are so vulnerable. 'Without a doubt, the main factor is the development standard followed by a majority of the countries, with high levels of poverty, socioeconomic exclusion and environmental degradation,' the study said. . . . One of the innovative elements in the study was its examination of the relationship between democratic government and the reduction of vulnerability. 'Weakness of political institutions and the democratic system are in many cases important causes of vulnerability to natural disasters because of inefficiency in public policy, the study said'" (IADB 2000a).

**2004** **Sovereign States and Their Organizations**
"Development of standards is easy but implementation often proves to be more difficult. Land use, planning and construction standards are most often decided and enforced at the local level. It requires both prudent decisions to be taken and the expression of public confidence in the perceived value of their application and affordability. The use of mechanisms and tools for enforcing existing building codes and zoning by-laws must be central to creating a culture of prevention among officials and within the local communities" (ISDR 2004).

**2004** **Sovereign States and Their Organizations**
"2. To urge Member States to adopt 'Hospitals Safe from Disasters' as a national risk reduction policy, set the goal that all new hospitals are built with a level of protection that better guarantees their remaining functional in disaster situations, and implement appropriate mitigation measures to reinforce existing health facilities, particularly those providing primary care" (PAHO 2004).

**2004** **Multilateral Development Banks**
"The 1990s saw growing recognition among the international community generally, and at ADB and among its DMCs specifically, that initiatives to mitigate the effects of natural hazards before they develop into disasters are essential. Thus, in addition to financing rehabilitation loans . . . ADB has provided DMCs with disaster-mitigation loans and TA. . . . In contrast with rehabilitation

projects, mitigation projects are inherently long term and are processed using normal ADB operation procedures" (ADB 2004: 12).

**2005–2014** **United Nations Hyogo Framework for Action**

**2005** **Sovereign States and Their Organizations**
"Actions are interventions that are undertaken before harm occurs that seek to avoid or diminish the harm. Actions should be chosen that are proportional to the seriousness of the potential harm, with consideration of their positive and negative consequences, and with the assessment of their moral implications of both action and inaction. The choice of action should be the result of a participatory process" (COMEST 2005).

**2005** **Multilateral Development Banks**
"Disasters occur when vulnerable societies or communities are exposed to hazardous events, such as a hurricane in the Caribbean, an earthquake in the Andean region, drought in the Southern Cone or floods in Central America, and are unable to absorb or recover from their impact. While these events are often described as natural disasters, both vulnerability and hazard are a result of human activities. Natural hazard events destroy development gains, but development processes themselves play a role in driving disaster risk. Reducing the number and impacts of natural hazards means tackling the development challenges that lead to the accumulation of hazard and human vulnerability that generate disaster" (IADB 2005).

**2006** **Sovereign States and Their Organizations**
"The absence of training in . . . mitigation in health facilities illustrates the absence of support or promotion of the subject at the country level" (PAHO 2006).

**2008** **Multilateral Development Banks**
"Development efforts are frequently disrupted by natural disasters which can sharply increase poverty and set back the pace of social and economic progress. However, country partnership or poverty reduction strategies tend to view disasters as interruptions to development rather than as a risk integral to development, even in countries that experience multiple impacts" (ADB 2008).

**2009** **Sovereign States and Their Organizations**
"Almost without exception, no sector has carried out mandated vulnerability and risk assessments of economic and social infrastructure and their related populations sufficient to define vulnerability and risk in order to guide development actions. This includes making the risk management information and choices made transparent to those who not only benefit from such actions, but who also depend on the provision of the related goods and services. Presently international vulnerability indexing initiatives using GIS and available national data help shape risk management decisions. They also make manifest if not facilitate manipulation of the indexing context and content" (HFA 2009).

**2009** **Sovereign States and Their Organizations**
"For international development assistance policies, programs and projects, the focus must shift from a reference on mainstreaming risk management in development to identifying and making visible the risk to natural hazards present in development actions throughout the sectors so as to reduce vulnerability in accordance with the Expected Outcome of the HFA" (ISDR 2009).

**2010** **Nongovernmental Organizations**
"One man's flood drain is another man's home. This paradox—the elimination of one risk to replace it with another—must encourage us to engage intelligently with communities struggling to survive along the fault lines of urban risk. In the long term, if we are looking after the vulnerable in our cities, we are looking after ourselves" (Geleta 2010).

**2010** **Nongovernmental Organizations**
"What we see as risk in cities, such as growth in informal or illegal settlements, inadequate infrastructure or services, building on sites at risk from high winds, floods or landslides, or building with flammable materials, is actually caused by a 'vulnerability gap.' On one side of the gap is the lack of knowledge or financial capacity and sometimes willingness of urban authorities to reduce vulnerabilities. Priorities in cities for economic growth, urban expansion and the fact that the well-off in cities may not be overly vulnerable to disasters thwart efforts to reduce risk. On the other side of the vulnerability gap are the poor urban communities, who do what they can to reduce their vulnerability, but ultimately are limited in

their financial and political capability to reduce the risk they face" (Johnson 2010).

**2013** **Multilateral Development Banks**
"Managing risk and building resilience as part of an incremental and iterative process, depending on the country context, specific needs, and capacities, are essential. An assessment of the levels of risk, a cost-benefit analysis of available interventions, and an inventory of existing capacity and financial resources can guide decision makers in the prioritization of the recommendations" (Jha and Stanton-Geddes 2013).

**2014** **Other**
"Of course, no code or regulation will ever serve its purpose well if it is not backed by robust enforcement, but there is enough anecdotal evidence to confirm that enforcement is usually the weakest link in the accountability chain. So even though the code is considered very necessary to minimise loss of life and property, it has to be accompanied by a strong inspection mechanism that will readily apprehend and ensure punishment of those who breach the regulations" (Gibbs 2014).

**2015–
2030** **United Nations Sendai Framework for Disaster Risk Reduction**

**2015** **Sovereign States and Their Organizations**
"It [Sendai Framework] aims to guide the multihazard management of disaster risk in development at all levels as well as within and across all sectors" (UNISDR 2015b).

**2015** **Sovereign States and Their Organizations**
"Consider recovery as part of the development agenda, to protect economic growth" (WCDRR 2015).

**2015** **Sovereign States and Their Organizations**
"SFDRR Seven Global Targets: (c) Reduce direct disaster economic loss in relation to global gross domestic product (GDP) by 2030" (UNISDR 2015b).

**2016** **Other**
"Emerging empirical evidence on disaster loss patterns and trends, however, unveils a radically different picture. Ballooning

investment in the disaster risk management sector at all scales has been accompanied by equally rapidly increasing levels of disaster related loss and damage, in particular associated with frequently occurring, localized extensive risks. Extensive risks are those that are most closely associated with underlying drives, such as environmental degradation, social and economic inequality, poorly planned and managed urban development and weak or ineffective governance" (Maskrey 2016).

**2019** **Sovereign States and Their Organizations**

GAR19 stated the following in relation to sovereign states' implementation of the HFA Priority for Action 4 (Reduce the underlying risk factors), the least implemented action item of HFA: "In general, institutional, legislative and policy frameworks did not sufficiently facilitate the integration of disaster risk considerations into public and private investment, environmental and natural resource management, social and economic development practices in all sectors, land-use planning and territorial development. Weak alignment and coherence in policies, financial instruments and institutions across sectors became a driver of risk. Few countries adopted frameworks of accountability, responsibility and enforcement and also appropriate political, legal and financial incentives to actively pursue risk reduction and prevention" (UNDRR 2019).

# Introduction

Since 1970 I have been involved in discussions about the impact of natural hazard events on the built environment, how those impacts come about, and how to avoid unwanted consequences. These discussions have frequently been in the context of development, which is often thought of as economic development and certainly as betterment for the population.

Over the fifty years of this discussion, numerous questions have arisen about how best to effect betterment, including how to protect resources. How should we carry out disaster risk reduction, and who should benefit from our efforts, when, and how? Anthony Oliver-Smith, a researcher who continues to contribute to understanding the relationship of disaster and society, has noted, "Since society is not generally the organization of completely equitable distribution of resources, every society is a dynamic arena of contesting interests organized along some lines of differentiation" (Oliver-Smith 2015: 40). Societies today largely dictate the use of physical space and create their built environment principally through what is called in current parlance "development."

But what is development, and does it always result in betterment, and for whom? This dynamic arena of contesting interests is all-encompassing, even if the goals and objectives that create the built environment are not always shared by all inhabitants. The point is that the built environment is the manifestation of a particular society in a particular location. That manifestation includes the built environment's vulnerability to natural hazard events in that place, which can often lead to death and injury and to damage and destruction of its related social and economic infrastructure.

Now as never before, the results of development are revealed through what are often described as disasters; the outcome of development is seen in the damage and destruction of the built environment and ecosystems following a natural hazard event. The global and local state of affairs is exposed by acknowledged mounting losses of property—and in many countries, lives—to natural hazard events.

Put another way, the shape of development since the 1960s and the beginning of modern international development assistance has fundamentally changed. Development is now a driver of risk, and to a great extent development is shaped by risk. The risk "topography" referred to in GAR19 (UNDRR 2019: iv) is related not only to loss of life and damage and destruction of economic and social infrastructure. Risk also encompasses financial and economic loss even if the built environment remains intact. Development constructs and reconstructs risk as it builds economic and social infrastructure in harm's way. And as never before, development and disasters are noted for their imposed conditions of dependency and interdependency on the affected society.

## Development as a Driver of Risk but Not Driven to Avoid Risk

This book identifies the actions of four major groups of stakeholders: sovereign states, multilateral development banks, public sector specialized disaster management and development agencies, and nongovernmental humanitarian assistance and development organizations. As themes from the Berghahn Books series *Catastrophes in Context* resonate throughout the discussion, examination of these four stakeholder groups offers a clearer understanding of approaches to dealing with the root causes of risk that bring about catastrophic loss to society. In focusing on these four stakeholder groups, we recognize that there are also other groups that play major roles in bringing about the built environment. As themes evolve in this book, the word "development" will be used with the understanding that it includes all components of the private, for-profit sector, the informal economy, the nonprofit sector, and community groups of all kinds.

Development will be presented as both a principal driver of risk and a potential principal driver of disaster risk reduction from natural hazard events, including the relationship of development to climate change and climate change adaptation. Moreover, the discussion will include questions of for whom, where, when, why, who pays, and who benefits. These questions are important, considering that today the vast majority of built environment components at risk to damage and destruction will also be at risk tomorrow, not only from catastrophic events, but also from chronic exposure to more frequent but less powerful events that are nonetheless damaging and reflect a lack of resilience.

These questions are also important because they highlight that (1) to eliminate all risk to natural hazard events in development is impossible; (2) society makes choices about the creation of risk; and (3) in the future, all natural hazard events might cause disasters of one scale or another because fewer segments of society will be able to manage their impact without outside assistance.

Since the early 1960s, development has been cast in economic terms as the creation, distribution, equitable distribution and redistribution of wealth, and access to resources. In 1990 the United Nations Development Programme (UNDP) introduced "human development" as a new way to advance human well-being. The human development approach enlarges population choices while still recognizing economic development. Human development is more than gross domestic product growth, or income and wealth, or producing commodities, markets, and accumulating capital. It focuses on improving people's opportunities and choices, rather than assuming economic growth will lead automatically to greater well-being for all. Income growth is seen as a means to development, rather than an end in itself (UNDP 1990: 1).

Overcoming underdevelopment has traditionally meant overcoming dependency of the individual, community, province, or nation on external assistance. But now development is increasingly embracing interdependency as a strategy while dependency continues in varying forms. Dependency, then, means that in addition to a subservient position, as in underdevelopment, it is also a sought-after relationship characterized as voluntary interdependence, such as between nations linked by economic and social networks that share goods and services either locally or globally.

Development has also been defined as betterment, which includes striving for the well-being of all people. Sustainable development promotes prosperity and economic opportunity, greater social cohesion, and protection and use of shared natural ecosystems both now and in the future. This is the stuff of a society's collective environments and actions.

In each country a version of the development definition has its own constituents. Development is discussed widely, but often left at the discussion stage are issues of betterment for whom and who pays. Not often addressed are issues of intended and excluded beneficiaries and to what resources and subsidies the target population will be given access. Most often not addressed are the underlying causes for risk to natural hazard events and resolution of the need for vulnerability reduction of what development builds: the economic and social infrastructure.

Some definitions, particularly those dealing with sustainable development, attempt to be all-inclusive, thus creating contradictions and mutually exclusive choices whenever real examples are examined. Almost without exception, definitions of development do not explicitly mention risk of populations or their built environment to natural hazard events.

## Disasters, Development, and Dependency

Disasters, like development, denote dependency. Natural hazard risk reduction aims to reduce if not control dependency. It is recognized that climate hazard risk management and disaster risk management of all other natural hazard events are also part of development, even though such actions may not ordinarily be undertaken or when taken are not visible as such.

The term "disaster" is often misused, but the term "disaster reduction" when applied to nations (sovereign states, countries) and by extension to their societies, including the private sector, has an important connotation: dependency. Following a natural hazard event, if the emergency situation, including humanitarian assistance needs, can be managed by the country itself so that a disaster declaration and appeal for international assistance is avoided given the impacted country's capacity to respond, then a form of dependency has been avoided.

Societies are becoming cognizant of the risk from natural hazard events to the lives of their citizens and to their economic and social infrastructure. Regardless of who may own or operate the infrastructure, society recognizes the role and extent to which infrastructure damage and destruction can cause harm. Their awareness comes from the interconnectedness of these infrastructure networks. The components are interdependent within a system. Systems themselves may be interdependent. Interdependency embodies dependency—designed dependency. But often population risk from natural hazard events has not been identified and is left unaccounted for, particularly in the case of those populations least able to deal with the consequences of infrastructure loss.

The distinction between vulnerability and risk is important when considering how and by whom their assessments are generated and how they are used. In addition, the distinction between the vulnerability and risk of a component of the built environment and the vulnerability and risk of an associated population is important in understanding the underlying causes of expected impact.

In many instances in this book, the term "vulnerability" or "risk" will be used to include both vulnerability and risk as well as hazard and exposure rather than stating "hazard, exposure, vulnerability, and risk." In other instances, these four components, along with loss, will be referred to as HEVRL. Doing so brings attention to both the qualitative and quantitative aspects of their respective assessment of impact on the built environment from natural hazard events. The discussion of loss will be emphasized in physical, economic, and financial terms, as this will figure predominantly in the discussion of risk management. When appropriate, loss will be identified using economic, social, political, cultural, or other descriptors.

This book focuses on disaster risk reduction of the built environment, that is, the avoidance of suffering economic and social infrastructure losses that necessitate external assistance to the impacted societal unit. It highlights the fact that not every natural hazard event impact results in a declared disaster and that disaster avoidance is a tangible development goal.

The discussion will deal with the existing vulnerable built environment as well as the economic and social infrastructure to be built and the reconstruction of economic and social infrastructure in the context of post-disaster recovery. It will come as no surprise that these three categories of economic and social infrastructure creation are all part of development.

## A Word on the Social Context of Disasters and Development

Declaration of a disaster and the response to it can lead to social change that benefits marginalized, poor, and vulnerable people. But why was development not addressing vulnerability before the hazardous event? More generally, disasters can have a positive, enabling effect that brings about change, but what did development actually enable before the event? Shocks brought on by disasters can open political space for contesting or concentrating political power, but what was the development power structure before the event? (Bender 2011). And so, without understanding the development context of disasters, what is really understood about risk and disaster?

Whatever the place or time, the development context prior to the disaster influences the politics and practice of what follows the event. Before every disaster, people are engaged in development efforts that involve resources and decisions on resource use and distribution. How do societies engage in debate, negotiation, positioning, and power? Who decides? Most development practitioners, policy makers, and researchers will now acknowledge that development creates vulnerability for some while lessening the risk of others—all kinds of risk. Risk reduction permitting sustainable, less vulnerable conditions for populations after a declared disaster depends to the greatest extent on changes to development theory and practice existing before the disastrous event.

On the one hand, economic development poses a deliberate creation of interdependency; on the other hand, disaster risk reduction focuses on reducing dependency. Creation of interdependency is desirable for various reasons, including profit in free market systems. Disaster reduction is desirable for various reasons, such as avoiding economic loss. But interdependency can also bring about risk and the probability of loss along with wealth and economic gain.

Under discussion is what is lost when risk management is primarily for the sake of economic gain and is not a principal goal for the health, safety, and welfare of the population. Development recognizes that disaster risk management consumes resources, particularly financial resources, and prompts change. It necessitates modifications to the built environment that only resources and change can bring about. The driving force of capitalism's competition along with often striving for monopolies or market domination is in contrast to resiliency's striving for redundancy and role of the community. Effective disaster risk reduction is not only an individual, but also a community approach to reduce the risk of damage and destruction.

Much will be said about varying positions held by different stakeholders and how those positions shape the risk of the built environment. Important to the discussion is how and why positions that lead to vulnerability were and continue to be chosen and what different positions might be chosen in the future. Consequently, knowing how to carry out vulnerability reduction is not as important as understanding the positions that bring on the vulnerability in the first place. Put into question are the choices that societies, whether global, national, or individual, make regarding risk. Engineering, architecture, land use planning, and the physical and social sciences must continue to research, test, and promulgate necessary assessments of hazards, exposure, vulnerability, risk, and loss. This will nourish monitoring, evaluation, reporting, regulation, and enforcement in order to lessen risk. Development must be willing to use these assessments and processes. Society must be willing to change values, priorities, goals, and objectives before its behaviors will reflect actions and outcomes of risk reduction.

## Sections of the Book

The first third of this discussion reflects on what has happened and continues to take place regarding development, disasters, and the built environment related to risk of natural hazard events. The middle of the discussion defines what needs to be done differently. What follows identifies specifics of the expected juxtaposition of the status quo with suggested changes. These sections include citations to help set context. The discussions are built on a reflection, not of any one country, institution, or type of building or natural hazard, but of the development, disaster, and built environment over the past five decades. The discussion does not include as broad a review of subnational, local, or individual roles in development and disaster management as it does for the roles of selected stakeholders.

Part I, "We Got Here for a Reason," is an overview of the linkage between disasters and development that explores facets of that linkage over time. The facets intersect, overlap, and obstruct each other. It begins with a description of the linkage (chapter 1); and goes on to deconstructing the linkage and identifying gaps in policy, practice, and knowledge (chapter 2); then to what has happened, given the linkage and gaps (chapter 3); to where the present linkage and gaps lead (chapter 4) with a particular look through the lens of recovery following a disaster (chapter 5); to arrive at comments on the statements of stakeholders about their actions in relation to disasters and development (chapter 6).

Part II, "Once and Future Disaster Risk Reduction" is a discussion of economic themes in disasters and development that lays out a framework for redefining the understanding of risk of the built environment to natural hazard events. It begins with discussion of a framework for alternative choices for taking on disaster risk reduction to the built environment (chapter 7); and goes on to natural hazard, exposure, vulnerability, and risk assessments in development processes (chapter 8); and to globalization and other prime movers of development in the face of disaster risk (chapter 9).

Part III, "Disaster Risk Reduction Will Be What It Is Conceived to Be," is a discussion of environmental themes that lays out a framework for refining understanding of environmental management issues in the disaster-development continuum specific to the built environment and risk from natural hazard events. First is examination of the sustaining nature through environmental management terms of the linkage between disasters and development (chapter 10); and next, the integration of disaster risk reduction and climate change adaptation issues, arguments, and proposals in development planning and practice (chapter 11).

Part IV, "They Who Call the Tune," is a discussion of assessments and processes for disaster risk reduction in development planning that leads to discussion of positions and actions built around the supply and demand for information in policy, planning, and practice. It begins with the offering, the call, and the use of hazard, exposure, vulnerability, risk, and loss assessments (chapter 12); next, analysis of how that information is used, whether in monitoring, evaluation, reporting, regulation, or enforcement processes (chapter 13); the role of international guidance in generating and using these assessments and processes in development and disaster risk reduction (chapter 14); followed by scenarios created in part using the back-casting technique, which demonstrates progress by describing changes that have come about on a number of fronts at some point in the future, and the steps taken (in reverse chronological order) to achieve that progress (chapter 15).

The conclusion ends on topics to facilitate change leading to disaster risk reduction. This includes some emerging views allowing for opposition along with mutually supportive and necessarily sequential actions. It entails mention of development, disaster, risk, and risk reduction with the focus on the built environment, and concludes with comments on willingness and the consideration of beginning again.

## In Sum

This discussion of disaster and development focuses on the built environment. It is not in any sense a memoir. Rather, it is yet another call for using development as the principal tool for disaster risk reduction. The focus on the built environment, and on dependency and interdependency, brings critical attention to the cultural context—the environment or situation relevant to beliefs, values, and practices in economic, social, political, and religious terms—of disasters and development.

Discussion of particular policies, programs, and practices shaping disaster and development do not contain extensive references of the subject matter in question. These particular references have been chosen to present and put into context varying dimensions of the disaster-development linkage and possible new approaches to defining and addressing disaster risk reduction. The ongoing recognition of vulnerability of the built environment and the mounting losses due to natural hazard events substantiate the qualitative contents of the chosen references. The theme of "disaster" risk reduction is taken deliberately and quite seriously.

Focus on the built environment brings the discussion to the differing human population groups that are directly and indirectly associated with each component of the economic and social infrastructure. It will also consider cultural aspects, precisely because disasters are socially constructed and interpreted according to cultural values and priorities, which also frame a process that creates physical risk through exposure and vulnerability.

This composite discussion will note the theme of disasters by design (Mileti 1999), but also development by design, dependency and interdependency, risk aversion and acceptance, risk transfer and profiting from risk, all by design. Throughout, the discussion is about including risk reduction in planning, designing, and constructing the built environment. The emphasis is on avoiding risk creation at levels that prompt disaster and reducing the existing vulnerability of the built environment. By understanding the choices made as to acceptable levels of risk of economic and social infrastructure that exists or is planned, stakeholders can also understand who decides and who benefits. This understanding also leads to recognition of the relationship between built environment risk and population vulnerability.

The discussion is not an announcement that vulnerability of the built environment can and should be somehow reduced to nothing. Instead, it focuses on societal decisions that lead to vulnerability so low that few impacts from natural hazard events will demand outside assistance by the impacted societal unit to cope with damage and destruction to economic and social infrastructure. In like manner, references to action or inaction leading to high levels of disaster risk of the built environment by stakeholders and other development participants, communities, populations, and societies should not be taken as condemnations. Such references reflect not only how risk comes about, but also identify the why, where, how, by whom, and for whom risk of the built environment to natural hazard events can be lessened.

# Part I
# WE GOT HERE FOR A REASON

# CHAPTER 1

# Linkage between Disaster and Development

Disasters can destroy development gains manifest as the built environment. Development can increase a society's exposure to damage and destruction of the built environment in the face of natural hazard events' greatest and smallest forces. Every component of the built environment—both economic and social infrastructure—has an associated population that is exposed to injury and loss of life, shelter, and livelihood. And other losses ensue: access to education, health care, food, potable water, sanitation, communications, transportation, even loss of community celebration. The losses impact the benefits that development claims to bring.

In 1984, early on in the discussion of the link between disasters and development, Gunnar Hagman of the Swedish Red Cross approached the subject in this way: "When a disaster has occurred, development agencies have regarded it as a nuisance and tried to avoid becoming involved; or even worse, the risk of existing or new potential hazards has been over-looked in the planning and implementation of some development activities. It is now being observed that intensive development may be the cause of many new disasters in poor countries" (Hagman 1984: 54).

At the same time Anders Wijkman and Lloyd Timberlake stated, "Most disaster problems are unsolved development problems. Disaster prevention and mitigation is thus primarily an aspect of development" (Wijkman and Timberlake 1984: 233).

The discussion at hand is about the risk of the built environment to natural hazard events through its relationship to development and how through gaps between knowledge, policy, and practice (Hoffman 2015), populations in various groupings deal with natural hazard events that are sometimes mistakenly referred to as natural disasters. The discussion also includes the relationship of populations to the elements of time, decision-making, and their built environment, expressed through societal units and their culture.

No matter what order might be given them, these three elements are not linear in their application. They merely describe how societal expression is created and used for thought and action. But knowledge, policy, and practice influence one another, overlap, and coexist—even when societal actions make visible contradictions among them. Their linkage is evident when known natural hazard events result in manageable loss; the gaps between them are evident when loss, particularly catastrophic loss, occurs. Examining these elements helps to understand a society's relationship to risk from natural hazard events, how it comes about, and what can be done to protect both people and economic and social infrastructure.

## Shaping the Linkage

The disaster-development linkage has evolved over the last fifty-plus years, and most profoundly so over during the past thirty-plus years. Deliberate economic development policies and practices separated and isolated the industrialized, emerging global economy agenda from middle and lesser developed countries' human development agendas, which came to the fore some three decades ago.

Through this separation, many countries were prevented from dealing directly with risk to natural hazard events as an issue related to development of the built environment. Such intentional actions, local, national, and international as they are wont to be, have created a theory and practice of disaster risk management that calls for humanitarian assistance but puts most effort into economic infrastructure repair and replacement. These actions occur alongside crosscutting issues such as sustainable development, environmental management, social inequality, gender equality, human rights, and the like. Disaster management as a sector is often viewed as at odds with or tangential to economic development. Through similar actions, disaster "specialists" have proclaimed disaster management and emergency management as sectors in order to lead participation and resource utilization in global (pandemics), national (earthquakes and drought), and local (flooding and volcanic eruptions) crises. Yet little mention is made of the built environment risk and risk reduction to natural hazard events unless it focuses on the trade-offs between development profits and gains, and risk reduction costs and disaster losses. Often development actions are discussed and presented both with and without the costs of investing in risk reduction.

The disaster management community has created competition for resources to address natural hazard risks. This includes risk posed not only by climate change, but also other atmospheric and hydrologic and geologic hazards. In addition, competition grows for expenditures for recovery and reconstruction, mitigation, prevention, preparedness, and early warning. Yet all these activities are usually defined as outside the goals, objectives, and responsibility of development actions.

The call, the case, and the opportunity for investing in reduction of disaster risk should be as much a part of every development decision as are the costs and benefits, winners and losers, and beneficiaries and benefactors of the development actions themselves. Unfortunately, many international development participants avoid discussions of risk to natural hazard events. They believe risk reduction organizations and other entities must be a partner with development organizations, preferably bringing their own financial support.

Investment in resilience can appear to be addressing the disaster-development linkage. In such cases, risk reduction may take place but without focusing on the underlying causes of its creation. Such investments have evolved, particularly in climate change adaptation, whereby project proposals and budgets are presented to reflect "with and without" risk reduction measures. Such investment is seen as development responding to potentially disastrous situations as an add-on rather than initially correcting a void, gap, or deliberate choice made through development policy and process. Identifying risk reduction measures can be mandatory to access financial support reserved for disaster risk reduction (DRR) and other "environmental" objectives. Such support often operates outside development paradigms and risk management policy, planning, and projects. It is to show parochial political entities that investment in resilience is occurring alongside the named investment in development. This is part of the international development community's now more than thirty-year accommodation with the "disaster" sector and the even longer recognition of the "environmental" sector. It has come about through partnering with even older separate programs—development assistance and humanitarian assistance—that exist separately (or at least in silos) by design and implementation in many organizations.

## Viewing Four Groups of Stakeholders

Four groups of prominent entities, all stakeholders in DRR, help frame this discussion. They are (1) sovereign states; (2) multilateral development banks (MDBs); (3) specialized international, regional, and national public disaster management and development agencies (DMDAs); and (4) nongovernmental international, regional, and national disaster risk management entities and development nongovernmental organizations (NGOs).

These are the major participants shaping policy, practice, and knowledge of disaster management and development. Admittedly this is not a comprehensive list of participants, but they are a significant portion of the stakeholders in international and national development and disaster management communities.

Sovereign states, MDBs, DMDAs, and NGOs define, shape, and operate in the fields of disaster risk reduction, disaster risk management, mitigation, climate change adaptation, resilience, emergency management, humanitarian assistance, and post-disaster relief, recovery, rehabilitation, and reconstruction, as well as all subjects and phases of development. Each has a unique role in shaping the built environment, yet each of their programs dealing with DRR are most often silos within their respective sectors and organizations. Each program can be seen as both cooperative and competing spheres of influence, support, action, and reaction.

## What Stakeholders Know and Do Not Know

Stakeholders largely know who is vulnerable and why, what can be done about it, who pays, and who benefits. They also understand from their development and disaster risk management (DRM) assistance how these policies shape knowledge and affect practice. Needless to say, they hold diverse positions. Their opinions are revealed in how they define the subject matter and deploy over time development project structure and content during pre-feasibility, feasibility, design, approval, and execution stages. Diverse positions held in stakeholder organizations are often the cause of discontinuities, sometimes created deliberately, between knowledge informing policy and policy shaping practice.

What stakeholders know about built environment risks and who is vulnerable and why is based mostly on experiential learning. Information often is closely held and thus disaggregated, and most often in noncompatible form. National security concerns have prompted sharing some of the gathered information—the location of critical economic and social infrastructure, for example—to facilitate emergency response and satisfy the public's right to know (if allowed). Information is often presented in forms other than natural hazard vulnerability assessments, such as documenting antiquated or failing infrastructure without mentioning risk to natural hazard events. Ample policy, knowledge, and practice demonstrate an understanding at all levels by all stakeholders that when chosen, risk management can and may take place. As to who pays and who benefits, these same stakeholders often make decisions that maximize benefits with the least cost possible to lessen risk. But they assume little or no responsibility or accountability for those decisions and for populations who are benefited or who will be impacted when loss to natural hazard events occur.

Vulnerability reflects dependency that detracts from a community's efforts over time to sustain progress toward development. The difference between the level of development or betterment and the level of vulnerability is part of the resilience of the community to disasters. When a natural hazard event forces a request for external assistance, the overall course of development may be altered for years to come. The disaster may create further scarcity, dependency, and loss of hard-earned development gains. Some vulnerability reduction issues, such as resiliency to earthquakes or hurricanes, can be addressed by the individual for the family home, community school, health facility, bridge, dam, or power plant. But in most cases vulnerability reduction is beyond the efforts of individuals. Actions are often best taken collectively and most effectively through community institutions. Lessening loss of life and reducing the economic impact of natural events must include public sector policy and include both public and private sector actions to protect ecosystems and the built environment.

## Accounting for Development's Losses Due to Disasters

There is an underlying assumption that knowledge, policy, and practice will lead naturally (as in the assumed evolution of public life, government, tradition, values, and individual action) to disaster reduction through disaster risk management. Unfortunately, there are few examples of a societal unit actually using these three elements individually or as a coordinated priority to achieve such a goal. On balance, it appears that societies do not lack access to knowledge, policy, and practice to reduce disasters. More often gaps exist between policy and practice because societies do not take the necessary, priority actions needed to reduce disaster risk.

The conundrum is straightforward. Calls for societies to use development as a tool— actually as the principal tool—for managing risk to natural hazard events are not new. Actual knowledge and practice used in policy formation has made direct contributions to reducing risk depending on the hazard type, population, and built environment component for achieving acceptable levels of risk to loss. But overall, the calls for disaster risk reduction have not been heeded. Development patterns continue to increase the vulnerability of the built environment—both what exists and what is added. Often development patterns contribute to the actual natural hazard event impact. Few examples exist where a societal unit has explicitly stated that disaster reduction is a priority of development, as shown in the country's own policy guidance that might include the national constitution, executive orders, laws and ordinances, budgets, judicial rulings, and building regulations and enforcement. There is no evidence that a particular form of national economy has consistently made physical risk reduction to economic and social infrastructure a societal priority.

## What Matters: The Ties That Bind

What matters is the link—the tie that binds—disaster and development. Risk is that significant link. Risk, which embodies exposure and vulnerability, is understood from gathered and analyzed physical science, engineering, planning, and architectural research. Risk is set in the context of social sciences (including economics), which observe and postulate over societal use, decision-making, and outcomes of policies and experience.

The subject of disaster and development is treated in research, teaching, and professional practice by multiple disciplines. These include disasters impacting development; development impacting disaster location, frequency, and severity; and the interaction of both. They are expressed as societal structures and functions, including economic, political, social, and cultural conditions. They also include the extent to which recovery aids development, or better said, the extent to which recovery resolves the misgivings and mistakes of pre-disaster development. And they include the extent to which development compounds the vulnerability of the population before, during, and after hazardous events.

But the specifics of natural hazard risk to the built environment, including which hazards affect what type of economic and social infrastructure, why and how the vulnerability comes about, and the actual impact from the natural hazard event—particularly physical and economic risk—are not common to discussions of development. Often only lifeline infrastructure and financial loss are discussed in development planning.

In fact, the type, location, severity, and frequency of natural hazard events as part of exposure and the level of vulnerability, risk, and expected loss to economic and social infrastructure are discussed almost exclusively for assessments by those specialists in economics, science, and engineering. These use data closely held by the owners and operators of physical infrastructure and risk management products.

Discussion of financial and economic risk and loss is quite different from that of avoiding physical loss. That discussion focuses on exposure and coverage of lent and borrowed capital, business continuity, and service interruption whether private or public. In development policy and practice there is far more interest in event outcome than in event occurrence and the causes of risk, particularly when the discussion refers to financial losses. This mirrors the situation in disaster management, where there is far more interest in disaster response than in disaster mitigation before the event.

> **The Relative State of Vulnerability and Loss in Context**
>
> In 1987, a meeting was held at the National Research Council in Washington, DC, to discuss "the big one"—a major earthquake along the San Andreas Fault and the anticipated death and destruction in the Silicon Valley in California. After several comments on the probable quantitative and qualitative impact of a large earthquake on the US computer industry and the economy in general, economist and disaster researcher Harold Cochrane quipped that actually a bad day in San Jose is a good day in Boston and Austin.
>
> (Author participation and observation)

## Whose Disaster Is It Anyway and Why?

Discussions about whose disaster it is and why should necessarily begin with a discussion of whose risk it is and why and should be built on themes of physical risk, economic risk, and financial risk. There are admittedly other types of risk associated with DRR. Indeed, the creation of "disaster" as a sector has done much to promulgate the theme of various types of risk and, by extension, vulnerability. These themes include economic growth, monetary income, education level, economic and social class, gender, age, education level, employment, health, and living conditions. The discussions are needed and useful, even when they do not include issues focusing directly on the built environment. This point is particularly important when the discussion includes risk and vulnerability aimed at identifying the impact of a unique set of hazards on particular components of the built environment, including those hazards associated with climate change.

Risk of loss to natural hazard events is not as high a priority to societies as other development challenges, such as access to food, education, health care, drinking water, sanitation, employment, transportation, and shelter (all traditional development objectives), along with the risk of impact from other events such as war, civil strife, ethnic cleansing, pandemics, religious persecution, racial intolerance, terrorism, and nuclear war.

## Dependency and Interdependency

Discussion of the disaster-development linkage also includes issues of dependency and interdependency in a globalizing world full of risks, including to natural hazard events. Most often the discussion focuses on the sovereign state, nation, or country. Manifestations of dependency, no matter the causal force, evoke notions of victims and benefactors. Dependency caused by natural hazard events includes images of suffering victims to which international agencies respond by sending material and technical resources and host donor conferences to sign up pledges. Dependency most often implies a one-way relationship from benefactor to victim. The impacted country often depends on such assistance.

From a development operations viewpoint, definitions of the Third World, Slow World, least developed countries (LDCs), and even middle-income countries imply dependency. The most blatant manifestation of a country's dependency can be considered a disaster declaration. The most obvious manifestation of another country's recognition of that dependency is humanitarian assistance. But there is another binding side to dependency: interdependency. In commerce and globalization, raw materials, labor, and production capacity are all dependent on some sort of infrastructure, which makes export markets possible. This interdependency also includes economic disaster relief to global economic partners, that is, financial, material, human, and technical contributions flowing to recipient impacted countries.

## Differing Senses in Time, Place, and Space

It is also useful to consider factors of time, place, and space. For example, there is a discernible temporal period of approaches to understanding risk and loss. An example is a transformative period that uniquely reveals the disaster-development linkage. It began around 1970 with the Peruvian earthquake and ran until the mid-1980s with the publications of Wijkman and Timberlake (1984) and Hagman (1984), along with the Mexico City earthquake of 1985.

Seen during this period was the juxtaposition of two powerful views of the nature of risk and society: one held by a widespread religious belief system in many societies, and the other held by an emerging group of individuals, communities, and organizations from various disciplines. Both views address the relationship between human behavior and loss due to natural hazard events. This was a watershed period for change worldwide in understanding people's perception of risk to natural hazard events, the

> **The Juxtaposition of Risk and Loss**
>
> In the first few days following the Peruvian earthquake of 31 May 1970, a newspaper reported a parish priest in Huaraz was arrested and charged with inciting public unrest based on his shouts from atop collapsed buildings that the people were being punished for their sins.
>
> Following the 19 September 1985 earthquake in Mexico City, the next day housewives in the southern part of the city complained about the scarcity of fresh produce at the markets. At the same time, the ruling PRI political party quickly called in E. L. Quarantelli, a pioneering researcher in the sociology of disasters, to speak to how university students could spontaneously carry out unsanctioned search and rescue operations and set up soup kitchens—all without prior professionally led instruction, simulations, or official authorization.
>
> (Author participation and observation)

root causes of vulnerability, and the consequences of disasters, as well as reconstituting international disaster assistance.

Future research can properly explore this period. But there was a change in understanding catastrophes. It occurred not only in developing countries, but also in First World and socialist nations. It was also a period of setting and resetting norms for international humanitarian assistance; the structure, function, and approaches for intervention; and dividing geo-administrative territory of the impacted country for relief actions in the "disaster" area, as shown in post-disaster assistance in Guatemala in 1976.

It was also the period when many DMDAs began or expanded beyond pilot programs their post-disaster assistance policies and practice, including those that focused on community service infrastructure (schools, potable water, health facilities and community health, self-help housing, access roads, and the like). These programs, which included technical assistance, volunteer service, local community development leadership training, and grant funding, were sponsored by multilateral and bilateral specialized agencies, private voluntary organizations (PVOs), NGOs, and faith-based organizations.

Over time, conditions before and after a disaster have brought sharply into focus the risk linkage of disaster and development. Perception of what happened includes review of development processes producing a built environment leading to risk of catastrophic loss; the loss of economic and social infrastructure; a reconstructed built environment that is possibly equally or more vulnerable as the one that existed before. This kind of temporal-based process happens repeatedly and is not bounded by dates or place, but by risk and development.

Also important is discussion of geographic place. It begins not from the site of the "disaster," but from using the sovereign state, nation, or country—the geopolitical place—and the physical place defined by the built environment and ecosystems. These are pivotal points of reference to both the universal and the particular of the disaster-development linkage, depending on the societal context. The structure and content of these places—whether politically recognized territory or river basins lived in and managed by associated populations—reveal much about the disaster-development linkage. Understanding the geographic place occurs precisely at the intersection of various economic, social, political, and cultural beliefs and the physical location of hazard zones by type, frequency, and severity.

And there is a technical space, not necessarily bounded by time or place, in which processes take place for creating, testing, and adopting in a cultural sense tools for managing natural hazard risk. Tools are used in a society as its culture discovers, creates, develops, adapts, implements, abuses, and discards those related to the built environment. How tools come into existence and are used relates to knowledge and practice. This is seen in customs, rites of passage and ceremonies, whether throughout society or particular and distinct within individual groups, depending on their experience in managing risk. But they are also revealed in development activities. Tools can be material or procedural artifacts. They are artifacts of science, engineering, and social sciences as well as arts and architecture. This discussion examines, then, risk and tools, and what has evolved between the aforementioned transition period and the present in the use of tools to create the built environment, how, and why.

Social space focuses both the universal and the local, as in the succinct words of Susanna Hoffman: "Yet while the misfortunes that occur are as different as survivors' faces and the calamities are as diverse as languages, among the cacophony of place, event, and process, it is clear that certain general themes do occur" (Hoffman 2015). All-embracing natural hazard exposure is part of the human condition. This exposure is according to observable fact, cultural traditions, and tribal and religious creation stories (Noah and the ark, for example). And there is control of one's immediate environment in the face of natural hazard threat.

## The Universal and the Particular at Distinct Scales

Taking into account these temporal, and geographic, technical and social spaces, society has universal or widely accepted ways to deal with risk—

that is, traditional materials and building practices, designs, spells, prayers, offerings, consultations, indentured labor, sacrifices, taboos, blessings, inaugural ceremonies, and the like. These may be cultural artifacts that are informal in the sense that they are not nominally part of official codes and laws governance. They serve as conditions or conditioners, and they may be an important part of governance.

Various types of tools may be considered universal in title and purpose but varying in design and use. These tools include building codes, hazard zoning, master planning, building plans, occupancy permits, insurance, inspections, citations, stop-work orders, and judicial appeals, as well as training and certification programs for architects and engineers, builders and craftsmen, fees, and monitoring, evaluation, reporting, regulation, and enforcement (MERRE). They are used as formal conditions or conditioners by a society most often through various administrative levels of government.

These cultural manifestations, whether informal or formal, are created, used, discarded, or disregarded through behaviors of concern, responsibility, accountability, leadership, knowledge, experience, technical competency, and control as well as ignorance, arrogance, error and omission, corruption, and greed. Methods for addressing risk can often be formed, nurtured, or protected by society and can become hallmarks of a society at the national, even global as well as local scale, while being led by individuals or groups.

At a broad geographic scale, behaviors related to the use of approaches and tools include social constructs with regulated and enforced behavior through formal governmental structure and functions brought about through the legislative, executive, and judicial branches of government. A society might have decided that leaders (elected or otherwise) may cooperate, collaborate, and conspire to bring about the built environment, whether through actions of an individual, community, or group public or private.

In contrast, universal, local, or community-based behavior reflects the cultural attributions of a society that is, for the most part, informal or otherwise outside formal governmental structures and functions. Certainly as powerful as formal government action, community-based behavior, particularly when it is bound to economic or religious beliefs, can result in less or more vulnerable economic and social infrastructure. Examples include housing structures that literally bend but do not break (collapse) or flood in a storm. On the other hand, a community may demand to build a school or health facility in a known flood plain or landslide-prone area; this may be to ensure proximity to the settlement, availability of a building site, or preference for having the facility as an integral physical part of the community.

## In Sum

The use of space in varying senses—temporal, geographic, technical, and social—whether at the universal or local scale, points to the important role of not only hazard exposure, but also vulnerability, and risk assessment with their data and information tools. Perhaps more important are processes to use those assessments through behaviors—monitoring, evaluating, reporting, regulating, and enforcing—related to creation of the built environment and the role of the risk linkage between disaster and development manifest in knowledge, policy, and practice. There is no disconnect between DRR and economic development; most often there is a difference as to the level of risk to be tolerated by a society in pursuing development goals and objectives.

Natural hazard events that destroy development gains may not be considered preordained as the role of human behavior in disastrous events is recognized, whatever its composition, scale, or level. Sometimes humans make decisions that create risk-prone physical environments, at least more risk-prone than they need be. These actions may be taken with forethought, but stakeholders can be quite oblivious to the gaps between what they want from development and what they have to consider when dealing with natural hazard events.

Development embodies risk as a result of preferences and supporting decisions. The risk to loss from natural hazard events can be summarized in development's policy and practices to the extent that society decides directly or indirectly, explicitly or implicitly, knowingly or unknowingly, on acceptable levels of risk.

Assessments and their tools, and MERRE processes and their behaviors come into play as they shape development efforts. The risk that links disaster and development can be deconstructed by viewing gaps that exist between knowledge, policy, and practice of risk management. Such examination will point to willingness to act on what is known, wanted, or preferred and carried out.

CHAPTER 2

# Deliberate Actions and Debilitating Outcomes—Gaps Appear

The linkage of disaster and development through risk can be seen in the processes that bring about the built environment. Risk reveals gaps between and within stakeholder policies and actions both individually and collectively in disaster management and development, between sectors, between levels of public administration, and between various population groups (Bender 2013b).

The interface of disaster and development constitutes two interwoven process streams. First is the development process that produces the built environment. It includes regional, national, subnational, and urban and rural planning, site selection, and infrastructure component design and construction. It also includes economic and social decisions by both public and private sectors.

The second is DRR. Some of its components are readily identifiable; some are not. DRR includes assessments of natural hazard, exposure, vulnerability, risk, and loss using tools often employed in infrastructure design and construction. Coupled with assessments are processes of monitoring, evaluation, reporting, regulation, and enforcement; they form the context and content of managing risk of infrastructure to natural hazard events. Formal management of natural hazard risk has existed throughout the history of modern development. But currently it is viewed as something brought into development processes through a best-case, cost-benefit analysis. The role of DRR has often been cast as an add-on, with and without option, based on the acceptable level of physical and economic—but most importantly, financial—risk after most development planning decisions have been made.

Development processes should include applying known risk reduction approaches for dealing with what is to be built, the risk encountered in post-disaster rebuilding, and the risk of existing economic and social infrastructure.

Deconstructing and understanding gaps in the disaster-development continuum is not a question of prescribing new remedies for resolving identified risk management problems. Instead, those engaged in the development planning process should be certain that the correct diagnosis has been made for necessary remedies. Most important is their willingness to address the causes of risk.

Before every disaster, people have engaged in development efforts that involved decisions about resources and their distribution and use. Anthony Oliver-Smith states, "These social processes and the risks they represent are all outcomes of human decision-making about how resources (including places) are used and by whom they are used. . . . The risks that we choose to see or not see for ourselves or for others are deeply embedded in the way our societies are organized and in the beliefs that sustain and perpetuate that organization" (Oliver-Smith 2013: 1). Who decides and how they decide are expressed through position, debate, negotiation, and power.

Gaps between knowledge, policy, and practice in the disaster-development continuum lead to vulnerability to natural hazard events. Gaps often result from discontinuity. They are sometimes more evident in societies that are moving toward stronger participatory democracies and free market economies. They can result from competing claims by groups using politics and government, social change, and economic development to achieve parochial ends. Policy approved does not mean policy implemented; gaps occur quite often, as the goals and objectives of DDR policy are not implemented through programs and practice. A gap can result from lack of funding, follow-through, staff knowledge and support, or lack of building regulation and enforcement (BRE). Also, sovereign states individually or collectively often take formulation and declaration of policy as actual practice.

Thus, lack of resilience is not often the product of chance. Issues of power, prestige, funding, and independence often cause—sometimes deliberately—discontinuities between knowledge, policy, and practice (Bender 2013), as can the feedback loop from practice to knowledge to policy. Individually, any of these three elements may provide a society with the wherewithal to manage risk and respond to an emergency. Yet there are no assurances that in any given instance any of these elements are positioned to effectively deal with disaster risk reduction. Nor is there any assurance that contributors from each of the elements will act in unison or that they will not be at odds with one another.

This linkage is best appreciated when an understanding of social construction of risk comes about through multiple points of view from involved sectors and communities. Moreover, development actions, with their complexity, shed light on how gaps promulgate risk. Deconstruct-

> **Understanding Physical Risk**
>
> Following the earthquake of 31 May 1970 in the Callejon de Huaylas in the Andes of Peru, villages along the principal road running the length of this high valley were examined. It became evident that something explained to some degree the vulnerability of adobe and masonry housing to earthquake damage.
>
> In some villages with housing almost entirely of adobe and the occasional brick or cement block construction, 80 percent of structures were damaged or destroyed. In other villages less than ten kilometers away, 80 percent of structures using similar materials were intact or had little damage.
>
> Further examination showed that for structures left standing (including schools and health facilities), knowledge, experience, and policy in some mix—such as using ring beams of reinforced concrete or wood that ran continuously in the walls at door and window lintel heights and again at the top of the walls—had created a seismic-resistant structure.
>
> (Author's participation as a Peace Corps volunteer architect and guide to John Meehan, Earthquake Engineering Research Institute reconnaissance team member advising on housing reconstruction to the Peruvian government)

ing risk, like the pathology of vulnerability, exposes deviation from an assumed or perceived normal state of risk-free, managed risk, or acceptable levels of risk to the built environment. Supposedly "natural disasters" occur, thereby disrupting the course of normal development actions. The progression of development is not interrupted by disaster. Rather, it is the "disaster" characterization of development—the "development of disaster"—that can lead to understanding and acting on risk that manifests itself through the gaps.

Up to this point the geographic scale of risk management has not been highlighted. This facet of gaps between knowledge, policy, and practice occurs because sovereign states often do not define geographic priorities for DRR. Consequently, assessments to address a specific hazard, exposure, vulnerability, and risk are often general in description and nationwide in geographic scope.

Loss estimates and post-disaster loss calculations often do not reflect specific subnational geographic contexts. HEVRL assessments are often the domain of independent technical units, operatives, NGOs, and academic researchers in varying parts of the country or region. The central government often assumes that local contexts are understood by involved stakeholders. On the one hand, local government is constantly struggling with challenges set by economic, social, physical change, and pressure from various constituencies. On the other hand, local government is the de facto implementer of central government's policies and political guidance. The result can be, and often is, increased risk, particularly for those who are least able to suffer the consequences of natural hazard events and for those who have little or no control over the creation or management of the risk that envelops them.

## Stakeholder Context of the Linkage-Gap Discussion

Gaps in disaster risk management and development between stakeholder groups come about through the distinct roles that stakeholders play in both DRR and development. Gaps also exist inside each stakeholder group, particularly when that group operates both DRR and development programs and projects within their institution.

In deconstructing the disaster-development linkage, a prime example of gaps between policies, practice, and knowledge manifests itself in the following way. Stakeholders who are aware of root causes of the disaster's vulnerability and risk operate development and DRR activities separate from one another. Each of these silos references a more or less shared list of themes, such as poverty alleviation, gender and racial equality, ethnicity, the "environment," politics, governance, social status, and economic and social infrastructure. Stakeholders' DRR actions may focus on omnibus solutions, such as an all-hazards approach to natural hazard risk mitigation.

This has given rise to many more words—declarations, frameworks, conventions, and initiatives—than actions. But by not specifying targets in a shared, actionable agenda of risk reduction of the built environment, stakeholders have political cover and maneuvering room. Stakeholders may aim to assist populations most in need of DRR assistance. At the same time, they have found that they can avoid acting on risk reduction of a specific hazard in a specific place for specific components of the built environment by attempting to address multiple hazards in multiple sites at the same time.

## Gaps Created by Not Addressing Gaps

In great part, gaps created by lack of specificity come about because sovereign states almost never define at the individual country or international level specifics of risk reduction action regarding the local type of infrastructure component and type of hazard. Most often, such actions are assumed to be the domain of subnational participants. Mention of regulation and enforcement almost immediately sends the discussion to science and engineering in designing and building infrastructure.

---

**Vulnerability Gap**

"What we see as risk in cities, such as growth in informal or illegal settlements, inadequate infrastructure or services, building on sites at risk from high winds, floods or landslides, or building with flammable materials, is actually caused by a 'vulnerability gap.' On one side of the gap is the lack of knowledge or financial capacity and sometimes willingness of urban authorities to reduce vulnerabilities. Priorities in cities for economic growth, urban expansion, and the fact that the well-off in cities may not be overly vulnerable to disasters thwart efforts to reduce risk. On the other side of the 'vulnerability gap' are the poor urban communities, who do what they can to reduce their vulnerability, but ultimately are limited in their financial and political capability to reduce the risk they face." (Johnson 2010: 45)

---

Authorities both public and private who own and/or operate vulnerable social and economic infrastructure, as well as those who own housing, usually bear responsibility and accountability for loss stemming from risk. Stakeholders can and sometimes do confuse policy and practice or use policy statements as the substance of progress reports. And their discussions of financial aspects of development often discount the benefits of reducing risk and highlight the costs of investing in resiliency. Their internal management structure does not address regulations coupled with enforcement. In most instances, whether policy or practice, the sovereign states, who collectively have limited capacity although sometimes specific power to effect change at the local level, believe that saying what is to be makes it so. They have deliberately laid aside or otherwise not recognized that what is purported to be achieved by policy and practice is in contradiction, competition, or contempt of other policies and practices they or others have also promulgated in the name of development.

For example, Western Hemisphere countries through the Organization of American States (OAS) work to forward policy and practice concerning disaster prevention, response, and humanitarian assistance. Their efforts include maintaining a vocabulary built around the term "disaster" despite member state participation in regional and international discussions concerning implementation of DRR and resilience and a risk-informed, integrated approach to sustainable development (OAS-DSD 2016; UNISDR 2015b).

Next is affirmation and reaffirmation that disaster risk management is a priority of national public policies and development strategies, along with the importance of issuing guidelines. The call for coordination among both peer groups and other organizations to avoid duplicating efforts in any and all spheres of activities follows, as does mandated continuance of effort by the organizations, but often using only non-regular budget resources. Invariably countries carry out the mandated need for periodic review, revision, and reporting of policy implementation mostly on inputs, but without specifying details of outcomes.

## Stakeholder Gaps

### Sovereign States

Pursuit of development is by and large the overriding preoccupation of nations. The public sector funds and constructs much of basic economic lifeline infrastructure as well as social service infrastructure. Moreover, sovereign states have reinforced the disaster risk management/emergency management sector by claiming oversight and responsibility for disaster reduction. The international community of nations charges each of its members with DRR through frameworks and thematic decades. Through individual country, subregional, and regional groupings, sovereign states have established several mechanisms to advance coordinated, joint action to reduce risk to natural hazard events, mitigate effects, and respond to declared disasters.

Initially sovereign state efforts focused almost exclusively on emergency management and humanitarian assistance. By the end of the past century, policies and practices began to include and then highlight the need for reducing risk of catastrophic loss in light of the mounting destruction of property. For the most part this shift was influenced by knowledge gained through practice by stakeholders responding to disasters and recovery.

At the national level, identification of the most vulnerable infrastructure is not often undertaken when national policy is preoccupied with and prioritizes proactive disaster preparedness for vulnerable populations. There have been policy declarations to address disaster loss and risk reduction of both populations and the built environment. These efforts resulted from sovereign states using their collective political organizations—often through declarations, resolutions, frameworks, conventions, funds (voluntary), committees, delegates, and representatives—to bring together entities claiming or wanting dominion over aspects of DRR. The gaps reveal how sovereign states use existing development and disaster management communities to garner external support as they either have minimal resources or choose to minimize use of national resources for DRR.

## Multilateral Development Banks

Institutions such as the World Bank, African Development Bank, Asian Development Bank, Central American Bank for Economic Integration, Inter-American Development Bank, Caribbean Development Bank, and their peers are primarily lenders to sovereign states, although sovereign states' primary source of borrowed capital for the built environment is now from private capital markets. Nonetheless, much of the lending of MDBs and bilateral lending to lesser developed countries is focused on poverty alleviation, whether through direct investment in social infrastructure and human services or indirectly through agriculture, communications, transport, and energy.

At present MDB efforts to bring substantive, coordinated knowledge, policy, and practice in natural hazard vulnerability reduction to borrowers' development actions is for practical purposes parallel to those development actions and reflect approaches of the private sector, often their major borrowing client. While MDBs lend and grant resources to repair and recover from damage and loss of assets in the built environment following a disaster declaration, much of such funding was originally extended for development programs. These stakeholders have a long-standing policy of nonintervention in national internal affairs such as land use zoning and building regulation and enforcement, except when sufficient international pressure is brought to bear (as can be the case in environmental management) or when their own financial position is threatened. No matter what the origin or causal factor of the risk of the infrastructure component built with their loan proceeds, MDBs most often assume no responsibility for the creation or management of physical risk.

Most often MDBs do not publicly identify the physical structures built with proceeds from their loans or grants. There are usually no bronze plaques naming names on bridges, schools, hospitals, and other public structures. While MDBs have long focused on financial risk management concerns, they have recently supported looking at economic risk. Financial risk is their primary concern because of its impact on the capacity of the borrower—whether a sovereign state or private sector entity—to repay development loans.

Support for reviewing economic risk comes with growing recognition that disaster losses of nations are most definitely decreasing the growth of impacted economies, disaster reconstruction funds notwithstanding. And avoidance of becoming involved in physical risk is to avoid any culpability in damage or destruction by leaving such matters to the borrower. MDBs call for the use of "best local practices," the sacrosanct social-political statement of MDBs concerning loans and sovereign state dominion over creating the built environment.

MDBs have not led creation of public policy risk management institutional capacity across sectors. Practice-based knowledge is available, and in some cases MDBs have on staff disaster specialists primarily for disaster recovery and reconstruction and for identifying exposure. Targeted sector investment strategy and the political expediency of attending to natural hazard-induced crisis management on a one-off basis has spurred the staffing. Natural hazard risk management is not yet defined as central to development practice, particularly as it applies to identifying and reducing risk of existing social and economic infrastructure. The gaps, then, are lack of direct involvement in physical risk reduction that are manifest in growing disaster losses, as well as lack of identifying and investing in risk reduction of existing vulnerable economic and social infrastructure.

## Disaster Management and Development Agencies

Risk reduction is now more broadly discussed in DMDAs, but effective policies and intervention schemes are only at an incipient stage of being a priority part of their development agendas. Presently DMDAs' most visible component—humanitarian assistance—fits a response to crisis situations with a necessary system for fundraising. DMDA actions are highly focused on doing well in the area of humanitarian assistance, as well as disaster relief and recovery, in order to raise funds for the next disaster response. This situation is juxtaposed with DMDAs' efforts to invest in risk reduction following a disaster and with climate change adaptation, which is often framed, promoted, and practiced outside DRM, DRR, and development policy frameworks.

A parallel situation is inclusion in the disaster management sector a broad range of risk reduction programs run by individual economic and social sector institutions that may also have their own emergency management capacity. Such actions involve specialized entities in most administrative levels in all sectors and between and among public and private institutions. Such a shift in policy increasingly calls development theory and practice into play, particularly as it addresses poverty, gender, civil society, and highly vulnerable populations targeted in global development framework goals. It calls into play the growing impact of other global population and infrastructure threats such as global warming, sea level rise, drought, pollution of air and seas, and habitat loss of flora and fauna. It also includes administrative decentralization, natural resource and land use management, governance, transparency, corruption, and accountability. The gaps are between DMDA policy for development and for their DRM programs.

### Nongovernmental Organizations

At the international and regional levels, NGOs may be further along than MDBs in discussing disaster-development linkages. But NGOs are constrained in the same ways as MDBs by existing approaches: managing natural hazard risk through focus on disaster assistance and as a need to "mainstream" DRR into development. Internal divisions and turf areas in both NGO and MDB institutions are built around funded and highly visible yet separate programs of development and disaster management. This is particularly the case with programs that deal with post-disaster recovery of economic and social infrastructure, such as schools, health facilities, potable water systems, rural transportation, energy, and agriculture. There is broader recognition of dealing with risk through programs specifically related to climate change adaptation. These are apt to be deliberately not identified as development or disaster risk management programs, but associated with environment and sustainable development actions.

International NGOs are among those publicly noting few precedents for evolving climate variability, flooding, drought, and sea level rise experienced in their target countries. Such climate-related hazards are increasingly identified as part of environmental programs with a sector identity and presence apart from development and disaster management. To their credit, most institutions dealing with climate change and climate change adaptation (CCA) began and continue to be clear about which economic sectors are contributing to climate change.

## Addressing the Gaps

Gaps between knowledge, policy, and practice that lead to risk are diverse in structure, process, and impact. They can involve one or more stakeholders and have applicable known remedies to address the majority of risk management issues in economic and social sectors with their accompanying infrastructure. The following are best described as process gaps that encapsulate the challenges of addressing risk as the link between disaster and development.

A focus on mainstreaming DRR into the center of technical operations in development processes is misplaced. It addresses a supposed gap between addressing and not addressing risk in the development process. Risk is addressed when undertaking infrastructure projects; mainstreaming as a dictated action has found limited acceptance. In general, the international development community has demurred from assuming overt responsibility for natural hazard risk reduction because its constituents do not demand it. Instead, the international development community accepts the claim by sovereign states for oversight and spearheading policy and practice of their individual national disaster risk reduction.

Risk to natural hazard events is recognized, particularly for economic infrastructure, but not always addressed in the sense that visible, transparent assignment of responsibility and accountability takes place. The resulting level of risk of economic and social infrastructure is not publicly disseminated. Nor is an acceptable level of risk to natural hazard events often articulated other than to say that local codes and standards are followed. The call for mainstreaming reveals that many entities outside the development community assume that those inside the development community do not consider risk. Risk to natural hazard events, particularly for economic infrastructure, is considered, but assessments to decide on an acceptable level of risk may not be present, at least in terms of physical risk of infrastructure components. In DRR processes, the gap is between available knowledge and experience and the willingness to reduce risk to avoid disaster.

The next gaps relate to globalization, which assumes little or no responsibility for risk to loss created by its forces to extract, transform, process, transport, and market goods. Such actions on a large scale, either nationally or globally, transform the landscape for extraction of raw materials or production of animals and crops and impact on ecosystems, movement and settlement of laborers, and coastal area development for commerce and workers settlements. Many development entities involved in globalization look for opportunities to participate in recovery, but such actions have often created vulnerability yet again. Globalization also impacts response to declared disasters and risk reduction through its participation in donations and in lending and borrowing between and among private institutions, countries, and sovereign states.

The next gap focuses on measuring the impact of disasters on development. The gap between disaster and development policy and practice is all too apparent in the lack of accounting for loss of development's gains due to declared and undeclared disasters. Beginning with GDP, development indicators do not account for the impact of loss from natural hazard events or for the exposure of existing economic and social infrastructure.

In general, no economic indicator accounts for the actual disaster loss, merely for a downturn in economic activity, which is often followed by a (most often modest) post-disaster reconstruction "boom." Increasingly visible is that the greater the reported economic growth, the greater the exposure of the society's built environment to natural hazard risk.

Next to consider is resource allocation related to disasters. The gap between national needs for international assistance and the international resources available to respond to disaster losses continues to grow. This gap includes distribution of scarce resources needed for post-disaster reconstruction and DRR initiatives and for development investment, social safety net initiatives, environmental management, and CCA actions.

Knowledge of risk at both the local and expert level is the next gap. One could assume that knowledge from experience with development policy and practice would inform recovery—particularly reconstruction—efforts on subjects of risk and DRR. But this is not necessarily the case, given the relationship of development as separate in policy and practice from DRR. In the nascent stage, post-disaster recovery spearheaded by some NGOs and DMDAs does now note traditional or historic development approaches reflecting use of risk-informed reconstruction discussions with expert guidance and local built environment experience and expertise.

Also DRM does not necessarily inform the development sector what was attempted and/or what was learned about avoiding risk in reconstruction. Development processes do not typically isolate, address, record, and monitor physical risk management in its operations—at least not to any degree commensurate with its managing of financial risk.

Another gap involves financial risk for lenders and financial loss exposure for borrowers. MDBs may be concerned about development loan repayment and public administration operational expenses after a disaster. This is followed by the gap related to locating risk management resources. The public sector uses public resources, beginning with the national treasury and international disaster assistance, to address financial, physical, and economic risk, in that order. The most glaring lack of resources is not related to financial risk, public or private. It is related to economic risk, particularly of the poor, who cannot locate risk management resources on their own and who often have no access to the decision-making processes. When health, education, water, transportation, and electrical energy infrastructure are damaged and destroyed, the poor suffer indirect and secondary losses that are often not calculated or addressed.

The vocabulary used in discussions of "disaster" constitutes a different type of gap. The vocabulary includes "the disaster cycle," "the window of opportunity following a disaster," along with "prevention," "mitigation," and now, "resilience." Each of these is commonly thought to be outside the domain of development. At best, stakeholders may want to exercise a "both-and" approach, that is, practice both risk reduction and development, but with no specific emphasis on identifying built environment-related risk to the population. When execution of DRM actions is concurrent with those of development to rebuild infrastructure, the name of the entity responsible and accountable for the resulting levels of risk is often not present.

Marginalization of root causes is another gap. Clearly identifying natural hazard risk in development processes, whether they pertain to planning new development, recovery following a disaster declaration, or reviewing existing economic and social infrastructure, makes assessment of hazards, exposure, vulnerability, and risk complicated. Natural hazard events are often little mentioned in shaping the development agenda unless catastrophic loss has recently occurred.

Throughout the development process there is a gap regarding the identity of owners and operators of specific components of economic and social infrastructure. They are not called out by name in relation to hazards, exposure, vulnerability, risk, and loss. They are even less likely to be called out for monitoring, evaluation, reporting, regulation, and enforcement of DRR actions.

A gap continues between emphasis on the probability of damage and destruction of economic and social infrastructure and the probability of occurrence of a natural hazard event. The emphasis on risk of natural hazard event occurrence, whether in DRM or development actions, obscures the more important probability of loss through damage and destruction. It highlights the lack of visible, transparent, and accessible knowledge of hazard and exposure.

Population movement—forced and voluntary migration—is often highlighted in natural hazard events, but often absent is a corresponding emphasis on specifics of such events that prompted the migration. Exposure and event occurrence are push factors for the role of population movement in dealing with DRR.

From the discussion of resilience comes increased attention to the gap between the capacity to prepare for anticipated losses from a natural hazard event, and the capacity to reduce vulnerability of the population and its associated infrastructure before the event takes place. It is one thing to prepare for losses that might take place. It is something else to lessen the underlying causes of the vulnerability so as to avoid to the extent possible damage and destruction of the built environment.

Finally is the gap between financial risk management and investment in DRR. Financial risk management related to natural hazard events demonstrates that along the DRR-development continuum, market structures and forces dictate compartmentalization of risk management options in order to package and sell financial instruments. This approach distinguishes between financial risk management, economic loss compensation, and physical infrastructure reconstruction cost reimbursement. Accessing financial risk management alternatives is not driven by nor often included in economic and physical risk reduction.

## In Sum

Numerous gaps exist between DRM and development processes that lead to risk, the primary link between the two. Correcting the existing diagnosis of what needs to be done to lower vulnerability depends on understanding what leads to creating the risk so as to correctly target risk reduction. There is no lack of existing economic, social, and technical solutions to risk reduction of the built environment. Unwillingness to address risk management of economic and social infrastructure in order to avoid a disaster lessens the demand for risk analysis. Disaster is to be understood broadly in the context of what development sets in place and the shape and content of the resulting risk.

CHAPTER 3

# What Development Has Brought and Disaster Wrought

*When you see a turtle in a tree, do not ask how it got there. Someone put it there for a reason.*

—Brazilian saying

## What Does Unwillingness Bring?

By the 1970s sovereign states classified as least developed countries (LDCs), with the support of the international development community composed of MDBs, DMDAs and NGOs, were expanding their built environment through grants, loans, and technical assistance. The theme of integrated regional development was established in theory and practice in the Americas (OAS 1984). Interdisciplinary planning and financing brought forth in the First and Third Worlds alike new economic and social infrastructure for progress wherever needed in the name of development.

But in many instances, development actions brought widespread exposure, vulnerability, risk, and loss of economic and social infrastructure to natural hazard events at all administrative, economic, and physical scales. These events, labeled as "disasters," wreaked destruction and disruption to what were applauded as development gains. As Iain Guest notes following Hurricane Mitch in 1998:

> In short, the sense of urgency that followed Mitch has evaporated. Even less is there a sense of new thinking—of new vision—from the governments affected or from the international community. This is deeply worrying, for if one thing was clear about Mitch it is that misguided, even abusive, policies were mainly responsible for the disaster. This was most obvious in the way that poor migrants from the interior were channeled into crowded, crime-ridden shanty-towns that clung to the slopes of Tegucigalpa, the capital of Honduras. Several of these barrios were swept away during the storms. It was also apparent in the slash and burn agriculture that denuded the mountains in the interior, or in the destruction of mangroves by shrimp farmers. Such practices made the environment more vulnerable, the poverty deeper, and Mitch more damaging. (Guest 1999: 2–3)

Disasters force examination of the structure and function of development, especially on the resulting vulnerability of infrastructure, life, and livelihoods. Today in most countries, what a society produces as the built environment is in the context of development by either design or its related impact. Depending on the development stage or economic development level of the country, the development processes to create the country's infrastructure might well be enveloped in governance and economic resource competition, but with no clear cultural mandate or tradition for societal control over natural hazard risk creation or reduction.

Disasters following natural hazard events are still most often considered unique experiences in the development continuum, separated in temporal, geographic, and administrative space even in countries cited for repetitive losses. Globally, more than 68 percent of all economic losses in the period 2005–2017 were attributed to extensive risk events—that is, low-severity, high-frequency hazardous events where communities are exposed to recurring localized floods, landslides, storms, or drought (UNDRR 2019: vii). The resulting loss of infrastructure created disastrous consequences, including declarations of disasters.

Consequences of those infrastructure losses often go beyond the event site itself. Most importantly, root causes for the exposure, vulnerability, and risk can no longer be considered unique. Often an increase in the exposure involves development actions (e.g., incursion into floodplains and floodways, unsustainable drawdown of rain-fed aquifers, destabilization of slopes through road and settlement construction). The underlying causes of increased exposure and vulnerability stem from shared (or similar) cultural, economic, social, scientific, and technical approaches to developing the built environment. These occur where risk management is dismissed or subjugated to other values, priorities, and behaviors. The missing diagnosis related to disasters is that development approaches are contained in contexts where risk reduction of economic and social infrastructure is often not a priority held by stakeholders or even communities and citizens.

This lack of willingness to carry out DRR focuses on the values and behaviors that have brought about the built environment in the first place. The issue is not whether more or less development is needed, but what role development is to serve for risk reduction of the built environment and by extension its associated populations. The moral and temporal challenges of recognizing people at risk are legitimate development concerns. On the one hand is recognition of the hundreds of millions of vulnerable people in low- and medium-income countries, often to multiple risks. On the other hand is an increasing interest in the scope and breadth of implications of vulnerability for each person at risk, no matter what the economic context, which is in addition to the vulnerability of the related economic and social infrastructure to damage and destruction. Such concerns shape to some extent the stakeholders' readiness to act on DRR to natural hazard events.

Also to be examined is the application of systemic assessments of risk to disaster risk reduction of known vulnerable economic and social infrastructure. Additional risks include catastrophic loss locally, regionally, and globally from natural and anthropogenic sources. The discussion leads to broad and deep discourse by development practitioners focusing on human survival that is manifestly steeped in a willingness to manage disaster risk reduction for all in the context of acceptable levels of risk from various threats. Not to be forgotten is that total global expenditures on arms and security vastly outweigh expenditures on development and DRR. Government expenditures on combating nuclear threats, terrorism, civil strife, and religious persecution continue to surpass the combined expenditures for (1) climate change adaptation and disaster risk management from all types of geologic, climatologic, and hydrologic events and (2) humanitarian assistance attending to pandemics, civil strife, ethnic cleansing, tribal conflict, and forced migration.

What development has brought and disasters have wrought points to transforming risk reduction of the built environment to the question of development as the principal process for addressing disaster risk reduction. Development is, or should be, risk reduction. This calls upon development theory and practice to include DRR as it addresses poverty, gender equality, and highly vulnerable populations targeted in the UN (United Nations) frameworks targeted for completion in 2030.

The international humanitarian relief community and its partner programs dealing with recovery, resettlement, and resilience have now recognized that repetitive disasters and the underlying risk factors make questionable the feasibility of continued effective emergency management on the scale that will be needed. This conclusion is in light of donor fatigue and the anticipated natural hazard events, including those related to climate variability and change, not to mention war, civil strife, forced migration, pandemics, terrorism, and religious intolerance.

A discussion continues as to whether increased losses related to natural hazard events are due to an increase in frequency and severity of events or to increased vulnerability through greater exposure of development-driven economic and social infrastructure, including risk brought about by reconstruction. Subregional institutions observe that risk has not been significantly reduced; rather it tends to increase and may increase even further in coming years, thus increasing economic, social, and environmental vulnerability. These declarations reflect continuing, reiterated vulnerability issues from one hurricane season, one El Niño–Southern Oscillation (ENSO) episode, one winter, and one summer to the next.

## Shaping the Disaster-Development Continuum

Since the 1980s, broad trends (presented in roughly chronological order) have shaped and continue to dramatically influence the disaster-development linkage of risk. From the beginning of that decade, a politically created and led disdain has grown for public sector planning, particularly land use planning. In many cases the public sector has chosen initiatives to adopt permissible land use to respond to private sector demands, wants, and needs, in that order. As Ulrich Beck (1992a), the sociologist known for his work on modernity, uncertainty, and the role of risk, has noted, at the beginning of the post–Cold War era a shift took place in societal tasks from primarily addressing wealth and income inequalities to addressing risk from "anthropogenic" and "natural" hazards. Exposure to these hazards cuts across traditional inequalities and across political, administrative, geographic, economic, and social boundaries.

By the early 1990s, declared economic losses attributed to disasters due to natural hazard events began outstripping non-reimbursable, non-military international development assistance. Economic and social infrastructure built with international assistance has been destroyed or damaged by natural hazard events, while unpaid loans from MDBs and bilateral development agencies remain. Much of the existing economic and social infrastructure built then continues to be vulnerable now. In international development assistance, formulation of crosscutting issues and creation of program silos continue to take place. At the same time, verbal cross-referencing of crosscutting themes and formal acknowledgment of each sector's program goals and aspirations also continue. Humanitarian assistance, disaster risk management, climate change adaptation, and resilience were preceded by civil liberty, livelihood enhancement, poverty alleviation, and governance initiatives, which in turn were preceded by gender equality and environmental management initiatives. All these initiatives now exist side by side, with development initiatives remaining foremost in the old-line sectors: agriculture, commerce and industry, communications, education, energy, health, housing, mining, telecommunications, transportation, urban and rural development, and water and sanitation.

Also since the mid-1990s, intentional transformation of disaster risk management interests into a sector alongside the development sector began. The sector has been guided by professional and institutional entities in government, academia, private enterprise, and PVOs and by political organizations and overseas development agencies looking for fresh themes to support in response to old challenges. Creation of the disaster sector has been bolstered not in the least by the UN thematic decade—International Decade for Natural Disaster Reduction (IDNDR: 1990–1999)—followed by two international framework agreements—Hyogo Framework for Action (HFA: 2005–2015) and Sendai Framework for Disaster Risk Reduction (SFDRR: 2015–2030).

Current calls from some practitioners are for increased discussion of the disaster-development linkage issue. They begin with assessment of the ever-greater increase of affected population and economic losses due to natural hazard events in coastal areas, even while recognizing a relative decrease in deaths due to natural hazard events (UNDRR 2019). These decreases are coupled with a decrease in access to financial and natural resources for humanitarian assistance and reconstruction support following a declared disaster and an ever-growing yet seldom met demand for resolving existing economic and particularly social infrastructure built environment vulnerability.

This situation exists despite the implications for countries with people of low and medium income at risk to loss of access to food, health care, shelter, water and sanitation, and education due to natural hazard events. There is also a call to identify the global implications of risk faced by individuals worldwide to a broad array of risk drivers, regardless of geographic place and political, economic, social, and natural hazard contexts. UN frameworks, agreements, and temporal goals created by sovereign states presently attempt to envelop these assessments, but without necessarily mandating action on the underlying contradictions and competition for effectively reaching the target populations. Yet when carried out, these vulnerability assessments will no doubt identify hundreds of millions of people around the globe facing risk in countries of all economic classification.

At the national level is a failure to systematically identify who and what is vulnerable to which natural hazard; where, why, what can be done about it; and who pays and who benefits. Moreover is the absence of appropriate risk management mechanisms to define and meet acceptable levels of risk, including policy and practices such as land use planning, zoning, codes, permits, regulation and enforcement, and insurance as a mandatory, visible, transparent part of development actions. These omissions have spawned an increasing call for international incentives and subsidies to make more palatable and pervasive natural hazard risk reduction measures. In the meantime, both public and private owners and operators of vulnerable economic and social infrastructure are not engaged in responsible and accountable disaster risk reduction except on a limited, voluntary, or mandated (through laws or access to financing) basis.

Beyond direct losses counted in deaths and infrastructure destruction, indirect and secondary losses from natural hazard events are growing. In addition to economic variables such as output, input, reduced exports and imports, and disruptions of supply chains are imputed losses related to lost school days of instruction, earning potential, and paid employment, as well as tools, material stocks, and physical places to work. There is also a negative impact on other crosscutting issues of living wages, income, gender inequality, poverty reduction, and sustainable natural resource use, all of which take place in the context of development.

## Development Actions as DRR Instruments

Sovereign state agreements pertaining to DRR, binding or otherwise, that call for specific ends or goals are often driven with good intentions but subsequently subjected to pressures from the development community. Moreover, governmental actions exist side by side those of the private sector, with varying degrees of coordination, collaboration, cooperation, and control. As Salvano Briceño notes, "Governance of risk (policies, legislation, and organizational arrangements) still focuses largely on preparing to respond to the hazards and planning for recovery. This leaves largely unattended the vulnerability component of risk, which is the only component on which change can be effected" (Briceño 2015: 1). The private sector may well depend on public infrastructure for significant if not critical components for its functioning, but the private sector focuses its natural hazard risk management actions on the infrastructure that it owns and operates and sometimes on the lifeline infrastructure of its employees in foreign production facilities.

At a broader scale, the international development community most often addresses natural hazard risk management as a separate rather than as an integral part of its development efforts. Faced with limited resources, the private sector and the international development community and sovereign states, no matter their form of government, continually define their preferred choice as "development" (with and without "disaster reduction" options) in financial and economic terms. This includes clearly defining development project options with and without expenditures on DRR and often further separating out CCA actions.

Until recently, due mostly to catastrophic results of natural hazard events that prompt repeated disaster declarations by the same national, provincial, and municipal governments, discussions have begun to define acceptable levels of risk in reconstruction. As Charlotte Benson and John Twigg have pointed out, "The identification and design of projects does not occur in isolation. Instead, it is influenced by the broader policies and objectives of an aid agency and its underlying ideology. If these do not stress the importance of risk reduction, then the issue receives little attention in appraisal and evaluation guidelines and is likely to be ignored in the design of many projects" (Benson and Twigg 2004: 145).

In many instances sovereign states acting through collective bodies do not succeed in effective DRR policy or practice. This is not to say that nations never address the issues involved. But at present the governance, economy, and culture of most countries are not generally poised nor predisposed to instigate effective policy and practice regarding natural hazard risk reduction if they challenge prevalent economic development policies and practices. Often DRR policy and practice does not specify the beneficiaries of its actions, nor the sector or those responsible for monitoring, evaluation, reporting, regulation, and enforcement (MERRE). And DRR policy may not be state mandates focusing on hazard type, built environment component, and administrative setting and location.

## Policy as Outputs

With reference to the gaps related to policy and practice, when national governments create agreements, binding or otherwise, that call for specific ends or goals, the countries often establish a reporting system that ultimately focuses—sometimes inadvertently—on means rather than outcomes. Reporting on policy-driven goals, such as lessening of the number of lives lost, population impacted, and financial, economic, and physical losses by sector, can end up being reports on the number and type of agreements, frameworks, committees and their meetings, laws, regulations and their dissemination, and information made available through public awareness campaigns, education, and training. The countries marshal resources for designated project inputs and work toward the identified outputs, while there is often little or no discussion of blame, blame agents, causal agents, exposure, identification of whose risk and who pays, and most importantly, responsibility and accountability. Neither is there discussion as to who gains and who is harmed by not dealing with risk, nor about behaviors, as when public and private sectors take risk-adverse, risk-neutral, and risk-prone actions.

As Benson and Twigg have noted, since the DRR debate is not part of the development debate, there is lack of understanding about the level of risk and the repetitive nature of events. They note the supposition that specialists deal with "disasters" and the immediacy of addressing development "owned" problems requiring a response to secure political votes. Finally, they note that donors and governments prefer to be seen at infrastructure ribbon-cutting ceremonies. At the scene of a disaster reconstruction site, they, ironically, gain public support (Benson and Twigg 2004).

In summary, convergence, duplication, and divergence surround disaster risk reduction policies, programs, and projects undertaken by political and technical entities. They form part of the underlying risk factors referred to collectively as a culture of disasters by design principally through development actions (Mileti 1999). Overall, progress varies sector by sector in disaster risk reduction, but for the most part at the national level, few discernible, quantified goals, measurable levels of achievement, or coordination between or among economic and social sectors exist. While there are some efforts through stakeholder participation related to climate change adaptation, there is little or no momentum through

---

### Stakeholder Policy as Practice

An example that has both added and taken from international actions of sovereign states to push forward policy and practice concerning disaster prevention, response, and humanitarian assistance is the *Inter-American Strategic Plan for Policy on Vulnerability Reduction, Risk Management and Disaster Response* (*IASP*), through the Organization of American States (IACNDR 2003).

Presented in a vocabulary built around the term "disaster," the plan contains little or no mention of risk except as qualitative risk of a humanitarian and infrastructure crisis. *IASP* does not focus on the context of the quantitative risk of loss and damage from natural hazard event impact on economic and social infrastructure. It does not affirm nor reaffirm that disaster risk management is a priority of national development policy. Other facets of the *IASP* are recognition of and adherence to sovereign states' efforts to carry out the following:
- Issuing guidelines;
- Coordination among peers and avoidance of duplicating any and all spheres of activity;
- Action by unanimous consent of the sovereign states, thus accepting the least common denominator as the level of effort;
- Mandated continuance of effort, but only using non-regular budget resources; and
- Periodic review, revision, and reporting on policy implementation, but without specific outcomes.

development channels of disaster risk reduction costs and benefits. For owners and operators of economic and social infrastructure, their respective stated predominant sector challenges are repair and replacement of components due to wear, tear, deferred repair, maintenance, and obsolescence. Component vulnerability to natural hazard events is not identified.

Collectively, sovereign states have called for progress along a path toward security from disasters. As policy, such a call is an example of political rhetoric to comply with or conjure up a commitment. In practice, the call is vague, whether the context is governance, the economy, or a manifestation of national culture. Moreover, sovereign states have reinforced the disaster risk management/emergency management sector laying claim to oversight and responsibility for disaster reduction. Thus, the development community gladly demurs from drawing attention for responsibility when governance, the economy, and the culture do not demand it. The development community instead accepts the claims of dominion by the disaster and emergency management communities.

## Careful Observation of the Development Sector

As the disaster sector has evolved under the watchful eye of the development sector, disaster management interests are often tasked with or seek responsibility for managing emergencies and recovery post-disaster, as well as overseeing risk reduction of the built environment using specialized agencies at all levels. But lacking is follow-through by governments plus a very parochial, reticent view by the private sector about managing risk in economic and social sectors. Moreover, funding shortfalls of sector budgets, both public and private, prompt requests for external counterpart participation in conventions and agreements, both national and international.

There has also been relatively little national investment in DRR of existing vulnerability of infrastructure. This is reflected in part by no assignment of responsibility and accountability of losses due to unmanaged risk. It also is the outcome of conditioning developing countries through development assistance. If the proposed action by an interested sovereign state is worthwhile as a priority by donors, it might well be supported. This is also true with the sector-specific international ministerial level organizations demurring from open and routine discussions on risk and particularly loss, assignment of responsibility and accountability, and approaches to regulation and enforcement. This follows the view that disaster and development management sectors often hold: "We are what we fund."

The list of what development actions have brought to vulnerability of economic and social infrastructure includes thwarting efforts to make risk assessment information, including loss, vulnerability, exposure, and natural hazard event history accessible to all and free as a public service. This kind of information is currently viewed as a market commodity to be bought and sold, particularly for financial risk management services. All along the development continuum, agencies demur from accepting responsibility and accountability in the absence of or through avoidance of regulation and enforcement for risk and loss.

The development sector may refer to "the environment," meaning an indivisible whole, where atmospheric, hydraulic, and geologic phenomena are seen as either good or bad in relation to populations and their associated built environment. On the other hand, the same phenomena are seen as having a direct bearing on the structure and function of ecosystems in any number of environments. And development actions do not routinely include environment-related economic and social infrastructure risk reduction needs assessment and associated technical assistance, training, and technology transfer.

After more than forty years of global efforts to support countries in disaster reduction, the stakeholders habitually convened by the international community are public entities responsible for emergency management, who are often also charged with disaster prevention and mitigation, and the entities responsible for national planning and budget. Also convened are researchers and academicians from various disciplines and international entities working in disaster management, emergency management, and humanitarian assistance. Habitually not present are the owners and/or operators of private and public economic and social infrastructure networks and representatives of associated population groups such as traditional sector organizations from agriculture, education, energy, health, housing, mining, telecommunications, tourism, transportation, water, and sanitation; private sector trade associations; public and private sector employee associations, including unions; and the for-profit risk management industry.

## Isolating Countries' Development Processes from Dealing with Risk

Investment in DRR has reached a stage, particularly when dealing with climate hazards, where project proposals and budgets are presented to reflect "with and without" natural hazard risk reduction measures. On the one hand, this can be required in order to access financial support reserved by the stakeholders for climate change adaptation, "environmental," or resilience objectives. Such support often operates by choice or political mandate outside the stakeholders' mainstream development and disaster risk management policy, planning, budgets and projects. On the other hand, it is often done to quantify for reporting purposes investment in DRR that is taking place alongside investment in development. The same can be said about investment in resilience and CCA in many countries and with many NGOs.

Risk transfer schemes usually built around financial risk management are emerging at the subregional scale and national scales to protect government fiscal solvency. Few risk transfer schemes, except in the agricultural sector, are being attempted at the subnational level. At both scales parametric insurance is touted for improved access to capital for disaster recovery, but economic and physical risk reduction comes about as a secondary objective, if at all. In addition, conditions precedent to access such insurance do not include requirements to lessen exposure, vulnerability, or physical risk. And not surprisingly, crosscutting issues such as governance, transparency, visibility, community participation, and environmental degradation are not prominent.

Risk reduction is now more broadly discussed in the international development community, but effective policies and intervention schemes are still not part of the core economic development agenda. Presently the international development community's rewards system—both real and imputed—seems to be at odds with efforts to invest in risk reduction. It is highly focused on doing a better job of development in terms of economic expansion, job creation, capital investment, and GDP growth.

In parallel, the transformation of disaster risk reduction into a development sector-centered approach, with each component of the development community having its own emergency management capacity in each sector, is best done at the beginning stages of discussion. Such a shift in policy calls into play development theory and practice, particularly as it addresses the poor and poverty, gender, civil society, and highly vulnerable populations targeted in the UN Sustainable Development Goals (SDGs). This shift in policy also calls into play administrative decentralization, natural resource and land use management, governance, transparency, visibility, corruption, and accountability.

At the international and regional levels, multilateral development banks, bilateral development assistance agencies, and NGOs are holding discussions, but they are constrained both internally and externally by the presentation of the disaster management-development link as one of "mainstreaming." These institutions are being told that risk to natural hazards—or as still often phrased, risk to natural disasters—is an issue that must be brought into development discussions. In reality, the risk issue has been there all along. It has been misidentified, not made visible, not acted on in a manner commensurate with significantly reducing vulnerability, nor addressed by using lower levels of risk tolerance.

Making disaster management an issue by creating specialized "disaster" or DRR agencies, conferences, and declarations has solidified such entities' presence in international and national discussions. But using the term "disaster" and focusing primarily on disaster events has also reinforced the use of the word "disaster" to describe the actual natural hazard event. Thus everything becomes a disaster, to the rather obvious disinterest, avoidance, and perhaps relief of those in the development community.

Addressing simultaneously the multiple natural hazards that surround a community as an "all-hazards approach" has facilitated avoiding the most basic element of vulnerability assessment of a component of economic or social infrastructure. That is, what is the specific natural hazard by location, severity, and frequency to which the infrastructure component is exposed? Creating specialized agencies, reporting mechanisms, international agreements and conventions, annual or biannual meetings, and dedicated program initiatives with or without dedicated funding sources gives sovereign states the sense that advanced, civilized, well-intentioned steps are being carried out. But left unclear in many cases is who gains from creation and maintenance of built environment vulnerability and why, as well as the consequences for losers and winners after a natural hazard event takes place.

Indiscriminate use of the word "disaster" has created in some instances the de facto policy of holding harmless (except perhaps in the case of financial loss of the powerful over the weak) those who own and operate vulnerable economic and social infrastructure in both the private and public sectors. It also has obscured the fact that humanitarian assistance and emergency management with their attending disciplines are legitimate professional endeavors with growing challenges and resource needs. These disciplines are competing for funding and opportunities alongside legitimate development disciplines dealing with their sector issues of vulnerability but seen through the lens of development winners and losers.

This situation has spawned competition among agencies to manage recovery, rehabilitation, and reconstruction funds and has highlighted the issue of the vulnerability of critical infrastructure and its role before, during, and after an emergency situation. But it mirrors the tragedy of the commons where individuals benefit by acting in their own self-interest at the expense of others dependent on the same resource. They sometimes do not expend their resources on reducing risk in society through collective means because there is no specific assignment of responsibility and accountability for protecting social and economic infrastructure. The result is limited exploration of the many paths available for effective risk reduction of those most vulnerable and least able to bring political, economic, and institutional weight to bear to reduce their vulnerabilities and cover their losses.

MDBs, DMDAs, and NGOs in many ways are in the same situation as their national counterpart governments. They use the creation of a disaster-event-centered institutional track growing out of disaster preparedness, response, and reconstruction experiences over the past fifty years. But that has been created alongside sixty years of development initiatives.

For countries, the result is that disaster risk reduction efforts are often unsustainable. Development assistance for DRR has been highly volatile, ex post facto, and marginal. It is miniscule compared with financing for disaster response. A total of $5.2 billion for DRR represents 3.8 percent of the total humanitarian assistance financing between 2005 and 2017. That is, for every $100 spent on population crisis/disaster support, less than $4 is spent on DRR (UNDRR 2019: iv).

Regardless of the origin or entry point of aid, including that under the banner of disaster management and resilience, international assistance continues to be triggered primarily by disaster declarations and crisis interventions. National priorities separate development goals from risk reduction. In the international development community, disaster risk reduction investment and technical assistance have become a separate, parallel track for professional advancement. There are, on a limited scale, exceptions to this in the case of climate change adaptation and building resilience, but even these examples are typically bound by the general development context, if not subsumed by development processes such as globalization, free trade, poverty alleviation, and access to credit.

## In Sum

What is wrought by disaster in large part lies at the feet of what is brought by development. Development's choices have created much of the existing vulnerability of the built environment to natural hazard events, choices selected through preferences for goals that allow toleration or even knowing acceptance of high levels of risk for damage and destruction of economic and social infrastructure. This risk has been created through growth, change, and lack of preference for resilience and management of risk as part of the development marketplace. Most of the world's vulnerable populations live in informal economies, often outside the support of formal government regulation and enforcement for DRR. But most of the vulnerable economic and social infrastructure by economic value and number of components is not directly related to the informal economy. Development stakeholders handle DRR through top-down approaches carried out by specialized agencies and programs within silos in their institutions through processes almost exclusively outside the development community's principal goals and objectives. Risk reduction is now more broadly discussed in the international development community (IDC), but effective policies and intervention schemes are still not part of the development agenda.

Next in the discussion is the apparent destiny of further prolonged exposure, vulnerability, risk, and loss of economic and social infrastructure to natural hazard events.

# CHAPTER 4

# Understanding Where the Disaster-Development Link Leads

In what might be called an overriding manner, development gives content to the life of a country. Stakeholders function where losses due to natural hazard events are only one of a lengthening list of crises and losses impacting development. The primary stakeholders to declare the losses are sovereign states, given all the constructs they have created for and by themselves. Current outcomes of the development-disaster risk linkage and its attendant gaps in policy, practice, and knowledge are increasing vulnerability of populations and their associated economic and social infrastructure.

Because of increased disaster preparedness efforts, the loss of human life is decreasing both in absolute and relative terms. But how long this trend will last is not clear. People are increasingly exposed to natural hazard events as they continue to occupy more natural hazard-prone landscape. But they participate in relatively less resilient economic endeavors and depend more on increasingly vulnerable economic and social infrastructure. As Andrew Maskrey has noted, "We are saying that the worst is yet to come because, in any given part of the world, most of the disasters that could possibly happen have not yet happened" (Maskrey 2013).

Arguably, development actions can lead to risk of avoidable, needless loss despite competition for development gains. Ironically, developers argue that disasters destroy development's gains while at the same time they claim that disaster reconstruction is good for the national economy.

Most important when examining culpability for such destruction is to identify change that should or might take place. This approach is central to a correct diagnosis of the built environment vulnerability issue. What are the pertinent themes related to (1) assessments of the hazard, exposure, vulnerability, and risk; (2) processes—the monitoring, evaluation, reporting, regulation, and enforcement (MERRE); and (3) behaviors as to how, when, and by whom these assessments and processes are used? How is it that lack of disaster risk reduction in its multiple forms appears as a gap between policy and practice despite knowledge, policy, and practice about hazard, exposure, vulnerability, risk, and loss?

## Where Present Outcomes Lead and Where Risk Reduction Can Reside

Three themes reveal the gaps between policy and practice as they relate to development and disaster. First are the differences between knowledge, policy, and practice evident in development goals that do not value DRR and values that guide DRR. Second are the differences between the values of those who have the most control over creation of vulnerability of the built environment and those who have little or no control over the vulnerability they face. And third are the differences between those who perceive DRR as part of the development process, those who see DRR belonging to the disaster sector, and those who see risk to natural hazards as primarily a measurable and marketable commodity for managing financial risk. Left unattended, these themes might well illustrate the destruction and mayhem that will dominate, if not replace in the years to come, the development agenda as originally envisioned (Bender 1989). Where the disaster-development risk linkage leads, and the changes needed to address gaps between knowledge, policy, and practice are discussed below.

### Powers, Super or Not, Challenging DRR Structure and Function

In much of development, risk reduction is viewed as an action to be managed, controlled in one way or another, and undertaken with the minimal cost possible. Financial risk can be bought and sold without reducing physical and economic risk related to damage and destruction of economic and social infrastructure. Beyond risk as a commercial commodity, some societies do not consider financial risk as something to be bought and sold; instead they think underlying physical and economic risk should be managed at acceptable levels determined through consensus from societal values, traditions, and collective actions.

Risk management can be considered a program silo supported by technical specialization, earmarked funding, and profit. Compartmentalizing development and disaster reduction efforts further amplifies managing risk through costs and benefits. A cost-benefit analysis often involves defining the expected costs if financial and sometimes economic risk is not lowered and the expected benefits in economic growth and monetary profit if risk management-related expenditures are minimized.

DRM might be said to assume the role of making operational a country's policy on risk management, thus allowing stakeholders the opportunity of having it both ways. That is to say, sovereign states proclaim policy and, backed by their own collective agreements involving the United Nations and regional political and technical bodies, have defined the bounds of their responsibility and accountability, individually and collectively. DRM entities carry out DRR unabated while informing policy through acquired knowledge (Bender 2014). The growing damage and destruction of economic and social infrastructure by natural hazard events makes apparent that development continues to create risk of the built environment while encouraging the DRM sector to attempt resolution of risk management issues.

Currently, there is little evidence that acquired knowledge of such practices is provoking policy changes in development's approach to DRR in any profound way. DRM's attempt to protect development from the constructed risk brought about by development's own actions is a schizophrenic behavior. Development, a social construction itself, is a risk creator, beginning with the creation of vulnerable economic and social infrastructure. At the same time, the development sector is asked to adopt disaster reduction actions in the name of mainstreaming, which have been codified over time as externalities put "into sets of institutional and administrative practices which now characterize an increasingly professionalized and structured disaster risk management sector" (Maskrey 2016: 5). This situation only reinforces (1) recognition of development priorities, (2) the perceived option of including or not including DRR actions in development and at what cost, and (3) needed risk reduction actions when addressing the consequences of infrastructure loss following a natural hazard event and existing infrastructure vulnerability. Countries have set up financing arrangements, and when the built environment is damaged or destroyed, they have defined processes through which "development" loan and grant funds can be reprogrammed for disaster recovery operations.

Mainstreaming DRR in development can mean continual consideration of risk in development decisions. Or it can mean assuming certain levels of risk to be constructed and addressing risk reduction as a development by-product after initial design and construction decisions have been made. The former is related most often to development policy; the latter is most often related to development practice. Stakeholders have a penchant for taking policy proclaimed as practice undertaken. Thus, they will adopt policy and consider the requisite practice as "in the works" or a fait accompli. International frameworks and proclamations purport "mainstreaming" DRR into development policy and actions.

But in reality, for most countries, risk in the building of economic and social infrastructure is accepted at various levels in various ways. Vulnerability of existing infrastructure is at levels far beyond the capacity—politically, economically, and socially—to rebuild and replace infrastructure without external assistance for most countries. Regardless of policy, there is little apparent will to make available necessary resources to alter development. It will remain so until development becomes the principal tool most responsible and accountable for implementing risk reduction, and thus risk reduction becomes in and of itself recognized as development.

## Underdevelopment and Dependency Written as Interdependency in Development

As DRM efforts work toward less dependency for post-disaster-event assistance, development efforts work toward greater interdependency for raw materials, labor, and commerce between sovereign states. Previously perceived benefactor-victim relationships between countries have evolved through economic development beyond "your risk is my concern" into "your risk is my risk," at least in areas of economic development. However, the issue of who pays for "your losses" when they occur is not always clear, even though who loses might be fairly well understood. Through economic and social infrastructure these relationships have a physical dimension of systems, interrelated facilities, and networks. Shared dependency by design can bring about shared risk, but not necessarily shared risk reduction.

Interconnectedness embodies globalization and is a characteristic of business and industry facilities as well as social services and lifeline networks. The interconnectedness is driven by various factors, including availability and scarcity of raw materials and labor, proximity to production facilities and transportation, access to IT and telecommunications, and access to markets and consumers. Each of these factors has a physical dimension that includes economic and social infrastructure as well as endowed natural resources.

Interdependency can bring about risk and the probability of loss, but also gain and the accumulation of wealth. Thus, the disaster-development linkage is bounded by risk management for economic gain on the one hand and for health, safety, and welfare of populations on the other. A facet of this linkage is that capitalism strives to eliminate competition and triumph via monopolies; risk reduction thrives on multiple options and redundancy to reduce the risk of impact, loss, and suffering and to enhance recovery.

## Disasters as Burgeoning Perpetrators of Development

The risk to economic and social infrastructure is endemic to development now. But in a future where more and more of what is built will be in response to loss (reconstruction) or lessening of existing vulnerability (retrofitting), disaster becomes a driver, so to speak, of development actions, which in turn are drivers of risk creation. In terms of loss and the resources needed to rebuild, on paper economic and social infrastructure reconstruction in particular and recovery in general will represent an increasing portion of a country's province, state, or urban development activities and requests for MDB project lending. Overall progress in disaster risk reduction varies sector by sector. Typically, however, at the national level there are no specific goals, measurable achievement levels, or coordination between sectors. The situation is cast to being one of integrating climate change adaptation, sea level rise, and drought and desertification risk reduction actions simultaneously across economic and social sectors.

## Understanding the Risk to Be Reduced by Development

Before every disaster, populations engage in development efforts involving resources and decisions concerning their built environment. There is, however, little understanding of natural hazard threats, due in great part to the paucity of hazard, exposure, vulnerability, risk, and loss (HEVRL) assessments. This promotes policies and practice driven by experiential learning, that is, the unfolding of actual disasters. NGOs, along with MDBs, sovereign states, and DMDAs, recognize the gaps between development and DRR that could be overcome to reduce loss to natural hazard event impacts.

As Benson and Twigg have stated, "The identification and design of projects does not occur in isolation. Instead, it is influenced by the broader policies and objectives of an aid [development] agency and its underlying ideology. If these do not stress the importance of risk reduction, then the issue receives little attention in appraisal and evaluation guidelines and is likely to be ignored in the design of many projects" (Benson and Twigg 2004: 16).

Early on, the science, engineering, and land use planning sectors recognized actions needed to reduce risk, such as inserting HEVR information in development processes (OAS-DRD 1991). But the DRM sector grew quickly around social sciences using the disaster event as the entry point for research in isolation from the economic development sector when it came to issues of natural hazard risk of the built environment.

Declarations and experiences, particularly content noting what is lost/damaged/destroyed and what is needed/requested/given following disaster declarations, are instructive in identifying preferred DRR tools and processes. Questions concerning which built environment components —whether public or private—are most impacted by what type of natural hazard; economic or social; professionally designed or artisan built; self-built or contracted; wood, concrete, or steel frame; financed or owned capital; permitted or illegal—are pertinent. Which decisions most impact the creation of vulnerable infrastructure components? What tools and behaviors shaped these decisions, and could they be different and changed, respectively, to lead to effective design and implementation of DRR actions in the future? What are the priorities for reconstruction assistance, for whom, by whom, with whom, why, and how?

In the past seventy-five years, more than half of all social and economic infrastructure, including housing, has come into existence. Efforts to deal with the risk to natural hazards have evolved from informal to increasingly dominant, formal tools. Policies, programs, and practices that create every piece of the built environment—from housing to places of public assembly, health and education facilities, and transportation, communication, and energy networks—are continually subjected to review and alteration. Which tools are chosen, when, by whom, and why, and which behaviors are employed are not always known. Decisions affecting tool selection are often not visible or transparent until risk assessments are completed. But choosing inadequate assessment tools and processes, or not using them at all, can result in constructing risk at various scales. Ultimately, formal and informal behaviors, whether using these tools or not, may dictate construction, reconstruction, and retrofitting of economic and social infrastructure, as well as the reduction of risk.

If risk is avoided or not permitted beyond acceptable levels, the risk might be referred to as self-selected, community-regulated, or administratively controlled. If the risk is not abated and goes beyond a society's ability to respond to the consequences of a natural hazard event—a disaster—the risk level might be called self-inflicted, community-condoned, or an administrative oversight.

It would seem that the majority of sovereign states favor using universal tools and processes to guide the assessment of risk and its reduction. This is the case if their proclamations, accords, frameworks, legislation, resolutions, and policies are taken at face value, particularly the SFDRR and *GAR19*. But when acting as a group, nation-states often avoid disagreeing with each other about application of their pronouncements. The official wording of their adopted policies respects individual sovereignty, so often each country does as it wants without retribution. Sovereignty explains how nations lay aside attempts at adopting universal standards and norms for everything from a constitutionally guaranteed freedom of citizens from disasters as part of human rights to a universal building code for one-story primary schools.

But closer examination shows that international and national policies do not necessarily permit or even prompt action at the local level. A review of the type, severity, and frequency of built environment losses reveals those that could have otherwise been avoided. Infrastructure components that suffer repeated damage or destruction include housing, schools, water systems, and health facilities as most vulnerable. But these are built environment components that are most often designed and built under absolute if not majority local authority, with community input into cost and construction, regulation, and enforcement.

Behaviors leading to a less vulnerable built environment—including concern, leadership, knowledge, and technical skills—are assumed to abound. The behaviors leading to a more vulnerable built environment—including ignorance, arrogance, error and omission, corruption, and greed—often do abound. So, what is it about behavior that decides the use of tools and their role in creating or abating vulnerability and risk? Behavior is based on cultural values, mores, norms, and standards. When it comes to vulnerability reduction of the built environment to natural hazard events, these vary greatly from society to society.

Populations may be in favor of, indifferent to, or in opposition to the use of certain tools and processes related to HEVRL and MERRE. Tools may or may not be used, or used effectively. Tools may expose unwanted information about vulnerability. So reasons for not choosing to use tools and processes at hand to reduce vulnerability are many. And the reasons for creating the tools are also directly related to behavioral characteristics.

Overlaying this context of tools, processes, and behavior is the omnipresence of poverty. When vulnerability of the poor is viewed at both global and local levels, it is understood that most often the poor have little or no choice but to accept exposure. They have few choices to control the processes that create the built environment most immediate and important to them: shelter, potable water, sanitation, streets, schools, health facilities, access to employment transportation, communication, and energy. The poor have few or negligible resources to lessen their vulnerability, whether those resources are knowledge, experience, technical, or financial. And they have the most limited access to resources for managing risk, whether physical, economic, or financial. This is true for the poor from rural, metro, city, town, neighborhood, residential block, or public housing settings.

Sovereign states make policies, but these do not necessarily lead to action. Whether or not they involve the three branches of government (executive, legislative, and judicial), policy implementation may never be put forward or possess required regulation, enforcement, or funding for action. Knowledge of risk does not ensure DRR action, particularly if it does not inform policy.

Society in its many facets and government in its many forms propose actions that are so reduced in effectiveness in order to reach consensual approval that they actually constitute a least common denominator. What happens if behavioral norms do not include or do not highly value DRR? Risk-prone conduct, particularly if no one is held responsible, may not be monitored, evaluated, reported, regulated, or subject to enforcement. Various groups (associations, federations, legal entities) who do not have consideration of DRR as part of their norms and standards may also not be held accountable. Risk may continue to be bought and sold in the marketplace.

## Development Life of Stakeholders, Development Life of Societies

Through debate, negotiation, and power viewed through varying perspectives, the development sector has been called upon—and sometimes called out—for three decades to be a driver, if not the principal driver, of disaster risk reduction. Considering the call for a shift from emphasis on disaster relief to disaster risk reduction and preparedness, stakeholders do not refer to their development programs as a principal instrument of risk creation or for implementation of DRR. Recognizing the importance of risk assessments and taking ownership of risk through the processes of DRR implementation are two separate issues.

In the context of development represented in great part by globalization, more is made of avoiding financial risk than of avoiding physical and certainly economic loss. If the costs of avoiding risk (up front, before the hazardous event even occurs) can be managed by passing the costs on, selling them, or simply not dealing with them, then short-term gains can be increased. Responsibility and accountability can be avoided. Physical risk reduction to the built environment is viewed as a cost to development that detracts from economic performance.

DRM presently uses strategies such as declaring absence or absolution from responsibility and accountability for loss while noting ongoing preparations for disaster assistance. Simply declaring insolvency or entering into a protracted legal process can negate having to pay compensation for losses should they occur. Practice trumps policy and knowledge.

For the public sector, avoidance of investing in risk reduction can take place in several ways. They include refusing to adopt and enforce levels of risk avoidance commensurate with the risk. Governments declare themselves self-insured, but with no dedicated revenue resources to compensate for losses and refusing to institute effective land use control of hazard-prone areas. Practice trumps policy and knowledge.

The call, the case, and the opportunity for investing in resilience should be seen as much a part of each development action as are the costs and benefits, winners and losers, and beneficiaries and benefactors. Unfortunately, the stakeholders are at a stage where at best they see investment in resilience—to reducing levels of loss that would not mean disastrous situations—as an add-on, not as an integral part of development.

The investment in resilience, particularly when dealing with climate change adaptation, has reached levels where project proposals and budgets are presented to reflect "with and without" risk reduction measures. On the one hand, such presentation of projects can be mandatory in order to access financial support reserved for climate change adaptation and other "environmental" objectives. Such support often operates outside

---

### The Universal and Particular of Disaster and Development

In 1992, Hurricane Andrew left much of Florida devastated and facing numerous challenges, including lack of a uniform, statewide building code and, in particular, insufficient enforcement of building standards. Proposed regulations and enforcement would have a broad, long-term effect on how and where future development would take place in Florida.

As communities began to rebuild their homes and businesses, they faced numerous challenges and delays. By 1998 a statewide code still had not been adopted. Following recommendations of a state study, the Florida governor's office sought institution of statewide standards for building safety and practices.

However, the newly created Florida Building Commission was challenged by conflicting interests of landowners, designers, builders, building material suppliers, real estate and banking interests, municipal and country governments, and home buyers, each of whom had a particular view of what was best for them. While statewide support was sought, local preferences thwarted adoption of a code.

After considerable consultation, in March 2002, the Florida Building Code, which supersedes all local building codes, was adopted.

standard development and DRM policy, planning, and projects. On the other hand, such an operation facilitates quantification of investment in resilience taking place alongside investment in development (Bender 2013b). Policy trumps practice.

Further observation of the linkage between disaster and development refers to the preparation period for the IDNDR, when the form and content of the "disaster cycle" were constructed from observation and experience around disaster events, including disaster relief, and the science and engineering needed to design and construct more resilient infrastructure for prevention and mitigation. The preparation for IDNDR did anticipate examining steps to better relate risk management to development. The disaster cycle is devoid of any indication of its relationship to the development context in which the disaster takes place. This is not surprising, given the macro and micro considerations bound up in the silos that abounded in creating a UN international decade and later framework agreements.

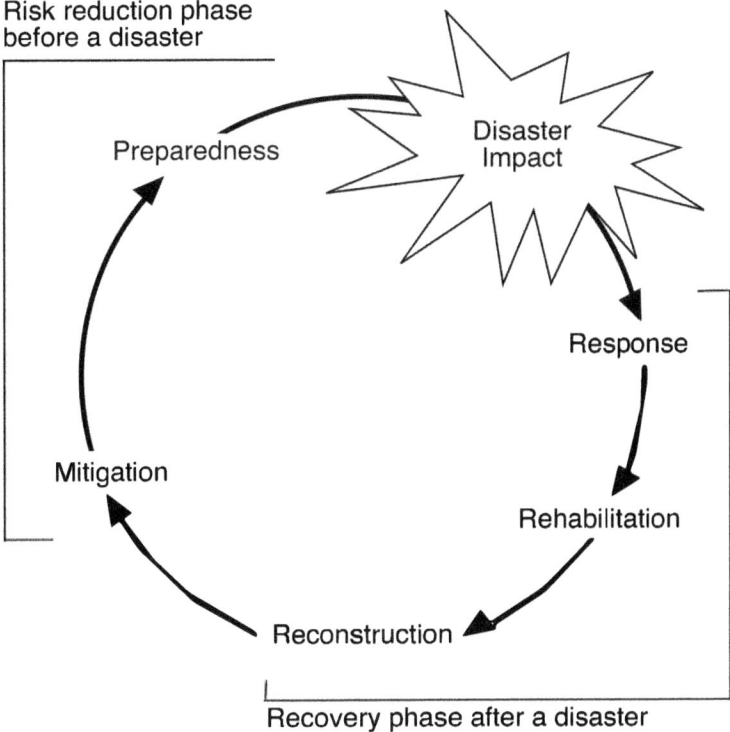

**Figure 4.1.** Disaster Cycle. Image composition by Stephanie Handy modeled after Pan American Health Organization. *Natural Disasters: Protecting the Public's Health*, Scientific Publication No. 575 (Washington, DC: Pan American Health Organization, 2000): 12.

## Implications of the Disaster Cycle and the Development Process

The understanding and implications of the disaster cycle image are often present in practice even if absent in policy statements, papers, and posters. This is manifest in the absence of references to the development process and its role in "disaster impact." The disaster cycle manifests the actual implementation of practice built around pre-planning and planning for crisis and fundraising on the back of the declared disaster in order to accumulate resources for the next crisis. For many nations with repetitive disasters, recovery is becoming the context, if not the content of development.

It is small comfort to say that development is present in recovery given its role in vulnerability creation before the disastrous event and the losses the nations have experienced. This makes all the more clear the view that risk assessments and DRR processes exist in broader societal contexts that include decisions and behaviors that manifest themselves in development. The challenge is not to further obfuscate the disaster cycle image and practice, but to recognize its relevance to the development process sector by sector.

If DRM was accepted as inside the development process, implications are that the disastrous event itself is not the entry point for development action, but that prevention and mitigation are part of development's responsibility and accountability. Moreover, monitoring, alert, relief, repair, rehabilitation, and reconstruction would be viewed as development players addressing a development need to reach a development goal: acceptable risk. Risk assessments and DRR implementation processes are not only part of development as their continual elaboration and application are the responsibility of development, for which development should be held accountable. The globalization model for development actually presents an approach not only for moving beyond the benefactor/victim and developed/underdeveloped paradigms. It also explains DRM as part of interdependence in development in the same way that commerce is a part of interdependence. In addition, climate change (along with other trans-global risks) may not merely demonstrate an end to the distinction between developed and developing countries as contrivances around definitions of advanced and backward economies, cultures, and built infrastructure networks. Finally, sovereign states, in part through reinforcement of DRM as a relationship of interdependence, may accept collaborative efforts within the global community as needed to ameliorate the anthropogenic causes or contributions to climate and other potentially catastrophic risks.

## In Sum

Transformation from a focus on emergency management to a focus on a development approach for addressing DRR is insipient, but difficult to advance at each administrative level, in all sectors, and between and among public and private institutions. Transformation calls not just for development theory and practice to address the poor and poverty, gender, and highly vulnerable populations targeted in the SDGs. It also means addressing land use management, administrative decentralization, governance, and corruption, as well as putting the disaster cycle into a development context. Risk reduction is now broadly discussed, but effective policies and intervention schemes are still not part of the development agenda.

Discussion about where disaster leads is obviously and necessarily about development. Disaster exists in development, linked by risk, and made apparent by the gaps between policy, practice and knowledge that do not deal advisedly with built environment vulnerability.

While the development community recognizes that disasters thwart development gains, at the same time it claims that disaster reconstruction can be good for national economic growth. It is not too much to say that nations have set up paradigms for owners and operators of their built environment, both public and private alike, where they influence if not control the bounds of responsibility and accountability for risk. Owners and operators certainly manage risk with an eye on short-term gain while anticipating avoidance of long-term loss or, at the least, responsibility for loss. Together with their stakeholder cohorts, they have set up financing arrangements to deal with loss, all this laid out in advance of the expected impact embodied in the disaster.

The disaster recovery process manifests very clearly how development and DRM sectors exhibit their capacity to gain support for addressing the needs of impacted populations following a disaster declaration. The post-disaster period also highlights unresolved issues between development and DRM that contribute to creating vulnerability before a natural hazard event occurs.

CHAPTER 5

# Disaster-Development Linkage through the Lens of Disaster Recovery

As laid out in the introduction, following a declaration of disaster, the response, recovery, and reconstruction can lead to change that benefits the marginalized, poor, and vulnerable populations. But given the existence of vulnerability brought about through development, how was development addressing the problems of these populations before the hazardous event occurred? It is possible that disasters can have a positive, enabling effect on addressing unresolved development issues, but what was development actually enabling before the hazardous event took place? Disaster shocks can open political space for contesting and concentrating political power. But what was the development power structure doing before the inevitable natural hazard event (Bender 2011)?

Understanding the context of development in which disasters occur allows for a broader and deeper understanding of the potential and shortcomings of DRR in recovery. It highlights issues within the disaster-development linkage that researchers of economic development and population betterment may not typically address.

Recovery following catastrophic loss due to a natural hazard event lays bare the actual tenets underlying development policies, programs, and practices, including construction of risk. In recognizing what disaster has wrought, the term "recovery" might well be considered "recovery from what development has brought." Much is revealed when both stakeholders and those impacted by disaster study what happens within development and recovery processes.

Recovery institution participants compete for post-disaster presence and effectiveness, which highlights the challenges for DRR and its place in post-disaster actions. Whether recovery is dominated by the development sector or the disaster management (DRM) sector, post-disaster operations reveal many choices to be considered within recovery. For whom, by whom, and at what cost does post-disaster recovery take place? As in the development process itself, DRR is not often seen as a principal goal of the recovery process. There are no generally accepted levels of risk to which recovery policy and projects are held. Indeed, best local practices continue from existing development policy, particularly when led by the development, not the DRM, sector.

## Recovery through Development or More Development through Recovery

Recovery can be viewed as part of development but must be examined in both the development and recovery sector dimensions. Such an approach reflects at least two observations about recovery: (1) "reconstruction must not be at the expense of transformation" (IADB 1999), where post-disaster situations are an opportunity for economic development change; and (2) "recovery is always in the context of a nation's development as the society created the past exposure, presently manifests the vulnerability, and assigns/negotiates future risk" (Bender 2016: 318).

In most cases the development sector undertakes post-disaster economic recovery, beginning with traditional sectors that are heavily dependent on large public infrastructure projects (energy, transportation, water and sanitation, communications). Recovery also includes NGOs and community groups supporting replacement and repair of social service infrastructure (public administration and safety, education, health, and social services). Development accepts the challenge and the burden of establishing reconstruction processes based on development's tenets and opportunities put forth by supporting stakeholders and the private sector. The pre-existing vulnerability that was part of the economic and social infrastructure has become evident, but reconstruction of useful and efficient infrastructure is paramount. In spite of the challenges of raising and matching donor resources with identified projects, DMDAs and NGOs are increasingly using community participation rather than the interpretation of outside participants. Beyond powerful and weak participants there are also absent institutions—would-be participants who have something to contribute. But given the trajectories of development and recovery before and after the natural hazard event, they are not present. Despite aspirations and efforts to the contrary, recovery is most often viewed responsible for producing a built environment that reflects a priority for the promotion and support of economic development. The theme "build back better" is cited. But usually it means building back through efficiency and expediency to promote economic growth. For some, but certainly not all participants in recovery and development actions, the theme does not include sustainability as a principal goal and objective.

Risk reduction is an increasingly visible issue in recovery policies, programs, and projects. It often comes at the insistence of international financing institutions and international donors, humanitarian assistance, and community development organizations. These participants have set up dialogues and shared experiences inside the recovery processes but outside development processes. This is similar to the CCA experience, where international donors want to avoid repetitive losses in the same geographic areas impacting the same populations and associated infrastructure. Donors expect those involved in recovery operations to build back more safely as a requisite for their giving support. In some instances, recovery has been defined, managed, and promoted as the bridge between emergency response and development. DRR, then, is often cast as an add-on or as initiating actions apart from both emergency management (EM) and development.

Whether the recovery or the development sector takes the lead, there is competition for resources. The competition is both internal and between participating institutions, not only for funding, but also for technical assistance and training. Contrasting with this are efforts to convert dependency between benefactors and disaster victims into interdependency through initiating and amplifying development opportunities most often tied to economic globalization. Such globalization efforts may include introduction of businesses, products, and services duplicating those already present in the country or the offer of new products and services that will compete with those already in the marketplace. These actions may be referred to as "disaster capitalism" (Klein 2007) or as part of the industrial-disaster complex (Svistova and Pyles 2018). Both approaches rely heavily on the declared virtues of trickle-down economics to provide opportunity and jobs to those who were outside of the formal economy before the disastrous event.

Other characteristics of post-disaster economic recovery are the development community's choice of approaches and participants for economic recovery regardless of the DRR content and its lack of differentiation between predominant hazard types and the risk to infrastructure to be reconstructed. Recovery efforts led by development entities also often tout an "all hazards" approach, despite DRR guidance that points to specific hazard risk reduction for specific components of economic and social infrastructure. This sometimes occurs from the dominance of outside experts and exclusion of local knowledge about natural hazards. Such an approach can also reflect the outside institution's most recent recovery experience in a different country.

Using local knowledge goes beyond relating to hazard assessment. Most challenging is the gap between local knowledge and professional expertise about risk to the built infrastructure (Mitchell et al. 2016). It could be assumed that knowledge from development policy through practice would inform reconstruction about DRR. But since development processes can differ from the local or national DRR processes, traditional and historic approaches to DRR are often overlooked by the development community. Anthony Oliver-Smith has noted previously that reconstruction becomes a test of the capacity of the system to respond to a clear demonstration that the major human and environmental destruction that takes place is rooted in the changes enacted in the social and environmental setting that took place in the distant and probably not-so-distant past before the disaster (Oliver-Smith 2009).

This lack of sharing experience about risk creation is followed, literally, by the development sector ignoring knowledge about what leads to resilience of economic and social infrastructure. Development planning and practice do not often address or monitor vulnerability of populations and their associated infrastructure in a visible, transparent, yet differentiated way. This is particularly the case when DRR information pertains to the poor and the social and economic infrastructure that serves the poor.

Available information about infrastructure loss is most often measured in economic terms, but the data are often not clear as to whether the loss is expressed in terms of net present value, replacement cost, or cost at the time of its construction. Sometimes a loss estimate (including estimates of social impact in indirect and secondary losses) of future economic activity is expressed in terms of GDP. Loss estimate information may be generated by a group of owners and operators, insurance, government, and stakeholder entities. Often loss estimates are offered by MDBs, DMDAs, and NGOs knowledgeable about particular past, proposed, or development projects under way in the disaster area. Thus, persistent differences and contradictions in loss data can be due to the various ways that stakeholders wish to use the information.

## Managing Risk in Recovery and Beyond

Responsibility and accountability for future damage and destruction of infrastructure are sometimes assumed as assigned by designated parties involved in the development processes. That assignment may not be visible, and it may not hold for housing, education, health, religious, and public building components. Responsibility and accountability may be a more accepted practice in the private sector and with public service utilities. But in general, their acceptance varies enormously from country to country and by public administrative setting.

Knowledge of vulnerability and possible damage of social and economic infrastructure does not always match the need of all prospective users. The knowledge of those who have experienced firsthand the impact of natural hazard events, conditioned by affect and emotion, is different from those coming to assist without such experience. Moreover, those who come to assist may not have acquired knowledge, practice, or policy guidance on associating the expressed knowledge of those impacted as relevant to a particular part of hazard, exposure, vulnerability, and risk assessments. Nor have these specialists necessarily been part of monitoring, evaluation, reporting, regulation, or enforcement of the actions for reconstruction or development. If the specialists do have such knowledge and expertise, they may not have the support needed for creating technical tools to increase public adoption and compliance with building regulations and enforcement.

Gaps between policy, practice, and knowledge include lack of vulnerability assessment information or urgency to restore social infrastructure such as lifelines and other social service infrastructure. The gaps demonstrate how DRR policy goals and objectives can interfere with providing immediate restoration of necessary services to those most impacted. Gaps in recognizing skill and capacity between construction contractors and risk management managers are revealed in the tasks they undertake. If builders are prepared to deal with DRR issues, they may lack authorization at decision points or be prohibited from presenting risk management issues at decision-making points (Malalgoda, Amaratunga, and Pathirage 2010). At the highest level, sovereign states that own the projects are monitoring MDB policies and actions. Sovereign states may also be board members of MDBs financing the projects. The MDBs exercise limited oversight of the technical content of projects they finance. That responsibility lies with the borrowing country or public or private sector entity.

Opportunistic, profit-driven motives in recovery are revealed in risk tolerance and emphasis on economic development. Simply stated, DRR cannot successfully compete as a crosscutting sector alongside development—let alone climate change adaptation, resilience, and sustainable development (Bender 1999).

Andrew Natsios notes that raising or lowering risk tolerance, which is described as flexibility, is discussed in development (including recovery) foreign assistance (Natsios 2009, 2010). The subject has been discussed most often regarding international development assistance partnerships and project management and administration in terms of responsibility and accountability. In the case of foreign assistance, risk tolerance does not necessarily concern levels of vulnerability of the built environment (or of the population) to natural hazard events. It often concerns the level of comfort that DMDA program management has with private sector vendors using the donor's funds. An example would be flexibility in spending budgeted funds on time and staying within cost-benefit guidelines for expenditures. In recovery there is an emphasis on building back quickly. It often results in a lack of risk assessment information generated or provided pertaining to the infrastructure components to be built. Without the necessary time and effort to produce and use risk assessments, reconstruction of vulnerable economic and social infrastructure may be created anew by those agencies and donors supporting the recovery.

## Understanding Underlying Risk Factors and Built Environment Disaster Recovery

Multidisciplinary research has been conducted for more than forty years in various countries, including "developing" countries, on the power structures before and after the disaster. Often such studies consider disasters as anomalies in the development history of the affected country. The disaster is often characterized as part of the "disaster cycle," now often called the disaster management cycle if the word "development" is inserted in conjunction with the "recovery" phase. Given that development as a process is not depicted as being part of the disaster cycle, such studies rarely define and discuss the built environment in terms of pre-disaster exposure, vulnerability, risk, and previous losses. Nor do the studies consider how specific structures sector by sector come to be vulnerable and what specific role development plays post-disaster in shaping a less or a more vulnerable built environment.

Arguably, following the disaster relief phase, impacted populations, particularly the most vulnerable, depend to the greatest extent on development rather than recovery for their well-being. This reflection has two facets. The first is that recovery, with its associated or segmented actions of repair, reconstruction, and resettlement, is burdened with the same questions as non-disaster-driven development. It includes not only questions as to who, when, where, and how the recovery agenda evolves, but also for whom, why, when, where, and who pays and who benefits. The second facet is that most stakeholders by their own structure and procedures define and manage their approach to recovery as something different from development. Despite recognition of desirable actions linking recovery to development—principally in economic terms—development most often stands apart from recovery in institutional policy and practice.

And therein lies the conundrum. It is nonsensical to think that the shortcomings of development actions can be overcome on the back of a post-disaster action called recovery. But it is precisely the process that should occur. The very development actions that contributed to, nay, constructed, the vulnerability must be identified and changed during recovery. Effective DRR requires reflection, discussion, and consensus building; and lessons learned should be brought forward quickly. Consensus may envelop decisions in the form of executive, legislative, and judicial positions. But often analysis of the political and economic implications of enhancing DRR now and in the future is not visible and transparent. And often the definition and acceptance of risk levels for economic and social infrastructure—that is, who is responsible and accountable for what construction standard, who pays, and who benefits—is not made clear.

## Stakeholder Support Created by Disasters: Long View and Private Sector

One theory cites overall positive economic effects to a country experiencing a disaster. Proponents of this line of thought suggest that more international assistance is given to a country following a disaster than would have otherwise been expected (Cavallo et al. 2010). While a short-term downturn in the GDP (the accepted measure of national economic performance) may take place, the infusion of external resources can precipitate a growth in GDP greater than what otherwise might be expected. In other words, experiencing a disaster can be good business from a GDP growth point of view.

Opportunities in post-disaster response relying in large part on the private sector come about in great part because the private sector builds and runs the greatest share of the built environment in the great majority of countries. With more privatization of ownership and/or operation of basic infrastructure and social services, this view is increasingly valid. Studies have shown that state and nongovernmental institutions "often seize opportunities afforded by crises to advance policies that strongly reshape economies, livelihoods, and affected populations' access to spaces and natural resources" (DICAN 2016). It is not surprising that post-disaster situations afford the opportunity to further place in the private sector pieces of the economic and social infrastructure that were traditionally owned, if not maintained and operated, as public sector goods and services.

This part of the free market economy can be seen as development, whereby an alternative approach to provision of goods and services merely takes place in the ambience of propitious transfer following a disaster. The post-disaster situation affords a period of transition, reorientation, and promulgation of policies and practices heretofore impossible to carry out. What is sought are new goals and objectives and often different beneficiaries and providers, usually with a profit motive built in. Instruments for carrying out post-disaster policies and practices are often mainstays of continuing the development agenda: funneling public sector administrative prerogatives and resources through financial instruments and offerings into private sector activities. After some disasters, the authorities in some countries may well respond by imposing reforms that would have been impossible before. These include (1) privatization of public property, making it unavailable to the indigenous people; (2) elimination of laws (deregulation) that include monitoring, reporting, regulation, or enforcement; and (3) reducing or eliminating programs for ordinary citizens needing public assistance ("austerity programs") (Fraser 2009). One person's or group's loss—anticipated, foretold, unavoidable or not—becomes another person's opportunity—awaited, prepared for, sought after.

## Construction of Recovery and Reconstruction of Risk

Post-disaster situations bring tremendous pressures on local, national, and international agencies to replace, preferably on the same sites, damaged and destroyed economic and social infrastructure. All too quickly risk assessment information and its incorporation into the recovery planning process, while evident, lack approval, as are resources for its generation and experienced staff to use it. As the severity and frequency of the damaging hazard event conditioned the exposure before the disaster, lack of risk assessment information often shapes to a very great extent the options for and outcomes of DRR.

Assistance from international and local institutions in constructing policies and programs and acquiring resources to nurture humanitarian assistance reveal how development can coexist in a crowded field ringed with special programs cast as sectors. The disaster sector inherits, so to speak, the outcome of vulnerability created by the development community. The development community takes possession of the reconstructed vulnerability of the post-disaster situation. As the disaster loss is socially determined (Oliver-Smith 2009), so is the reconstructed vulnerability.

The noted inequalities in the population both before and after a disaster are in great part the outcome of tools, processes, and behaviors brought on by pre-existing economic and social configuration (Riederer 2015). Inequalities are created by deliberate choices and lack of choices. Starting at the local level, DRR is a choice, even when such actions are in opposition to values, norms, and standards held by some in society. For example, there are reasons for not choosing and using in recovery the assessments and tools at hand to reduce vulnerability. And there are reasons for emphasizing the need for creating new tools for needed applications of known approaches to DRR. Looking at national disaster declarations and what is requested and what is offered as aid, the documentation reveals which tools are in demand, by whom, and why. It also becomes more clear which behaviors lead to losses and to loss reduction and why (Bender 2014).

Along with the type of hazard impact, the institutional and geopolitical setting significantly conditions recovery. The array of involved institutions working at various levels may have little or no policy, practice, or knowledge of appropriate natural hazard risk reduction for social and economic infrastructure in recovery and build back better. They may be unfamiliar with intricacies of the natural resource setting in the impacted area. They also may be unaware of the composition, alliances, and differences within the political landscape. These institutions may have little or no experience dealing with hazard, exposure, vulnerability, risk, or loss assessments or with DRR monitoring, evaluation, reporting, regulation, and enforcement. Following the disastrous event, their lack of experience becomes evident. If involvement in recovery is primarily by economic and social sector-specific institutions, then the risk assessment process may be mostly shaped by that sector's pre-disaster approach.

On the other hand, institutional involvement might be multi-sector, such as settlement recovery with housing and community service infrastructure. Involved institutions most likely will depend on one or more outside or international advisers for risk assessment and reduction. These advisers may have a voice but usually not a vote in risk reduction decisions. Thus, by default or design, whether a single institution or a group, frequently there may be limited knowledge or competent risk reduction practice involving the affected area, its population, and its local public and private economic and social support groups.

When reconstruction includes resettlement, lead institutions—whether existing or new, local or from afar—may be apt to adopt, follow, or expand familiar, existing pre-disaster development policies and practices. Build back better may not fare any better with resettlement efforts than with recovery of devastated communities in situ. The situation is fed by a lack of compatible DRR actions undertaken by involved institutions such as relief, recovery, or development agencies. And given the temporal pressure for completing economic and social infrastructure reconstruction, stakeholders may have not placed pertinent risk reduction technical dimensions on the agenda for post-disaster institutional boardroom decisions. This is particularly the case when land ownership, land use planning, and proposed natural hazard zoning become issues. Political expediency often dictates risk reduction measures be delayed, put aside, or undertaken as optional actions. Moreover, the history of preparation and use of risk assessments, and even verifiable loss information, may have little influence in the final outcome of social and economic infrastructure projects. Such a history includes the roles of public and private institutions regarding whether DRR is seen by the development community as integral, discretionary, parallel, or an add-on to the repair, rehabilitation, and reconstruction of social and economic infrastructure, particularly lifeline and social service infrastructure.

The degree to which the government will make decisions transparent and take on or assign accountability for the resulting level of risk of economic and social infrastructure varies enormously. Government decisions concerning DRR, often carried out with controversy and discussion, are most visible in deciding the level of regulatory and enforcement processes that control planning—particularly land use planning, building design, and construction during recovery.

Issues of speed versus quality and of rights versus sustainability are certainly real in recovery. These are also, however, the pitched battles of development in general that highlight the values, goals, objectives, and power of the competing participants. It follows that stylized images and slogans of heroes and villains used by competing recovery participants discourage an observable understanding of risks. Moreover, images and slogans are most often built around recognizable approaches such as build back better, and these exist before as well as after the disaster occurs.

## DRR and Development-Driven Recovery

Risk reduction to natural hazard events can be identified as relevant, recommended, and even mandatory to address economic and social infrastructure. Raising or lowering the risk tolerance may not appear in the building design process until after major project decisions have been made. DRR might be assumed part of the recovery process for infrastructure projects, invisible but explicitly or implicitly part of, if nothing else, regulation and enforcement. The use of hazard, exposure, vulnerability, risk, and loss information from the immediately preceding event may not be visible or affect the recovery process. Such information might be used in one-off instances of a specific building type (school), hazard (earthquake), and construction type (reinforced concrete with masonry infill).

On the other hand, at the Third United Nations World Conference on Disaster Risk Reduction Ministerial Round Table on Reconstruction after Disasters, including the theme of "build back better," its summary report stated, "Consider recovery as part of the development agenda, to protect economic growth," in its final point on measures in support of the implementation of the adopted post-2015 SFDRR framework for disaster risk reduction (WCDRR 2015: 51).

---

**Questions for the Recovery Sector about the Recovery Process**

Public and private discussions regarding several pertinent subjects can prove difficult. They include:

(1) Acknowledging scarcity in reconstruction is politically and epistemically produced but not absolute;
(2) Distinguishing who is the client and who is served;
(3) Questioning the "non-negotiables" of reconstruction;
(4) Identifying and implementing reconstruction practices that directly address the socially disruptive and materially destructive impact of geophysical phenomena; and
(5) Peculiarities of historical, material, environmental, sociocultural, and political contingency of both disaster-affected populations and ideas, and techniques of stakeholders intervening to assist in reconstruction. (Barrios 2017)

Moreover, discussion of various subjects may occur when involved participants are not present. These subjects include:

(1) Acceptable levels of risk of loss, and to which natural hazard events;
(2) Cost, use, and benefit of generating HEVRL information amid limited institutional capacity;
(3) Natural resources, land tenure, zoning, codes, and taxes, along with building regulation and enforcement; and
(4) Scientific and technical data collection and review.

Experience has shown that including these topics in discussions of economic development can have unintended consequences. This is particularly true if they relate directly to relationships in and between stakeholders, and between stakeholders and the impacted communities.

---

Pressure to build back quickly is often foremost from local citizens, but often from international and national stakeholders as well. There may be recommendations to use previous building sites due to social and economic ties and legal titles or the absence of alternative sites. All too quickly the need for incorporation of natural hazard, exposure, vulnerability, and risk assessments is forgotten or discarded. Even when such information is sought, the result may be less than what is needed to properly make a determination of risk levels related to building back and certainly to build back better. In fact, pressure to begin recovery may be so great that stakeholders determine time is insufficient to permit or provide necessary resources for such assessments. This is particularly true if hazard, exposure, vulnerability, and risk information was not part, in the first place, of the original development project design/approval and implementation processes.

## The Window of Opportunity with No End in Sight

Disaster risk reduction in recovery can be illustrated by two juxtaposed images. The first is the "window of opportunity" following the "disaster." The second is the intolerable situation with no end in sight for those suffering through the post-disaster recovery, something akin to what is described in Sartre's play *No Exit*. Recovery lays open issues in the disaster-development link of risk, whether in examining shortcomings in planning, design, and construction of the built environment before the natural hazard event or experienced in the recovery.

In the aftermath of a disastrous event there is supposedly a window of opportunity to enlist international assistance, government and local support, and private-sector involvement for vulnerability reduction. The overwhelming impact of losses and resultant exposure of pre-existing vulnerability are assumed to enhance opportunities to make more effective disaster risk reduction possible. Ian Chistopolos states, "The basic reason that the seemingly common sense assumptions regarding the window of opportunity fail to materialize is that, although post-disaster recovery creates a DRR window, it also creates a myriad of other pressures" (Christopolos 2006: 2). From his perspective, humanitarian principles do not mesh well with DRR, which can mean that humanitarian principles and DRR do not resonate with development goals and objectives.

In a broader perspective, the pressure for sharing certain principles comes from choices to be made in competing claims. Misconceptions about the presence or absence of risk management in development continue, whether before or after a disaster. Risk to natural hazard events is dealt with even where it is not reduced or when responsibility and accountability are not assigned. As for evaluating DRR policies and practices in the rush to recovery, there are both those that led to the vulnerability of failed infrastructure components and those that if carried out in recovery can avoid repetitive losses.

> ### New Normal Bound by Painful Choices
>
> Heather McIlvaine-Newsad writes, "After extensive research in areas that were flooded in 2008 Casagrande (*David G.*), Jones (*E.C.*), and I (2015) discovered that despite internal conflicts, socio-economic, and/or political differences, people were able to identify vital components of their community they needed to protect for survival. Once the levees breached and the flood waters receded leaders had to make painful choices about what they wanted their community to look like in the future. Would they rebuild in vulnerable locations or reorganize and re-imagine their community based on the 'new' normal? Additional research shows that in order for communities to rebound there must be people in charge who are not afraid to make difficult and unpopular choices. Communities who have approached this task mindfully are more successful in the long run than those who have been reactionary and worked against each other" (McIlvaine-Newsad 2016: 1).

Considering the imagery of no exit as the post-disaster situation, hellish as it can be, communities evolve through a series of well-known experiences—demands, initiatives, confessions, exposures, failures, competitions, and disagreements. In the end it is readily apparent that the built environment—or what is left of it—and the natural environment with its ecosystem structures and functions do not actually constitute all of the suffering. Participating in the reconstruction, both victims and benefactors, with their social, cultural, economic, and religious beliefs and subsequent actions, also constitute each other's hell.

"Hell is other people" is the message of Sartre's play. Yet society with its participants, whether they are participating in recovery in the name of development or development in the name of recovery, must go on. Sartre's play concludes with, "*Eh bien, continuons*" ("Well, let's get on with it").

## In Sum

Disaster losses truly bring penetrating insight into the role of development in risk creation. Losses make visible the disaster-development link and gaps related to vulnerability in recovery and reconstruction that span images between a window of opportunity and no exit. These images exhibit the gap between acting on awareness of risk in development and the impact of natural hazard events stemming from that risk.

Across the spectrum of public and private endeavors, institutional weaknesses are revealed and addressed in unexpected and unimaginable ways. Often stakeholders and local inhabitants least expected to push forward a DRR agenda become champions in reconstructing pieces of the social and economic infrastructure. The development and DRR communities, committed verbally to take up anew risk reduction in an effort to "build back better," find ways to bridge gaps beginning in their own institutions and make bridges with new partners. This includes creating opportunities for synchronized humanitarian assistance and reconstruction agendas involving communication, coordination, and cooperation. Key to these efforts is recognizing that DRR requires evaluating, prioritizing, supporting, and executing actions, whether posed in the humanitarian assistance or recovery or development actions. The willingness to act and to be observed acting is stronger than in the pre-disaster era. The remaining built environment is by definition an example of what can be accomplished. In place of risk-prone preferences confronting knowledge, knowledge leads to preferences through generation of new practices. The challenge is to advance development policy so as to use DRR to resolve previous development practice shortcomings.

Key stakeholders' decision-making positions may or may not ensure DRR actions in recovery as development continues. Stakeholder governance includes technical and political dimensions. Technical content shaping goals and objectives for DRR goes into loan and grant review meetings for reconstruction; political decisions to promote economic development as the priority often come out.

Gaps present between DRR policies and development actions before the disastrous event can remain or appear during the recovery. It is not an issue of too little time. At issue is the objective, purpose, and product of recovery when the needs and wants of those most directly impacted by the disastrous event, particularly the poor and disadvantaged, are not the primary concern. The often-announced strategy to carry out DRR in recovery alongside development actions is not only formidable, particularly in global development policy and practices, but also misspoken and questionable, given development's role in constructing risk. Perhaps how, where, why, and to what ends stakeholders and societal units deal with DRR during reconstruction serve as an excellent indicator of their intent to carry out DRR actions in the vulnerability reduction of existing economic and social infrastructure and of new infrastructure to be built.

# CHAPTER 6

# Continuity in the Name of Constituents

Overall, the development sector approach to DRR for the built environment evolves from responding to disasters and the call for physical science and engineering to answer vulnerability issues. Stakeholders, who are part of the development community, recognize the impact of disaster events and the opportunity for the disaster sector to garner support. The evolution of DRR, and in a broader context DRM, is from responding to identifiable constituents: victims impacted by disaster and donors who come to their aid. Yet built environment vulnerability brought about by development often continues. Exposure in each economic and social infrastructure sector varies according to types of hazards, physical settings and geographic scale, sector administration and ownership, and impacted population groups.

Those who shape the disaster-development continuum—that is, stakeholders and other entities both public and private who finance, design, and build at all geopolitical and administrative levels—have created interlocking, intertwined, or contrasting policies and actions. The actions are part of development or disaster management, or both, and are supported through considerable effort. Levels of risk of loss of infrastructure that will prompt a disaster declaration are present in all countries and are not likely to disappear any time soon. All of these examples demonstrate the disaster-development continuum in the name of their respective constituents.

Stakeholders maintain traditional development sector silos, along with their crosscutting issue sectors. Plans are drawn up, budgets are prepared and approved, loans and grants are drawn down, and social and economic infrastructure is created. For stakeholders, creating sectors and funding is a facet of carrying out policy, programs, and practice.

Historically, development and DRM sectors may be coming to recognize risk creation as "what development was doing before the disaster."

Beginning recently, approved international development loan programs focusing on the built environment and other actions often include provision for emergency financial assistance in case of a declared disaster. Disaster-related international financing in its broadest definition is limited, typically representing about 2 percent of total international development assistance. This disaster-related financing during the period 1980–2009 was approximately divided among emergency response (70 percent) and reconstruction (25 percent); the remaining 5 percent was for disaster prevention and preparedness (World Bank 2012: 31). Stakeholders believe such financing needs will continue to grow, so they create sectors and funding silos to entice and secure disaster and development programs under a variety of banners and slogans.

The growing need for reconstruction financing related directly to increasing disaster declarations brings several observations. The first is that additional disaster-related financing might be taken from programmed development assistance: international assistance may become a zero-sum game. Second, as MDBs respond to SFDRR and put more emphasis on DRM rather than reconstruction, that may also impact non-disaster-related financing because it might include greater investment in retrofitting vulnerable existing economic and social infrastructure. Third, greater emphasis on either or both DRM and reconstruction may leave attention to retrofitting existing vulnerable economic and social infrastructure with proportionally even less resources than are presently available. Literally, infrastructure would have to be damaged, destroyed, or targeted for special DRM treatment. And fourth, the total sum of international and national financing may constitute only enough resources to carry out a "development as survival" strategy where all public infrastructure expenditures are either for reconstruction or retrofitting.

Considering the side-by-side existence of development and various crosscutting sectors, stakeholder groups see strength in maintaining disparate, even contradictory policies and practices within the same institution. For example, the OAS initiated programs in many of these areas in the 1980s through direct technical cooperation, training, applied research, and participation in international conferences and workshops. Such initiatives demand financial support from donors of all types. In the case of DRR, inducements to gain needed support include three elements: (1) changes in how donors perceive governments and collaborating technical cooperation agencies address natural hazard assessment and mitigation issues; (2) incentives for stakeholders experiencing vulnerability to undertake analysis of risk; and (3) assignment of accountability for losses (CIDIE 1988).

## Origins of DRR as a Destination for Support

*Entre bomberos, no se pisan las mangueras.*
[Firemen don't step on each other's hoses.]
—Well-known saying in Latin America

Examining silos and DRR helps to better understand development's role in construction of vulnerability of the built environment and why risk reduction of the built environment is lacking despite disaster risk management initiatives. Specialized disaster-related humanitarian assistance and reconstruction programs, led by the stakeholders and later the United Nations, took place from the 1970s to end of the 1980s, followed by the International Decade for Natural Disaster Reduction (1990–1999), with its focus on disaster response and preparation. Attention to prevention-focused risk management was highlighted in the Hyogo Framework for Action (2005–2015), followed by the Sendai Framework for Disaster Risk Reduction (2015–2030), with its emphasis on systemic assessment of all types of catastrophic risk.

Programs at all levels generally prioritizing post-disaster and risk identification have become increasingly effective institutional actions, as has the fundraising by the programs' institutional sponsors. Presently through SFDRR, stakeholders have chosen to act with crosscutting sectors alongside development actors on disaster reduction issues. To do so, they have amplified and diversified their programs and target areas, and identified specific needed resources and geographic target areas. Only general published policy is visible, but the evolution of policy and program is as much about respecting self-proclaimed roles and turf areas within and among the stakeholders as it is about questioning development's role in creating risk.

Beginning in 2000, discussions about "mainstreaming" DRR into development clearly targeted both sovereign states and MDBs. Sentiments ranged from "development already considers risk" to "specialized entities and mandated responsibilities are being put in place to deal with disaster management." Perhaps UNDP's strategy for mainstreaming DRR and CCA into the development process (Planitz 2013) is the most prominent recommended approach by the UN and its collection of sovereign states, also echoed by most stakeholders. By using a lineal approach similar to that of economic development, hazards and risks are identified, and alternative DRR and CCA options are identified and prioritized. There is only a general call for development processes to include sustainability and resilience, but not as a principal goal and certainly not as a principal driver of DRR. Mainstreaming DRR in development processes is not mandated. Preferred options for DRR action at the national and local level are proposed for incorporation into sector plans, programs, and projects.

Many stakeholders have followed a stair-step agenda of national development plans and strategies, preparation of budgets and regulations, and ultimately enforcement. Thus begins the DRR actions, but these are not defined as specific goals and objectives of development actions.

With risk to natural hazard events magnified by climate change and tied to development, progress for disaster reduction and climate-resilient development is said to hinge on pursuing disaster risk reduction, climate change adaptation, resilience, and sustainable development as commonly supported goals. Risk reduction is to be considered an essential investment in all four endeavors. But the cost is often identified as an option or adjunct to development programs or projects. Some development stakeholders recommend financial disaster risk reduction to cover costs should a disaster be declared but without defining the acceptable level of risk in physical, economic, or financial loss. This is visible when development program and project budgets isolate approval for the cost of not only DRR, but also CCA and resilience actions.

It is important to remember that each of these four crosscutting sectors (DRM, CCA, sustainable development, and resilience) are well established with calls for mainstreaming DRR and CCA using DRM national authorities, policy, legislative frameworks, and databases. Putting resilience into practice necessitates a broader base of action because it goes beyond DRR. Throughout this construct, development is not, per se, a self-selected instrument to implement DRR; development is a receptor. DRR is not usually offered through development programs. This reflects DRM's status as a sector seeking support under its own banner, and the development sector accepting DRM as responsible for all things "disaster."

When recovery is viewed as an opportunity and entry point for DRR, it reflects development as apart but coexisting with recovery and DRR as something brought to recovery. Fostering integrated approaches across disciplines is needed to address risk—where "disciplines" becomes the code word for economic and social sectors. Inside recovery actions, policies and programs are measured in monetary units for reporting on progress. Quantifying even the number of physical units or monetary value of more or less vulnerable infrastructure is not always carried out. Economic and social sector participation is targeted, yet defined as a recipient, not a driver, of DRR, CCA, sustainable development, and resilience. And it is not common to have an overt decision about the acceptable level of risk to loss for economic and social infrastructure to natural hazard events as part of development projects to rebuild, as well as retrofit infrastructure components.

## Participants as Constituents

In most cases the disaster risk management sector oversees national disaster risk reduction, including that of the built environment, through specialized agencies. For more than forty years, global efforts have continued to directly support countries in disaster risk reduction through EM and DRM. Following the requisite declaration of disaster following an event, those habitually convened by the international disaster management community to discuss DRR are public sector entities responsible for emergency management. They are also often charged—by choice or mandate—with monitoring, regulation, enforcement, and alert. The public entities are usually national and responsible for national planning and budget. Other participants convened in the DRM sector include researchers, academicians, and politicians. At the international level, usually PVOs, NGOs, and specialized UN, regional, and national agencies working in disaster assistance following natural hazard events and other types of crisis are convened. Most often not present at international, regional, and national meetings are the owners and operators of vulnerable economic and social infrastructure and associated population groups from traditional sectors such as agriculture, communications, education, energy, housing, tourism, transportation, social infrastructure, and urban lifeline infrastructure. Rarely is there participation by organized community groups whose identification is based on geographic place, income, or ethnicity.

Some countries now have broadened their emergency management and vulnerability reduction agenda, often using participation in subregional, intergovernmental organizations and their associated disaster risk management specialized agencies. Subregional (multinational) intergovernmental agencies have proved to be close enough to national and subnational government entities to help identify and propose action on national issues. The scope of these agencies is also broad enough to address intergovernmental issues and provide economy of scale to support collective action by countries with aid from the international community. They are forming de facto subregional platforms alongside those formally created by the United Nations Office for Disaster Risk Reduction (UNDRR).

With HFA and now SFDRR and regional disaster-related frameworks as a backdrop, the focus on acquired commitments and implementation of some regional, subregional, and national initiatives now increasingly includes "reducing underlying risk factors" as a priority action. At varying levels of policy support, such initiatives are unveiling the breadth and depth of individual country and subregion vulnerability, their existing risk reduction capacity, and the need for structural, financial, and operational change in how development takes place and the built environment comes about.

Lack of follow-through by national governments is manifest by not specifically mandating natural hazard risk reduction sector by sector or not providing funding needed to carry out mandated or approved risk reduction actions. National and sector budgets have funded relatively little investment in disaster risk reduction to be undertaken by the owners and operators themselves, whether public or private. This is in part the result of conditioning many countries that if it is worth doing, the international development community will be supportive. In some cases, there has been little national government capacity or interest in mapping, data collection, monitoring, and evaluation to support disaster risk reduction, all of which are or could be part of a national government DRR strategy.

A parallel situation exists at the international level. Sector-specific ministerial meetings that proclaim policies and promote programs receive little attention and even fewer resources to evaluate, define, choose, and implement acceptable levels of risk in existing vulnerable infrastructure, new project initiatives, and post-disaster reconstruction and resettlement projects. International action through professional and private-public business associations and working groups exists in some cases. But in post-disaster reconstruction, DRR by traditional economic and social sectors usually takes place at the local level in the very visible DRM, community development, and humanitarian assistance organizations.

When stakeholders defer from following agreed-upon actions, they have to provide their own protective political cover. By creating specialized agencies, stakeholders can argue they are indeed taking action, but through the specialized agency mechanism. This explains in part why some stakeholders support specialized DRR agencies and accept them as so named "crosscutting" issues such as environment operating separately and distinctly from traditional development sectors.

Meanwhile, the strategy of seeking support for DRR implementation through collaboration with subject areas identified as sectors (and operating as silos) continues. An example is a timely and well-intentioned effort to include protection of populations from natural hazard events as part of the Universal Declaration of Human Rights. This would name specific sectors to deal visibly and publicly with loss of life and property through UN specialized agency ministerial forums and declarations (e.g., education and health).

While vulnerability of populations to natural hazard events is certainly a health, safety, and welfare issue, it may not become part of the intentionally tightly bound basic human rights discussion, given sovereign states' management of human rights policy at present. Some argue that until currently accepted basic rights are respected, social vulnerability to disaster victims ought not to be added to human rights demands. In addition, calls for expanding official international intervention in disaster relief and recovery illuminate the mostly still unfinished discussion by stakeholders as to what extent DRR of economic and social infrastructure is part of humanitarian assistance.

Finally, there is the subject of sovereignty. Sovereign states and other stakeholders call on each other to negotiate and then sign and ratify accords. The accords define a prescribed yet usually bounded, conditional range of actions to be taken. Accord signers may or may not demand consensus, but whatever the acceptance level, it represents a least common denominator of actions individual countries are willing to implement. Accords are only as valuable as the signers' actions to follow through.

Some accords on DRR, if followed, would bring progress in vulnerability reduction. Some countries take less DRR action and could perhaps suffer some consequences, given the international response following a disaster declaration—usually financial. Not only sovereign states but other stakeholders often attempt to have it both ways: committing to an accord, then doing as they see needed by taking a position of exceptionalism, budget constraints, referencing a previous agreement accepted by consensus or at least the majority, deferring to "best local practice" for technical guidance in reconstruction (e.g., building codes covering earthquake and hurricane impact), or simply withdrawing from the accord.

In attempting to follow the both-and approach (development with risk reduction), sovereign states' actions for people's betterment and well-being appear to depend more on reducing economic and physical loss through resilience in addition to addressing the priority risk of financial loss. This is in contrast with the economic development practice dealing with the built environment, which posits "with and without" DRR approaches. Moreover, differentiation between universal—whether called global, regional, or national—policies and practices, and local actions is often revealed in whether DRR choices made reflect "either-or" rather than "both-and" approaches as determined by social and political preferences as well as availability of resources. In the end, sovereign states are quite capable of calling for development and for DRM without combining or even coordinating the two sets of choices.

## Development Actions in Context

Recognizing networks that make up the built environment is a principal part of understanding DRR in development. Their physical components include emergency and social facility lifelines, trade corridors, telecommunication networks, potable water networks, transportation waterways, hydroelectric power generation and transmission, and health facility networks. Many network operations depend on some form of "just in time" delivery of parts or services and shared staff. Regardless of their relationship to the systems, people are becoming cognizant of these networks and their components. People are also aware of their dependency on the networks, particularly when they fail, whether at the local level as part of international networks that operate in the regional or global economy.

From an industrialized country's perspective, an obvious use of globalization is to gain market dominance—dependency by others on its marketed products and services. And for poor countries, an obvious objective is making industrialized countries dependent on its raw materials and capacity for production of goods and services, along with increased purchasing power.

Contemplating the cost of effective DRR is often a challenge. Some national governments question whether they can afford DRR in the same way that they question whether they can afford environmental safeguards and other mandated actions—e.g., avoiding destruction of the structure and function of natural ecosystems large and small—while pursuing development goals and objectives focusing on expansion, globalization, and profit. Thus, in the name of development, failing to include disaster risk reduction, which prompts in some cases avoidance of declaring a disaster following a natural hazard event, countries continue to put more and more people in harm's way, engendering disasters from development and the development of disasters (Bender 2012).

No matter the form of stakeholder participation, the concern is formation of policies that will shape how decisions will be made. From global to local politics, decision-making depends to a great extent on the vocabulary used and how natural hazard event frequency and severity are framed. Decision-making also depends on how the disaster "story" spreads in both generic and specific event reporting about the actual natural hazard event. That may include science-based governance or government-directed science, which may well be part of what does or does not form part of the natural hazard risk discussion and official decision-making processes. The hope is that the FORIN methodology will be more widely applied as a mainstream instrument in disaster risk research. On the subject of researching risk, FORIN states, "Only when the lens of research shifts in focus from analyzing the effects of exogenous events to the causes of endogenous risks will it be possible to assign responsibility to social actors for managing disaster risks" (Oliver-Smith et al. 2016: 6). In addition to its social sector actors, the development process needs to present participants from all other appropriate, applicable development activities when discussing assignment of responsibility for the built environment. Understanding risk construction, not just the breadth and frequency of hazard types, can and should lead to success in achieving targets and expected outcomes of the SFDRR.

The disaster story may include the role of the disaster moment, but the construction of risk must be also discussed. That will include the juxtaposition of belief, faith, certainty, and doubt concerning exposure, vulnerability, risk, and loss, along with the level of acceptable risk that affect development decisions. Also, often missing is discussion of low-value interventions in DRR (as in low-value interventions in health care), no-regret DRR actions, and how the human condition of exposure is frequently presented only in relation to the "disaster cycle."

## Openings in Disaster Recovery

Disasters play a role in opening development processes to address change, create political space, and modify the structure of power. But the very execution of recovery in development can thwart change in capturing potential opportunities and overcoming shortcomings in knowledge, policy, and practice of DRR in development.

It is common to view the post-disaster response as relying on the private sector, given that the private sector builds and runs the greatest share of the built environment (DICAN 2016). It is not surprising that post-disaster situations give the private sector access to owning or managing even more pieces of the economic and social infrastructure that were maintained, if not guarded as public sector goods and services. Part of a development-driven recovery looks for opportunities to transfer the provision of some services of various kinds from the public to the private sector. The post-disaster situation affords a period of transition, reorientation, and promulgation of policies and practices heretofore not possible to carry out. Sought are new, different goals and objectives and often different beneficiaries and providers—usually with a not-for-profit or at least a program-sustaining motive built in. Instruments for carrying out post-disaster policies and practices are often the mainstays of continuing the development agenda: funneling public sector resources through tax exemptions, including development bonds, grants, and subsidies into private sector activities.

Policies and actions related to resource allocation affecting DRR can amplify as well as lessen vulnerability of economic and social infrastructure. Such resources may be economic, social, human, physical, natural, or political. Armin Sparf, an international fire suppression specialist, has shared his thoughts and noted that resource-related universal and local actions evident in differing economic models may involve (1) various risk transfer schemes; (2) market mechanisms and business practices that amplify or diminish risks of damage and loss; and (3) illegal and corrupt practices by those in power that affect all facets of building regulation and enforcement (personal communication, Sparf, September 2018).

Discussion about opening opportunities for improved risk reduction is not only about political support. The challenge is to have society committed to identifying links between knowledge, policy, and practice that allow development decisions to focus on acceptable levels of risk that include stated responsibility and accountability. Whether profits are pocketed by the many or the few and subsidies in the form of risk are born with or without assignment of responsibility and accountability, they are to be undertaken with visibility and transparency. Regardless of the economic model, the vulnerability of post-disaster economic livelihoods and community infrastructure can fare better or worse than what existed before the disaster. Whether following disastrous natural hazard events, retrofitting existing vulnerable infrastructure, or in new development, investing in vulnerability and risk reduction benefits someone.

## In Sum

This discussion includes the concept of disaster capitalism, which is spawned from the same free market system that prompts much of the buying and selling of financial risk instruments related to the built infrastructure. Disaster capitalism, a free market economy, or any other economic form should be subject to a visible and transparent process of choosing whose risk is reduced, how, why, by whom, and who pays. Wealth ownership might still be a social challenge, but risk management, including to natural hazard events, is an overarching issue no matter what the economic or social class. Perhaps wealth in the form of physical assets is best viewed by considering the vulnerability of those assets to natural hazard events—and now to other catastrophic events. There is no evidence that a particular form of national economy has consistently made risk reduction a societal priority.

The discussion now proceeds to a response to the need for a new framework for DRR in development and will explore how the very work of risk management presents choices, including use of HEVRL assessments and MERRE processes, as well as a broad array of participants across many disciplines in the assignment of responsibility and accountability. Next the discussion will focus on HEVRL assessments of natural hazard risk as an integral support to MERRE processes that inform decision-making and application in development. From there the discussion will examine DRR in current and emerging economic development forces generating the built environment.

# Part II
# ONCE AND FUTURE DISASTER RISK REDUCTION

CHAPTER 7

# Redefining Disaster Risk Reduction in Development of the Built Environment

Discussion of the disaster-development linkage to this point has focused on risk with a multidisciplinary view of vulnerability, natural hazard events, and loss. Also noted were the disaster-cycle paradigm, creation of the disaster sector by its various constituents, and creation of vulnerability of the built environment.

As discussed earlier, the science and engineering communities built their approach to disasters on the strength of their design and construction knowledge and experience. The social science community built its approach on inadequacies and inequalities of postcolonial development revealed in various forms of societal risk, including disasters resulting from natural events. Social scientists also used the disaster event as a way to participate alongside stakeholders in humanitarian assistance and emergency management. The emerging disaster community, responding to the growing number of disasters around the globe, was able then and continues now to reinforce its institutional and operational presence in terms of political visibility and financial support.

There is a conditioned presence of disaster risk reduction carried out by development sector participants, including the stakeholders of this discussion, who often hold no responsibility or accountability for the ensuing level of risk of the built environment. GAR19 notes that risk from natural and man-made hazards is the core rationale for the call to integrate DRR into development. Development-based drivers of risk threaten reaching the Sustainable Development Goals (SDGs), and disaster impacts point to unsustainable development gains. Furthermore, GAR19 points to a required shift to systems-based thinking in mainstreaming risk reduction within development and points out that progress will occur at entry points such as policy, planning, budgeting, technical review, stakeholder engagement, and finance (UNDRR 2019: 354).

**Disaster-Development Linkage in the Language of Development**

In 1988 the Committee of International Development Institutions on the Environment (CIDIE), the group of international development institutions brought together by the United Nations Environment Programme (UNEP) to work on emerging environmental management issues, published *Incorporating Natural Hazard Assessment and Mitigation into Project Preparation*. As a development "insider" stakeholder, CIDIE was formed to identify and discuss environment-based challenges to the development community on themes stemming in part from the UN Conference on the Human Environment (1972 Stockholm Conference).

The OAS considered natural hazards to be an integral part of subjects to be discussed in the preparation of an environmental impact assessment (EIA) and environmental impact statement (EIS). The discussions reviewed the earliest EIA-EIS subjects, which analyzed not only the impact of development efforts on environment(s), but also the impact of ecosystem structure and function on development efforts. The OAS–Department of Regional Development, the CIDIE member responsible for preparing the volume 2 document, provided technical assistance services to OAS member states that included pre-investment project identification studies based on natural resources. Issues of natural hazard exposure and vulnerability analysis were included in preparing pre-feasibility projects for financing.

Publication of the CIDIE volume 2 document was groundbreaking, if not naive, in stating that (1) natural hazard management is part of environmental management issues; and (2) natural hazard risk is a development issue.

In the years following 1988 it became apparent that, particularly with creation of the IDNDR, the disaster management community, not the environment community, was claiming dominion over vulnerability and disaster risk reduction. DRM became a sector apart from development. Confronted with demands for stakeholder-led actions through UNEP and the Intergovernmental Panel on Climate Change (IPCC) as well as the IDNDR, CIDIE's call for incorporating natural hazard information during the development investment project formulation process was lost. CIDIE members and their partners turned their attention to the UNEP and IPCC to address environmental matters and to IDNDR, which clearly described the issue facing nations and populations as part of a disaster cycle, but without reference to development.

CIDIE participants included the African Development Bank, Asian Development Bank, Caribbean Development Bank, Central American Development Bank, Inter-American Development Bank, Organization of American States, World Bank, United Nations Development Programme, and United Nations Environment Programme. Observer institutions included the Canadian International Development Agency, United Kingdom Overseas Development Administration, and United States Agency for International Development.

## Redefining DRR in Development

Most stakeholders present a nuanced call for a new approach to DRR through development. Such a needed new approach, however, means laying aside the misnomer that risk management is absent from development and therefore must be brought or "mainstreamed" into development policy and practice. A new approach also requires development to take responsibility and accountability through visible and transparent risk management practices.

Such an approach does not call for the elimination of risk or pretend that such a goal is possible. It does call for identifying and working for risk reduction to acceptable levels, meaning the affected society understands and is willing to confront the consequences of that level of loss. It is a call for distinguishing between the anticipated risk of loss to the built environment components, the designed level of risk through customs and norms, and the level of risk in existing and completed new construction, including in post-disaster reconstruction. There is no questioning the existence of risk drivers, but there is a need to identify and assign responsibility and accountability for each risk driver.

All development embodies risk and through its policy and practice does consider at specified times actions to eliminate, abate, transfer, or assume certain risks. What cannot be taken for granted is risk accountability and responsibility. Risk may be created without being recognized. This call for a new approach to disaster risk reduction focuses on risk with assigned responsibility and accountability using tools and assessments that lead to development choices lessening disaster risk.

Decades ago, development theory and practice were responding not only to opportunities for transforming frontier and colonial expanses through vibrant economic and social occupation of the landscape, but also as timely response to an increasing number of natural and human catastrophic events. The opportunities offered economic growth and societal choices; disaster responses focused on timely efforts to reduce loss after the event. Disaster relief was not intended to become synonymous with development assistance, with depletion of scarce financial resources destined for new investments. Institutional divisions were not to be created between disaster management and development assistance, particularly for the poor (Bender 1989).

In 1994, Alberto Giesecke noted, "However, I believe that much remains to be done: evaluation of natural risks (estimations of severity, frequency and location of natural phenomena that could cause disaster); studies of community vulnerability, be it structural, social, economic or cultural; estimation of losses; research that leads to a better understanding of the factors that contribute to natural phenomena; prediction methods... and social studies to identify human activities that exacerbates the impact of natural phenomena" (Giesecke 1994, punctuation added for clarity).

Disasters are not confined to poorer countries, although they do impact poorer people disproportionately in rich and poor countries alike. Presently efforts to reduce and control damage and loss are outweighed by processes generating new risk in societies, as Allan Lavell and Andrew Maskrey (2014) have noted in their policy research on disasters and their underlying causes. Addressing the central question why this increase is happening despite much greater scientific knowledge and technical capacity related to risk and disaster was begun by Gilbert White, a geographer and founding proponent in the early 1940s of floodplain management based on human activity adaptation (White, Kates, and Burton 2001).

## Diagnosis and Misdiagnosis

This chapter will focus on redefining DRR in development, in which development policy and practice will be a principal, if not the principal, instrument dealing with the vulnerability of economic and social infrastructure to natural hazard events. DRR of the built environment in development is thus proposed as a choice about whether to join, supplant, or supersede current priority development goals.

When preparing for the IDNDR in the mid-1980s, the organizers of the decade promulgated the diagnosis that there was a lack of knowledge about risk of natural hazard events pertaining to populations and the built environment. More importantly, it was proposed that application of science and engineering knowledge was the way to create economic and social infrastructure to withstand natural hazard impacts. Additionally, natural hazard events, no matter the extent of their impact on the built environment, were often referred to as disasters, as in, "the disaster struck at such and such time and place."

The emphasis on disaster reduction was on what was to be built as new development, not on what was to be rebuilt following declared disasters or on the existing vulnerability of economic and social infrastructure. In other words, the diagnosis called for support for infrastructure design and research and its application through professional practice in development actions, as well as improved disaster management whenever a disaster occurred. Questions remaining for social scientists to answer were who is impacted by disasters and why, and what happens to those impacted after a disaster, whether declared or undeclared.

In most cases the present lack of DRR is not due to the absence of social science, engineering, architecture, and physical science knowledge and experience. This misdiagnosis occurred in part from the consequences of how risk was and is managed. Risk was not identified in a visible, transparent way that encompassed decision-making related to development or acceptable risk and assigning responsibility and accountability for risk in creating the built environment. This lack is precisely because development processes, which have many stakeholders as participants, address risk management only through the development paradigm. The development participants avoided naming, blaming, or most importantly, visibly and transparently pronouncing the level of acceptable risk and accepting a defining role in being responsible and accountable for creation of risk of the built environment.

In the 1970s and '80s, physical, economic, and financial losses continued to mount from natural hazard events, revealing a separation between commitment to both catastrophic event response and natural hazard risk reduction (CIDIE 1988). Under the blessing of the development sector, responses to such catastrophic loss increasingly became part of recovery led by humanitarian assistance participants but were off-budget, and therefore separate from development actions. DRR became a loss management issue distributed among financial and economic areas of the impacted economy to be dealt with by political and donor mechanisms. For many stakeholders, disasters are considered a problem for development, yet they do not view development as having created the problem.

## Diagnosis to Treatment

The proposal for a new framework for DRR implementation comes from correcting the misdiagnosis. Now recognized is the need to consistently and appropriately not only identify but act on the level of risk to natural hazard events for each component of economic and social infrastructure. Whether that infrastructure exists or is to be built or rebuilt through post-disaster recovery, the level of expected risk of damage and destruction must be determined. The appropriate risk reduction actions including the identification of what or who is responsible and accountable for the chosen level of risk of loss in a visible and transparent way must be undertaken.

Correct diagnosis includes using the knowledge and experience of not only available professionals, but also artisans and traditional craftspeople; they can retrofit existing economic and social infrastructure and apply their knowledge and experience in all built environment design and construction. Acquired and new knowledge can be applied to both formal and informal development processes for investment in DRR, targeting components by hazard type, location, and frequency.

Demanding responsibility and accountability does not contradict the announcement in GAR19 that the era of hazard-by-hazard risk reduction must give way to understanding the systemic nature of risk (UNDRR 2019: iv). Recognizing the macro dimensions of risk is needed—for the perilous state of populations at risk to a variety of calamities from various causal factors impacting populations around the globe. What must also continue is micro engagement of DRR at the national, subnational, and local levels. Meeting the DRR challenge to the built environment occurs through recognizing the physical, economic, and financial risk of the constituent parts that constitute the whole of society.

DRM, CCA, resilience, and sustainable development sectors continually examine their relationship to development. They cast themselves as apart from the development sector. Guiding documents of these crosscutting sectors call for mainstreaming DRR into development. Sometimes the guidance casts itself as a distinct alternative to current development policies, programs, and practices. On the one hand, crosscutting sectors comment on target populations impacted and losses of associated economic and social infrastructure. On the other hand, the development community focuses, operates, and measures progress in economic terms.

There exist many solutions for infrastructure vulnerability problems that have been identified. But discussion of the goals and objectives of the IDNDR, HFA, and SFDRR point to the need for solutions if only the existing problems of vulnerability were recognized. For example, in the mid-1980s to 1990s risk reduction issues of existing vulnerable schools and hospitals related to collapse or severe damage from natural hazard events were understood. Components to be retrofitted or reconstructed were identified or could have been identified. Tools and practices to deal with these risks were known. Then, as now, discussion should not have been about developing new macro assessments of risk, but one of making sure that the correct DRR action was being executed at each vulnerable school and hospital site.

In the past fifty-odd years, physical science, engineering, and architecture provided most of the tools and practices available to reduce loss of life and property of economic and social infrastructure. They focus, most simply, on the physical aspects of natural hazard impact of infrastructure. They were known and applicable—some in earlier forms during preparation for the IDNDR and HFA. However, discussion of what was and still is needed to lessen physical risk of the built environment has been avoided.

Reframing DRR in development means redefining development nomenclature and discourse. This reframing includes a different discussion and list of development goals and objectives that reveal how risk to natural hazard events is to be considered and addressed. The reframing will help development institutions, public and private at whatever scale, become more likely to consider risk reduction as a principal measure of development progress.

---

**Address Very Real and Likely Global Threats**

Over several decades, Terry Jeggle worked as a learned, experienced, and gentle practitioner of humanitarian assistance in many regions of the globe. In one of our exchanges about populations at risk, he wrote, "There is also a need to recognize the complicity of established political interests of individual governments and many of the organizations which comprise the 'international development community' in maintaining such persistent failures. Ultimately in the language of the discipline involved, there is a need for a framework with assigned and acknowledged responsibilities to be created, and resourced to address the basic human needs of people exposed and vulnerable to the very real and likely global threats of the 21st century" (personal correspondence, December 2013).

---

## Moving from Response to Risk Reduction

Further discussion of problems and solutions in DRR includes the observation that solutions do best when they embody policy built on knowledge and practice. Susan Cutter writes that needed is "a re-framing of current programs and policies away from response to more pro-active and longer term emphases on hazard mitigation and enhancing resilience at local to global scales" (Cutter 2014b).

But when the problem is intentionally or otherwise misidentified, known solutions can be more readily ignored. How were the underlying causes of vulnerability created in the development process, not only those of physical design and construction, but also infrastructure siting, maintenance, and unintended residual risk? Prescriptions for risk reduction should be part of the development process.

The proposed framework for managing the disaster-development linkage of the built environment includes using hazard, exposure, vulnerability, risk, and loss (HEVRL) assessments, and monitoring, evaluation, reporting, regulation, and enforcement (MERRE) processes, sector by sector, component by component.

> ### DRR as Bottom-Up or Top-Down
>
> Concerning discussions on a possible program approach for the proposed UN International Decade for Natural Disaster Reduction (IDNDR) for the 1990s, Robert Hinshaw has written,
>
> "James (Ken) Mitchell, former Chicago student and research associate of (Gilbert) White's, agreed to chair an ad hoc committee on the subject under the National Research Council of the NAS. The committee's draft reports focused on improving the use of existing scientific information rather than on the development of new research and development initiatives. . . . Gilbert had joined a short-term study in the Yucatan, Mexico, on attitudes and approaches regarding hazards and their mitigation. An example supplied by the Yucatan schools impressed Gilbert with its ingenuity and simplicity: re-hang the doors of schools to open outward rather than inward, as was the custom so that earthquake rubble within the room would not prevent the occupants from opening the doors and escaping from the building. From this suggestion, Mitchell's ad hoc committee agreed that increasing the safety and security of schools would be an appropriate theme, since school personnel are already available in any country and represent comparatively comparable samples, at least in terms of socioeconomic status" (Hinshaw 2006: 178).
>
> A bottom-up effort at school vulnerability reduction around the globe would have provided a robust research opportunity and actual risk reduction to be carried out by local groups through a demand-driven approach. The proposal prepared by the ad hoc committee appointed in 1986 by the National Research Council and presented in 1987 was not approved. The task force was dismissed.

## Framework Evolution

The new framework centers on development's ownership of risk and risk reduction based upon an acceptable level of risk. Acceptable risk to loss, damage, and destruction of economic and social infrastructure involves two facets: (1) understanding the expected loss, given specific natural hazard events that impact specific components of the built environment; and (2) including societal actions that actually review and carry out visible and transparent decision-making as to what is acceptable risk. MERRE processes help define responsible and accountable actions using HEVRL assessments in determining potential loss. With direct involvement of international finance institutions, bilateral agencies, and NGOs of the international development community, risk reduction to natural hazard events must be redefined through development processes that include DRR policies, planning, programs, and practice (Bender 2009b).

## Practice Over Acquired Knowledge and Vocalized Policy

Although present approaches to risk measurement and management are considered in some circles inadequate to deal with the interconnectedness of hazard, exposure, and vulnerability (UNDRR 2019: iv), vulnerability of specific components of economic and social infrastructure is often known. This is not the same as knowing the vulnerability of the population associated with a specific component. Reducing the vulnerability of built environment components can present win-win situations, even when erring on the side of caution, particularly when the risk management issue is life safety and provision of lifeline services.

DRR policy formation to guide CCA, resilience, and sustainable development efforts reveals how the impact of natural hazard events on the built environment comes about, the potential for such events in the future, and strategies to avoid their disastrous consequences. Yet government and the development sector are often reluctant to adopt such policies. This is in part a direct result of preferred actions to maximize market interventions and minimize government interference in transactions that impact creation of the built environment. This knowledge of how to avoid or negate policy mandates reinforces minimal use of DRR actions. Practice trumps knowledge and policy.

A society might believe that public service infrastructure—education, health, transport, communications, energy, water and sanitation, and places of public assembly—is developed to standards that ensure life safety, if not continuity of service, when natural hazard events occur. This is not necessarily the case. The public sector, conditioned by societal forces, is just as apt as individuals and private corporations to relegate risk management to low priority. Building to a high level of acceptable loss of infrastructure usually translates into initial cost savings, reduced taxes, making possible additional infrastructure, and responding to political pressure. Practice trumps policy and knowledge.

At the international level, both public and private sector participants acknowledge the evolving shift among governments to recognize the explicit and implicit costs of disasters. They note that governments are now more attuned to citizens' rising expectations of their government's capacity to manage emergencies and respond to disaster losses. Administrators understand the political price to be paid for getting disaster management wrong. Yet despite increasing use of insurance and other risk transfer mechanisms, public sector uninsured losses of infrastructure due to natural hazard events continue to rise, as does the extent of government liability. Practice trumps knowledge and policy.

## Framework for Both-And

Calls for a framework where development takes responsibility and accountability for DRR force the development community to undertake "both-and"—that is, doing what is commonly referred to as development's work (economic growth, expansion, and betterment) plus ensuring inclusion of DRR per society's understanding of acceptable levels of risk.

But what is to be expected from this framework? Proponents of both development and DRR implementation point to the imperfections and difficulties of rapid inclusive economic growth (Levy 2014). For those looking for DRR to be included in the built infrastructure segment of that growth, creating risk to social and economic infrastructure is not merely more chaos in the medium term. Creating such vulnerability is continuation of development characterized by monetizing risk at the expense of social safety and well-being. Without social, legal, or cultural governance to recognize, accept, and mitigate physical and economic risk, financial risk management will continue to be the surrogate DRR through orchestration, transfer, and assignment.

Examining the nature of vulnerability (hazard plus exposure) in creation of the built environment must continue in order to select which actions should be readily avoided and discover yet unknown or misunderstood actions that contribute to vulnerability. They undoubtedly include both top-down and bottom-up examination given that so many HEVRL and MERRE actions are carried out at the local level by both individuals and national or international initiatives. Using the both-and approach, development is an instrument of risk reduction by presenting DRR for discussion and decision through including HEVRL and MERRE in policy and practice.

## The Framework for Willingness

Ownership of risk demands a framework built of willpower and willingness. Willpower is a combination of determination and self-discipline despite difficulties, including opposition. Willingness is being prepared to do what is deemed needed.

Lassa et al. (2018) propose that societal resilience—which includes DRR—is about political commitment, which means a commitment of authority—public or private—acting to reduce vulnerability of the built environment. Lack of political commitment often looms large in MERRE processes. This lack is seen in preferences for short-term gain (including monetary and political) in lieu of long-term infrastructure resilience. As identified earlier, worldwide declarations and frameworks by sovereign states (who are in authority) and by other development participants may include demands for factual "alerts" for equitable access by all to a less vulnerable built environment (truth to power and justice to truth). They call for approaches integrating disaster-related reduction measures into development. However, these are not expressions of will for development to take ownership of responsibility and accountability for constructed risk. Needed is an explicit policy change by the development sector as to disaster risk management of the built environment for those least able to lessen their vulnerability to natural hazard events. Seizing such opportunities for honest and comprehensive conversations will depend on leadership and on how questions are framed. As noted earlier, leadership combines risk-taking and inspiration, along with ability to navigate politically.

Many in the DRM, CCA, resilience, and sustainable development communities understand that DRR is not a final state. Like development itself, DRR is dynamic; it has a set of conditioning factors and employs processes. But lessening vulnerability of the built environment demands an understanding of risk related to infrastructure not only in physical science, engineering, and architectural terms, but also in social, economic, and cultural terms. Resilience, adaptation, and risk reduction prior to a hazardous event (prevention) and during (managed disruption) and after the crisis (achieved revitalization) are not presently reflected in the development vocabulary. Discussion of a redefined framework for disaster risk reduction in development is not so much "how to" carry out the needed DRR activities in a technical sense, but when, where, by whom, and who pays and who benefits in an operational sense.

## Vulnerability Reduction at the Expense of . . .

Prioritizing DRR of social and economic infrastructure in development is not meant to be at the expense of DRM, EM, humanitarian assistance, CCA, sustainable development, or even development proper. Such misunderstanding would challenge the work of disaster resilience, which has been described as the ability to handle the impact produced from the natural hazard event, of disaster preparedness and response, and of rehabilitation and reconstruction (the ability of individuals, communities, organizations, and states to adapt to and recover from hazards, shocks, or stresses without compromising long-term prospects for development) (Rodin 2014). Redirecting development goals toward more resilient economic and social infrastructure may redirect some business activities and benefits. Less risk to natural hazards and other events can be the mark of successful development, regardless of economic disruption of present development processes.

As for adapting to avoid natural hazard event impacts without compromising long-term prospects for development, therein lies the seeming conundrum. Given GAR19's spectrum of catastrophic risks and need for their systemic understanding, long- and short-term survival is through development (UNDRR 2019). What level of effort by a given societal unit does not compromise the long-term prospects for development if that level is dependent upon declaring a disaster? Resilience is not per se vulnerability reduction unless development's principal goal becomes risk reduction of loss to an acceptable level. Otherwise resilience (to a plethora of risks) is one of the allied or parallel crosscutting sectors viewed as available but considered optional to address the outcome of natural hazard events. Survival in any timeframe is a looming development goal, given GAR19's spectrum of catastrophic risks.

## The Point of View

DRR is subject to scrutiny and evaluation from numerous points of view. Not all stakeholders seeking disaster risk reduction share the same values. A framework for redefining disaster risk reduction through development addresses the desired results of assessments and a MERRE process that reflects consideration of public (including community) views, choices, and the implementation of acceptable levels of risk. Such a framework avoids intentionally or inadvertently increasing risk or creating new risks for selected population segments.

For successful development actions, DRR before natural hazard events take place, rather than catastrophic event response, is the defining parameter in an economic, social, and moral sense. DRR is the need. It should be mandated, and that is the challenge. Enfolding disaster risk reduction within development allows for identifying and tracking who benefits and who pays. Being engaged in interdependency to the point that declaring a disaster is unnecessary or unknown says less about the degree of loss and damage, and more about responsibility and accountability. It refocuses risk management on when, where, and how the impact of hazardous events will be revealed. Willingness to carry out DRR in development of the built environment has to be an inside job.

## Development Status in the Face of Predominant Threats

A shift in perception is required regarding what constitutes development as economic growth, the role of forced migration and resettlement of populations, and attending to the poor and dispossessed, particularly related to economic and social infrastructure. There are now settled populations, as well as vast numbers of people in residence, in transition, and resettling due to globalization, forced migration, labor markets, poverty, natural resource exploitation, war, civil violence, religious persecution, ethnic cleansing, and, of course, natural hazard events.

In 1988 CIDIE identified the conditions for increasing local, national, and international attention to disaster risk reduction issues, including mitigation of existing vulnerability as part of the development process. The more developed a country's planning institutions and processes, the more easily natural hazards, HEVRL, and MERRE issues would be addressed. The more experience a country gained in assessing specific hazards, often following a major disaster, the more likely it would request assistance for continuing such assessments. And the more scientific, engineering, and prevention-related information available to countries and to donors, the easier it would be to use HEVRL assessments and MERRE processes in development programs and projects. The more experience governments and donors have with the kinds of DRR measures that are most cost-effective and implementable, the less reluctant countries would be to include such measures in policies, planning, programs, and projects. And the more experience and confidence there is in evaluating mitigation measures at various points in the development cycle, the more likely that the staffs of national development agencies and international development assistance agencies would be prepared to undertake work necessary to address DRR (CIDIE 1988).

Or so it was believed if those conditions came into existence. To date, conditions have evolved to where a country's planning institutions and processes have focused on what brings economic development acceptance, support, and gain, rather than on vulnerability reduction to natural hazard events, notwithstanding existing vulnerability. The experience most noticeable in addressing vulnerability reduction has been financial risk transfer related to financial loss. The increased availability of HEVRL and MERRE information has gone primarily to feed the financial risk transfer markets and the disaster management sector for crisis response. Defining costs and benefits to implement DRR measures has primarily been used in consideration of development plans with and without DRR actions. Experience and confidence gained in dealing with DRR measures has not transformed development into a driver for DRR implementation.

## Beyond the Move from Response to Disaster Risk Management

Lack of reducing natural hazard risk through development actions reflects squarely on causes and outcomes of the disaster-development gap at all societal levels. The losses incurred are often little understood except in the sense of financial risk management. The losses anticipated are often part of risk as a development subsidy, risk transfers, and a risk reduction agenda identified as add-on options to economic and social infrastructure projects, externally funded, and considered a cross-sector action similar to economic development-environmental management actions. Eva von Oelreich wrote in 2004, "Disaster reduction pays off in terms of lives saved and livelihoods protected but urgent action is needed by the governments of disaster-prone countries to invest in disaster risk reduction measures" (von Oelreich 2004).

If development is ready, willing, and able to simultaneously create risk and address constructed risk in the built environment, certainly disaster research might well help unveil "the social construction of risk that could potentially contribute to a profound redefinition of DRM" (Maskrey 2016: 5). More importantly, it might well force examination of development's role in the creation and reduction of risk seen not only through the lens of social, but also economic, physical science, engineering, and architecture points of view.

In the Forensic Investigations of Disasters (FORIN) conceptual framework, "all disaster risk is socially constructed. From that perspective disasters are not merely *not natural*, they also *don't exist* independently as things or as objects. They are only moments of space-time compression within broader social and historical processes" (Maskrey 2016: 5). For risk reduction of the built environment, certainly these broader processes must clearly identify in the language of development risk reduction for whom, where, when, why, how, at what cost, and who pays and who benefits. Causes and effects of natural hazard events can already be found in development decision-making, even when they are not visible and transparent in the decision-making process, even when no responsibility and accountability is assigned, and even when speaking truth to power falls short of speaking justice to truth. Consideration of risk to the built environment is consideration of cause and effect; certainly consideration of hazard, exposure, and vulnerability is essential to not only social disaster research, but also economic development research.

## Progress on Risk Assessment

The recent Paris Agreement on greenhouse gas (GHG) emissions' mitigation, adaptation, and finance, adopted by 190-plus UNFCCC signers (February 2019) includes statements referring to the probable continuation of global warming and intensification of climate abnormalities for some time after the agreement's goals for emissions are met. Climate change will result in loss, damage, and destruction even as the best efforts of this consensus—a manifestation of the practice of the least common denominator adopted by sovereign states—are under way (UN 2015).

Discussion of such accords increases the focus on risk from various natural hazard events, whether affected or not by anthropogenic development actions. Creation of new vulnerable social and economic infrastructure still leads to yet-uncalculated (but not incalculable) loss, damage, and destruction of the built environment and associated populations. Worldwide, average annual addition to existing physical economic and social infrastructure is approximately 2 percent. Up to 60 percent of all loss, damage, and destruction of economic and social infrastructure during the next twenty years will most likely be part of 2020's existing vulnerable infrastructure.

The framework presented in the FORIN 2 document is an important approach for understanding how vulnerability as a social construct in economic and social infrastructure occurs (Oliver-Smith et al. 2016). The framework also highlights lessons for choosing levels of risk for what is to be built. But most importantly, new social science research can examine what might well be FORIN's greatest contribution: identifying existing vulnerability of the built environment before natural hazard events take place. The framework offers a systematic method to view existing vulnerability, identified by, if nothing else, hazard and exposure of economic and social infrastructure and its associated populations for use through MERRE in development.

## In Sum

Reframing DRR in development embraces policies and processes where change is to take place. The change will address creation of vulnerability that is a choice made by society, not merely an accumulation of market decisions. Civil discourse and political positions will inform societal actions through participatory decision-making. Whatever the vulnerability produced, it will come about through knowing and understanding who is vulnerable, why, who pays, and who benefits. Vulnerability issues will be resolved by socially responsible decisions based on objective facts, through the willingness to choose whose vulnerability is part of society's quest for care and community rather than domination and wealth. Risk reduction becomes an integral part of a changed development process.

If an operable window of opportunity exists following a disaster, one might argue an equally viable opportunity exists before the natural hazard event occurs. How to open that not-often-mentioned window presents the same challenge as the opportunity development presents in other circumstances of risk. As in the post-disaster experience, unknown is when or how that window of opportunity existing prior to a natural hazard event will be slammed shut.

CHAPTER 8

# Making Risk Information Visible

Use of the word "disaster" to explain the root causes of losses that occur obscures the role of risk in the disaster-development linkage. Why not manage risk to natural hazard events in such a way as to avoid having to declare a disaster following a natural hazard event? While all natural hazard event impact is not avoidable, catastrophic loss and damage are often avoidable when managed through development policy, planning, and practice to reduce risk.

Discussion now focuses on assessments of hazards, exposure, vulnerability, and risk (referred to collectively as risk assessments) and how they become part of processes that inform risk management decision-making and application.

The development community recognizes vulnerabilities in economic and social infrastructure. It avoids risk to lessen dependency and may share risk to strengthen interdependency in development relationships and makes risk management choices accordingly. Ironically, the same development processes of the private and public sectors use HEVRL assessments and MERRE to produce highly vulnerable economic and social infrastructure components.

Heretofore, using language other than that of the development community, stakeholders have considered how DRM, CCA, resilience, and sustainable development could bring DRR to the built environment. They have considered rethinking the concept of bringing DRR into the development process in order to reduce risk. Now the discussion on making DRR effective will use development's own terms and language. This requires understanding when and how DRR can take place in the development process.

More than thirty years ago, Ulrich Beck first noted, "In contrast to all earlier epochs (including industrial society), the risk society is characterized essentially by a lack: the impossibility of an external attribution of hazards. In other words, risks depend on decisions, they are industrially produced and in this sense politically reflexive" (Beck 1992b: 183). Today in most sovereign states, what society produces as the built environment is called "development." Land use planning, design, and construction are enveloped in governance, management, and economic competition. Too often this occurs with little or no consensus or cultural mandate regarding acceptable levels of risk.

Discussion now moves from disaster avoidance to the use of data and information in constructing risk. It also focuses on the three instances of vulnerability of economic and social infrastructure: (1) construction of new infrastructure components, often implicitly if not explicitly deemed the principal target of DRR; (2) reconstruction of infrastructure through repair, reconstruction, and replacement (all in the name of recovery) following a natural hazard event; and (3) retrofitting existing vulnerable infrastructure, the largest group of vulnerable components to be addressed anywhere in any generation.

Information on vulnerability and risk can and should address not only the physical infrastructure component of a structure and its site, but also specifics of the associated natural hazard event. Hazard together with the component at risk constitutes exposure. Exposure does not inform to any significant detail the level of risk. It should be noted that in many instances when initiating DRR, it is not always clear or qualitatively defined which two elements of exposure—the hazard or the physical component—will be considered for risk reduction action. For example, flood hazard reduction of a school may focus on site selection rather than on elevating the school structure above the floodplain. In addition, the decision to proceed with DRR actions is often based solely on the hazard and exposure assessments without preparing vulnerability and risk assessments in qualitative and quantitative terms, respectively. If an exposure assessment is made, or if outside participants produce such an assessment, how and to what use will subsequent vulnerability and risk assessments ensure consideration of an acceptable level of risk?

## Assessments and Processes in DRR

Development planning contains two risk management-related constructs. One is HEVRL assessments—the research, discovery, preparation, analysis, and formulation of objective information. These multidisciplinary analyses are to inform the decision-making processes of development. The assessments identify existing, desirable, and achievable levels of risk of loss of the infrastructure component through research and analysis of the component in question and past and probable events. The second construct, MERRE, deals with understanding and choosing an acceptable level of risk between approaches and their positive and negative aspects, while also focusing on economic and social issues, moral imperatives, culture, governance, custom and tradition, and social relationships.

As seen in the structure, operations, and content of the HEVRL assessments and MERRE processes, decisions concerning acceptable levels of risk are complex. Often the actual level of risk of an economic or social infrastructure component is the result of root causes, whether technical, social, economic, or political. These are revealed in public and private discussions, construction management decisions, social preferences and beliefs, technical and legal documents, and economic conditions that shape the physical location (hazard zone) and resilience (physical construction) of the infrastructure component. The decisions are not the result of simply applying physical sciences and technology. HEVRL as data and information transformed into assessments form the basis for understanding the origins and subject matter of risk. They are not per se value laden, even when there is physical and social science input that, for example, categorizes characteristics in ascending or descending order to draw attention to a particular HEVRL element. MERRE processes form the basis for acting on the risk. They are inherently value laden in that they include decisions about preferences, rights, privileges, law, and order, but all these in the context of human behaviors through formal and informal mechanisms.

## Structure and Function of Hazard, Exposure, Vulnerability, Risk, and Loss Assessments

HEVRL assessments are particular in their design, content, generation, and presentation due in great part to the disciplines involved in their preparation. They reflect knowledge, policy, and practice. The content of the data, information, and resulting assessments flows from contributions of the physical sciences, engineering, architecture, and economic and physical planning, as well as administration and financial management. Natural hazard information contains specific natural climatic, atmospheric, hydrologic, meteorologic, geologic, physiologic, and geographic observations related to the events. By design, a hazard assessment can contain specifics about place, severity or magnitude, and frequency of possible and past events. It can be presented in various formats and most often informs parameters of space, time, and characteristics of forces (e.g., wind, water, tides, ground-shaking, ash, lava, smoke) at play. In some cases, the hazard information is based on data models from previous hazardous events and records from monitoring the forces that spawn the events. Sometimes natural hazard information based on modeling dealing with hazard is not legally admissible as part of land use planning and infrastructure design and construction.

In tandem with the hazard assessment is identifying the infrastructure component of interest. This initial assessment is prompted by the likely impact of a prevalent natural hazard event on the component. The site and its propensity for natural hazard events is considered in conjunction with the structural characteristics and condition of the infrastructure component. This constitutes exposure: the existing or possible placement of an infrastructure component in harm's way (see table 8.1).

Next considered is vulnerability of the natural hazard event's impact on the infrastructure component, usually expressed qualitatively by type and magnitude—wood-framed houses will be flattened by the wind, concrete-block structures will be cracked and possibly toppled by an earthquake. Vulnerability can be expressed as a worst-case scenario: the anticipated maximum impact of the natural hazard event and resulting degree of destruction of the infrastructure component. It can also be an event that does not threaten life safety but impacts use of the component—rising water covering a bridge that blocks entrance to a settlement, school, or hospital, for example.

This is followed by the risk assessment, which is the quantitative probability of the degree of expected loss, that is, damage or destruction, negation of use given a specified natural hazard event by location, magnitude, and frequency. Loss assessment is the quantitative and qualitative description of actual damage or destruction of an infrastructure component. It is most often expressed in monetary terms and can include quantities of specific types of infrastructure components (e.g., the number of damaged and destroyed schools), but with few details. Increasingly, loss assessments attempt to qualify and quantify economic, social, and other types of direct, indirect, and secondary impacts. Populations impacted may be identified by gender, race, income, education level, nationality, legal status, and the like. Loss of education, health, water and sanitation, transportation, and communication infrastructure most often impacts associated populations far beyond direct physical injury or loss of life. Economic loss is seldom publicly reported.

Access to HEVRL information has long been proposed as a public good, but not often presented as free or open source information. Recurring public expenditures to prepare assessments in recognition of evolving health, safety, and welfare of the public are necessary. HEVRL assessments could be, but not always are, a visible or much discussed part of the economic and social infrastructure owners' and operators' approach to design and risk management considerations of the project. Here is where responsibility and accountability are important—not only for the preparation of information (as in the case of modeling possible hazard events), but also for the choice of risk levels adopted—and the levels of loss anticipated from natural hazard events. Whether the HEVRL assessments are proprietary, held closely for security reasons, accessible by authorities on a need-to-know basis, or part of public information, each sector's preparation and use of the assessments condition the decisions that lead to the amount of risk carried and the possible losses incurred.

Within development processes, and prior to initiation of the policy, planning, or building project activity, lack of established parameters for the limits of acceptable risk—expressed as financial, economic, and physical risk—and identification of the entity or person responsible and accountable for making those decisions concerning risk management become glaring.

Each step within development planning processes nominally involves tools and actions that deal with natural hazard risk reduction (see table 8.1). For example, a generic development project begins with a preliminary mission or consultation, followed by a development diagnosis and project program definition that includes specific components of the built environment and geographic composition of the specific site. Next comes the project formulation, action plan definition, or project preliminary design, followed by project final design and implementation.

Throughout the process, key decision points include viability of the plan or project considering the prevalent natural hazard threats, assignment of technical, financial, and structural options to manage risk, followed by the DRR strategy to be used (see table 8.1). With each phase of the project, analysis of costs and benefits of managing the risk at a specific level becomes more detailed. Using HEVRL assessment information during early stages of the development process, such as including natural hazard mitigation measures, is less costly than attempting to modify a project in its later final design or construction stages or after construction is completed. Because of the economic and social dimensions of choosing an acceptable level of risk, cost-benefit analysis is increasingly used to inform the decision-making process.

Far too often in the initial planning stages of an infrastructure project, the only analysis carried out is creating a list of previous "disasters," often natural hazard events that have affected the general or specific geographic area of the proposed or existing development project and that may or may not have become declared disasters. This is often done with no reference to a detailed geologic, hydrologic, or climate hazard composition of the specific site. These disastrous events are discussed as to the severity of the hazardous event itself (e.g., magnitude 7.8 earthquake, category 4 hurricane, 500-year flood). Such descriptions rarely contain specifics of damage or destruction to infrastructure such as structure type, location, materials, and construction technique.

Considering HEVRL data and information consumes financial and technical resources. Therefore, the information provided at each phase should match the need for making decisions in that particular development planning stage. The critical factor for successfully incorporating appropriate natural hazard risk management into each phase of project preparation is the ability of planners to access and effectively use hazard information (OAS-DRD 1991). A focus on such incorporation reflects how behavior over the past decades—in this case technical competency—can shape data and information.

## Structure and Function of MERRE Processes

MERRE processes are meant to use HEVRL assessments in forming and making decisions about an acceptable level of risk and implementation. The breadth and depth of choosing an acceptable level of risk with assignment of responsibility and accountability can be narrow and shallow (general and open to interpretation) or wide and deep (specific permitting both normative and adhering to performance standards). All require human, technical, and monetary resources—gathering HEVRL information and carrying out monitoring, evaluation and reporting, compliance, and subsequent regulation and enforcement.

MERRE processes are typically conducted through public sector auspices based on legislative mandates, executive administration, and judicial action. They are part of the formal sector that requires professional preparation of programs and plans followed by licensed construction. They can also be part of culture, custom, tradition, and mores of the informal sector. MERRE processes are increasingly the subject of social science and NGO observation, research, and advocacy. This is particularly the case when working with people who have little or no control over their physical environment, beginning with their settlement site. Much of their built environment comes about through the informal sector, where professional or licensed resources play a small role or none at all. Nonetheless, at the community level, particularly with housing, education, and health facilities, creating the economic and social infrastructure may be subject to learned, gratuitous, and unrequested MERRE-like practices as part of accepted—or not—citizen behavior.

As to what risk is acceptable, with few exceptions the implicit level of acceptable risk is assurance of life safety, no matter the type, function, or use of the infrastructure component. At this level, no deaths or serious injuries are expected if evacuation from the at-risk building or other infrastructure component is carried out in a timely fashion. For some public and private infrastructure elements, the expressed acceptable level of risk is continuity of service. This means that with or without modest repairs the impacted infrastructure component will remain in service or can be made serviceable within predetermined acceptable time and cost parameters.

When choosing an acceptable level of risk, the desired level (or resilience) to physical damage and destruction is only one of three facets. The other two facets are (1) knowledge of the expected financial and economic loss, given specific natural hazard events impacting specific components of the built environment; and (2) steps in the development process that actually review, discuss, and carry out decision-making as to the acceptable level of risk and how it will be achieved.

The "how" of acceptable level of risk is to be achieved begins with discussion of risk reduction for whom, where, and why. This invariably includes discussion of who benefits and who pays. There is also the question of management of the acceptable level of risk (by whom) in contrast to the "desired" level of risk (why). A third element not often identified is the actual resulting level of risk of the completed infrastructure component (how did it happen). Brought together, these three facets of risk assessment show the importance and role of exposure in HEVRL.

Choosing a level of risk requires cooperation and designation of priority action. To achieve both, stakeholders need adequate access to general and

---

**Building Regulation and Enforcement, and Risk Creation**

"By far, the greatest growth in earthquake vulnerability in the world is the consequence of rapid urbanization and the universal use of poor quality reinforced concrete frame residential structures to maximize density for cheap urban housing. Reinforced concrete is the cheapest means to store poor people in urban areas. Unfortunately, reinforced concrete construction is more demanding than it appears. The result is that we have created and continue to create an enormous stock of high occupancy, highly vulnerable buildings in active seismic areas of the world. This is particularly the case in the developing countries where design, material, construction, and regulatory standards are inadequate. This represents a failure in technical education, plan review, site supervision, labor-force training, materials testing, site inspection, and building standard enforcement. The improper use of cement and steel in reinforced concrete construction is the primary cause of death in most recent earthquakes." (Krimgold 2008) local information on hazards. National and regional planning institutions and sector agencies must undertake the necessary hazards assessments for the decisions to be made and formulate policies for nonstructural mitigation. Such actions, in turn, are part of identifying and preparing planning and investment projects that donors and lenders should review for support. Finally, the risk reduction measures should reflect an efficient and appropriately balanced use of risk avoidance, reduction, adoption, and transfer approaches.

It is important to remember that MERRE is built on a behavior-knowledge continuum. It should be a user of, not complementary to, HEVRL assessment information. MERRE processes define and force (sometimes under legal mandate or political duress) decisions concerning an acceptable level of risk using mechanisms that society deems appropriate responses.

## Development Planning Processes as Receptors of HEVRL and MERRE

DRR processes, formal or informal as they might be, are familiar to the development community and are considered as allowed in broader development. But HEVRL assessments and MERRE processes may not be considered; or when they are, the assessments and processes may be prepared and presented by external participants who are not directly involved in making development decisions affecting infrastructure at risk. Sovereign states and other stakeholders are well versed as to the impact of those people external to the project participants in MERRE processes. The stakeholders also know how individuals and groups approach financial, economic, and physical natural hazard risk management through use and misuse of HEVRL assessments and MERRE processes. As Cassidy Johnson has written, broader-scale definition and mandates for DRR-related assessments and processes have taken place, but local (subnational and below) administrative jurisdictions, accompanying private businesses, and settlement inhabitants must often bear the brunt of DRR political, technical, and administrative implementation and a significant part of its economic and social costs (Johnson 2011).

Also at a broader scale, the dominant global disaster management participants are comfortable with maintaining that DRR actions be brought to the development sector. There is no lack of encouragement to review adopted DRR frameworks that identify opportunities and barriers to integrated governance into development. Notwithstanding the dominant role of the private sector in the creation of the built environment, UNDRR

**Table 8.1.** Generation of DRR Information and the Development Planning Process for Creating the Built Environment.

| Phases in Development Planning Processes | Risk Assessment Step Data, Analysis, and Information | | | | |
|---|---|---|---|---|---|
| | Hazard | Exposure | Vulnerability | Risk | Loss |
| Preliminary Mission | x | x | | | x |
| Development Diagnosis | x | x | | | |
| Project Formulation and Action Plan | | x | x | | |
| Project Design and Engineering | | | x | x | x |
| Finance | | | x | x | x |
| Approval | | | | x | |
| Construction | | | | x | |

refers to SFDRR as a truly sovereign state-owned enterprise in a sea of risk management that is only "supported" by the private sector (UNDRR 2019: ix). Truly, DRR is needed as a principal action of the development sector, not assigned solely to government or the private sector, but with each of these two playing their responsible and accountable parts.

## Risk Assessment—Taking HEVRL to Economic Measures

Less risk of physical loss generally means (somewhat) greater financial investment in natural hazard mitigation measures for the infrastructure component, whether it is for new economic and social infrastructure, retrofit of existing vulnerable infrastructure components, or reconstruction of infrastructure following a disaster. Excluding much of the housing and local community service building structures around the world, most economic and social infrastructure is designed and constructed with some level of risk assessment. Much of the infrastructure that lacks risk assessment input is built to high levels of acceptable risk of loss.

Development community participants and particularly stakeholders acting on risk information may be thought to do so primarily by responding to physical loss. In fact, they most often act first on expected financial loss, then on economic loss, and only then on lessening risk of physical loss (damage or destruction of capital stock). This is seen in the creation of financial risk management products using asymmetrical knowledge (when the seller in an economic transaction has greater material knowledge than the buyer, or vice versa) of the risk in question. Producers of insurance instruments, risk pools, indexes and the like generally know as much or more than owners, operators, and development lenders about infrastructure components at risk. This comes about as risk is managed (the sale of purchased coverage) from those who aggregate risk information from individual risk-prone owners and operators and from actual losses.

As DRR is increasingly considered a public sector responsibility—often by default—perhaps the more likely schools and hospitals, for example, will be constructed or retrofitted to have lower acceptable risk of loss and less vulnerability. But the more losses to natural hazard events appear to be indiscriminate as to where they strike, and unpredictable as to when, the less likely societies appear committed to selecting particular components of economic and social infrastructure—particularly those owned and operated by the public sector—for special DRR attention. The less visible and transparent the underlying causes of risk and accompanying responsibility and accountability, the more likely recovery will be deemed a broad public responsibility. In the end, the less detail available about HEVRL assessments and MERRE processes, the less likely DRR will be considered as a role for the development community. These positions stem in part from economic and political pressure, recognition of a growing presence of large-scale catastrophic risk to populations around the globe, the public impact of questioning risks related to climate change and sea level rise, and deeply divided opinions by societies on the role of government in resolving a variety of population-related economic and social problems at home and abroad.

## Absence and Presence of Justification for Investment in Disaster Risk Reduction

Development has its own nomenclature to identify goals and objectives readily paired with development problems. These goals and objectives, such as the UN Millennium Development Goals and Sustainable Development Goals, place the concept of human progress center stage, but with an understood backdrop of gain—usually economic gain—driven by development actions. Calls persist for better measures of development that focus on human progress (see, for example, Vernon and Baksh 2010; Beachy, Shank, and Zorn 2013). They envision a society with greater local participation working for growth and change, but inside a political and economic paradigm that values husbandry of natural resources, and opportunity and equality of access to growth and change. This both-and approach demands careful examination of the actual measures of development progress, which must reside in both the socio-political and the scientific-technical domains of knowledge, policy, and practice. Growth should include greater security, not increased risk. Quantifiable development growth measurements are a means to understand human progress, not an end that substitutes for sustainable betterment.

## Dealing with Existing Risk

The foregoing description of the development planning process and treatment of DRR is applicable to the issue of existing risk of economic and social infrastructure, similar to addressing pre-existing conditions in the heath sector. Rather than focusing on multiple underlying causes of risk creation, the primary concern is how to reduce existing risk of loss. As in the health sector, HEVRL assessments with their baseline information—the diagnosis—are needed to identify, prioritize, and act on risk reduction. Who will assume responsibility for risk reduction actions (treatment) once the extent of the vulnerability is known? What mechanism will pay for those risk reduction actions? How will priorities be established for addressing existing risk, particularly for public sector economic and social infrastructure that is in disrepair or in impoverished urban and rural areas?

## In Sum

Development—with economic development at its core—is a creator of risk and the primary force that gives form and function to the built environment. Given the current generation of natural hazard risk assessments, manifestation of progress in DRR in development should take place for development's own good. The tools available for identifying and recognizing the risk of natural hazard events can be used to achieve extremely specific ends through knowledge, experience, behaviors, policies, processes, and practices. Indeed, risk management itself is an increasingly visible part of the globalization of economic progress, sustainability, and survival. Increasingly apparent are conditioning factors and conflicting approaches that affect not only the willingness to address DRR, but also on whose behalf, why, and through what means.

Chapters 9, 10, and 11 will explore three conditioning factors—economic forces, environmental issues, and climate change adaptation, respectively, before HEVRL and MERRE are addressed in more depth in chapters 12 and 13.

CHAPTER 9

# Risk within Present and Emerging Economic Development Forces

At the highest international level, sovereign states met and declared DRR a goal (UNISDR 2015b). Within the statement, which includes a focus on natural hazard events, climate change, and sea level rise, "risk reduction" was bounded on one end by reference to local participation. It was bounded on the other end with some of the most intractable issues of worldwide concern: inequality of access to housing, education, health care, a living wage, and increasing vulnerability to all types of naturally occurring and population-induced hazards threatening catastrophic impacts, some leading to annihilation.

Causal factors of risk are development as a process, as a sector, and as a business community. The vulnerability of the very economic and social infrastructure components thought of as development gains is of global proportions. Moreover, by and large SFDRR does not challenge economic development participants to carry out DRR by using development resources.

Many current efforts to reduce risk to the built environment, both inside and outside the development community, focus on reducing financial risk regardless of the level of effort to mitigate physical and economic risk. Within traditional social science disaster research, vulnerability of the built environment is addressed separately from social, economic, and other types of vulnerability. These perspectives of risk are important when considering DRR, not only for physical risk of the built environment, but also for population risk of family, community, nation, and society.

This chapter will explore risk and traditional development sector actions within globalization and other economic development forces, and the tools, processes, and behaviors used to manage vulnerability from natural hazard events. The issue remains that actors embedded in economic development efforts lay aside or simply do not reduce risk—particularly physical risk of the built environment—to natural hazard events. Their economic development decisions often do not identify who is responsible and accountable for the residual risk to infrastructure components once completed. Accountability is often transferred or missing from globalization, local government, and private sector efforts. To understand how lack of accountability affects loss of economic and social infrastructure requires analysis of whether and how the impacts of natural hazard events are measured.

Managing loss is identified as the concern, but often without specifying the type of associated risk. Unless otherwise indicated, DRR for physical infrastructure components is in financial and economic terms, particularly when discussing benefit and cost of physical infrastructure risk reduction. Physical infrastructure includes existing infrastructure (globally, the most pressing DRR issue of the built environment at risk), building infrastructure components as part of new development (often assumed to be the core issue as posed by physical sciences, engineering, and development planning entities), and reconstruction of damaged and destroyed infrastructure following a disaster.

## Economic Development and Globalization: The Least Common Denominator for DRR

Globalization is not another name for development; it is a style of development. The commonly stated goal of a sovereign state is economic growth and expansion through private and public sector actions, while promoting betterment for citizens and participating in a global economy through interdependency. This goal appears to be the first choice of the development community. Through globalization, its role in shaping the built environment and adding risk to economic and social infrastructure is enlarged and increasingly apparent.

In the post–Cold War era, globalization strengthens the development sector's ability to place identifiable program initiatives into silos, even as existing, new, and proposed issues between the programs play on within the same sector or institution. Essentially, this is development by program—a nation wills economic investment and return on investment through expenditures both public and private in the name of development.

Globalization as a process creates vulnerable economic and social infrastructure, sometimes knowingly. Given that the economic development sector may make DRR investment an option, those participants skilled in identifying and marketing financial risk have not always made investment in physical risk reduction an economic priority. But they often include monetary reserves as resources in nations seeking development lending to deal with secondary and indirect economic loss in a disaster.

For participating countries, acceptable risk of loss through financial risk management becomes the least common denominator of economic development and its dominant market economy. Such choices define the greatest acceptable level of risk of infrastructure to natural hazard events. The risk is expressed in financial, economic, and physical terms, in that order of priority. Globalization, then, includes dealing with disaster management among nations, financial institutions, and private businesses in a manner that is similar to dealing with other development challenges.

Globalization makes markets for financial risk management in the context of development processes. Globalization pursues its interest in contributing to recovery as a development action. Globalization also impacts the response to declared disasters and risk reduction by affording private sector opportunities for increasing financial donations and facilitating remittances, as well as lending and borrowing between and among private institutions, businesses, and sovereign states.

Actions within and between nations at whatever level are always viewed as a prerogative of the sovereign state. To varying degrees, groups within private sector operations may well depend on public service infrastructure (energy, health, telecommunications, transportation, water, and sanitation) for significant if not critical operation of components of economic infrastructure. The private business sector generally focuses its development processes, including DRR actions, on the built environment it owns and operates and, more recently, on the local service and lifeline infrastructure that serves its employees.

Through globalization, as disaster recovery issues become increasingly indistinguishable from issues of development, disasters are often handled via relationships between private sector economic players as well as NGOs and sovereign states. International disaster assistance from stakeholders may take on varying dimensions, depending on whether the recipient entity is in the public or private sector and whether the objective is relief or recovery. This reflects the increasing presence of private businesses as they define and drive commerce and trade. They are participants less concerned with spatial and political territories than with internationally integrated production, markets, and economic opportunities. Often the private sector is the operator and sometimes the owner of traditional components of public infrastructure: energy, health, telecommunications, transportation, water, and sanitation. These are coupled with the role of labor migration (both unskilled and highly skilled) as part of both "push" and "pull" factors in economic actions including globalization, recovery, seasonal labor migration, and local sector-specific development programs.

## DRR an Unlikely Development Goal

Meanwhile, other development participants, particularly from the DMDAs and NGOs, bring their various programs to build economic and social infrastructure inside and outside public sector development planning initiatives. DRR is rarely a visible goal of these initiatives, and both international entities and individual governments address disaster management as a separate, rather than integral, part of their development efforts. Development participants cite access to limited resources as a conditioning factor for choosing between options in order to maximize efficiency in economic activities and to protect the country's population and infrastructure from natural hazard event impact.

Development participants discuss various DRR issues but usually take little action to define or accept certain levels of risk, even in countries with repeated calls for international assistance. The development participants will consider certification of risk reduction actions related to specific components of the built environment, mainly through energy and transportation infrastructure projects, particularly those related to terrestrial trade corridors. They voluntarily accept international standards, depending on the sources of financing and the international certifications required by participation in the corridors. Such DRR actions are similar to development actions in that they are structured around profit-driven motives and provide a return on the investments made within the project.

When disaster losses occur, both private and public sectors, regardless of the economic or social sector involved, often have financial liabilities covered by explicit or implicit financial risk transfer mechanisms. Rarely do these mechanisms include actual assets, capital stock, or services as collateral. Public sector financial risk reduction mechanisms most often use financial assets such as the national treasury or bonds, insurance, and reinsurance, externally financed contingency funds, and international disaster assistance for disaster-related financial support.

The development forces cited above are intertwined with global actions for post-disaster recovery and reconstruction. They often choose to follow the traditional development patterns used prior to the disastrous event, but with emphasis on broadening or deepening the participation of the private sector. Disaster recovery interventions are sometimes referred to as disaster capitalism or actions of the disaster industrial complex (see chapter 5). The structure and content of these actions are not identified as part of sustainable development actions, environmental management, CCA, or DRR approaches by DRM advocates.

International development assistance agencies and MDBs are many times in the same situation as their national counterpart governments: they use their disaster event specialty agency to participate in disaster recovery. When the international agencies partner with national governments in DRR, they often find that national and local counterparts, both public and private, cannot or do not want to sustain DRR actions in recovery once the outside recovery support is consumed.

In international disaster assistance, collecting resources for DRR support is often tied to specific disaster declarations. Long- and even medium-term continuance (if not completion) of DRR must come through development programs. Even though declared responsibility for DRR and recovery is within the public sector, most national priorities do not include these as a specific development goal. In most instances the national government is the actual, if not declared, "self-insurer" for publicly owned economic and social infrastructure. Rebuilding housing for the poor and homeless due to a natural hazard event, along with accompanying critical service and lifeline infrastructure, is most often a major, largely externally funded activity of the public sector in most poor- and middle-income countries. Rebuilding damaged and destroyed economic infrastructure requires additional investment funds from development capital sources. Often the decision is not to build back better, but rather to accept a higher level of risk of loss in order to fund more projects or build back more quickly. When the public sector finances site-specific risk reduction reconstruction efforts—for example, flood protection for industrial parks—then the private sector sees an easier path to deal with physical and economic recovery investments as part of recovery and development.

Ample calls targeting development sector participants to implement have been made for including climate change, GHG emissions, ecosystem degradation, pollution, and natural hazard vulnerability to measure development gains in globalization and other development models. To date, such measurements have been conducted through specialized economic development reviews and studies. The measurements are most often created and applied in development practice through negotiation, regulation, enforcement, judicial ruling, and sometimes legislation, depending on factors related to the negative impact on economic performance and the source of financing.

At present, such measurements are not part of official national accounts, nor do they appear in MERRE information from the public sector, nor are they integrated (mainstreamed) into sector development planning studies used by most stakeholders. MDB sector managers and task team leaders working on development have specific responsibilities while recognizing the presence of specialists for DRR effort who operate in parallel programs, tasks, and teams.

## A Special Place for GDP

How does development measure itself in terms of economic growth, wealth, capital stock transfers, return on investment, and employment generation? The first tool used for measuring economic development is at the macro scale: the national gross domestic product. GDP is the globally accepted metric for development gains, particularly at the national level, through short-term economic output, usually on an annual basis. But as mentioned in chapter 2, such economic measurements exclude loss, direct or indirect, due to natural hazard events, as well as accounting for the existing vulnerability and risk of damage and destruction of the built environment and environmental degradation. There is no accounting for loss related to climate change, sea level rise, drought, and risk of loss in the future. What GDP measurement does include are all expenditures to deal with recovery from the abovementioned losses and expenditures following losses from all other human and natural happenings. From divorces to funerals, acute and chronic medical treatment, and on through to recovery from major catastrophes such as earthquakes, hurricanes, flooding, tsunamis, and volcanic eruptions, the expenditures count toward GDP growth. To put it simply, what counts is an accountable economic transaction notwithstanding the reason for the expenditure. As will be noted later in the discussion, investments in DRR show up on balance sheets, including when related to transfer of financial risk.

Published theory and post-disaster recovery practices led by some MDBs highlight possible overall positive economic effects of a country experiencing a disaster (Cavallo et al. 2010). In the short term, a downturn in GDP may take place in the impacted country because of foregone economic activity. But infusion of external resources can precipitate a growth in GDP greater than what otherwise might be expected. Thus experiencing a disaster can be seen as a gain for a country from the point of view of GDP growth. But often entities that finance infrastructure development projects, particularly MDBs, no longer have their names inscribed on dedication plaques as sponsors, as was common before the 1990s.

## Accounting for Natural Resources

Green accounting, otherwise known as natural resource and environmental accounting, is inclusion of natural resource stocks in national income accounts. Its purpose is to recognize the productive role of natural resources in capital formation, including the presence of capital stocks (ecosystem structure) and services (ecosystem functions). Unlike GDP, green accounting calculates the presence and loss of those stocks and services in monetary terms. Natural events, the hazards they pose, and their impact on landscapes are part of the evolution of ecosystems and their measurable, natural resources. They are therefore part of green accounting for use in national income (and loss) measurements.

Green accounting includes demand and scarcity. For example, landscapes that are less, rather than more, susceptible to natural hazard events are therefore sought for development. The cost of reducing vulnerability of the development site is minimized, while the return on investment is maximized for delivery of the same level of development. Naturally occurring mitigation elements in ecosystems that control flooding (forests, wetlands, and marshes), reduce coastal wind and wave action (reefs, beaches, dunes, and mangroves), or stabilize the soil (woodlands, hedgerows, and prairies) are typically in finite supply relative to the time frames in which a country or community wishes to exploit them in their natural state. Some landscapes become more vulnerable to natural hazard events because naturally occurring mitigation elements protecting them have been altered or damaged by natural hazard events. More common, however, is damage and destruction of naturally occurring mitigation elements by "man-made" forces, often through development actions. Environmental degradation often results in commercial gain for some development entities exploiting certain landscapes, but loss for others because of destruction of the protective services the same landscape offers.

Green accounting does not consider the destructive impact of ecosystems per se in normal evolution of their structure and function. Erosion, drought, and periodic flooding can impact economic and social infrastructure when they occur. In that sense, green accounting differs from how the climate change community measures loss. That community looks at climate-induced impacts on economic and social infrastructure and the society at large (see chapter 11), but also on ecosystem goods and services.

## Risk as Subsidy

Economic and social infrastructure are vulnerable to known, predictable natural hazard events but are efficient and profitable during their period of use. The subsidy created by avoiding when and where possible an investment in reducing risk to natural hazard events plays a large part in that benefit and profitability. Entities that otherwise might be charged with the responsibility and accountability of responding for the damage or destruction and those entities that ultimately suffer the physical loss when the natural hazard event occurs are both financial beneficiaries of risk as subsidy, at least until the moment of loss.

Using risk as a subsidy until having to pay for the loss is often preferred, rather than investing in DRR and lowering the acceptable level of risk loss. The cost of risk as subsidy manifests itself as payment for response, relief, and recovery and includes repair, reconstruction, and replacement of economic and social infrastructure. The subsidy also comes due for payment to cover the cost of alternative goods and services made necessary following the natural hazard event (including price escalations—also known as price gouging), as well as foregone use of goods and services that may not be replaced. The concept of risk as subsidy also applies to carrying forward high levels of risk related to access to natural resources (see chapter 10).

## Risk Transfer

In disasters and development, risk transfer as part of DRM is a robust subject for discussion of both tools and behaviors. Financial risk transfer is the process of formally or informally shifting the financial consequences of particular losses from one party to another. Risk of financial loss can be reduced, while physical losses from a natural hazard event and the economic consequences of the impact of the event may not be subject to mitigation or reduction.

Financial risk transfer schemes are emerging at the subregional scale to protect national government fiscal solvency. There are a few financial risk transfers being attempted at the local level, such as business interruption insurance. The agriculture sector attempts large-scale risk transfer strategies using insurance and commodity futures' market mechanisms.

Employing risk transfer strategies has become commonplace in order to shift, minimize, or eliminate responsibility and accountability for risk. This is most evident in monetary quantification of not only expected loss, but also the calculated cost and benefit for transferring risk—a market economy taking on the dimension of a market society. Financial risk reduction becomes a monetary decision, not a moral decision, subject to cost and benefit. But not clear or visible to the public is risk reduction for whom, where, when, how, and why. There are few instances where both the cost and benefit of infrastructure built to a specific level of physical risk are publicly known.

Financial risk transfer can pose a moral dilemma, because governments and businesses must make decisions on how much risk they are willing to retain or transfer, with the understanding that by transferring some of the risk rather than reducing the risk through physical mitigation, they may still be confronted with loss of life and damages to social and economic infrastructure. Placing monetary value on how much financial and economic risk can be transferred or retained is a complex process involving use of technical and scientific data and social and economic analysis, as well as examination of political ramifications. Not surprisingly, crosscutting issues such as governance, transparency, visibility, public participation, and environmental degradation are not high-priority issues for examination when the impact of financial risk transfer schemes is viewed. Putting an estimate on potential losses often involves placing emphasis on the three Ds: deaths, dollars, and downtime (Comerio 2013).

## Insurance

Insurance measures the risk of something happening (probability) to set parameters for determining the cost of coverage and the payout for loss. The parameter may be the actual loss or the occurrence of a triggering event that might lead to loss (parametric insurance). Coverage constitutes a transfer of responsibility for the payout from the purchaser of the insurance to a guarantor of payment should the parameters be met. Insurance is about risk and possible loss, but it is also about gain—usually financial, in the context of whose risk, whose loss, and who pays.

Traditional hazard insurance covers anticipated loss to specific components of the built environment (e.g., housing, roads, schools) from specific natural hazard events (e.g., floods, earthquakes). Calculations of premiums paid by the policyholder and policy payouts to the policyholders suffering losses are based on robust databases and information about HEVRL to set rate rates and profit margins. Given the exposure of some economic and social sectors, particularly infrastructure owned and operated by government, what kind of risk, how much risk, and to whom it might be transferred become dominant themes. Those who offer insurance gather extensive data and information on HEVRL. Products are designed to match recognized risk situations with coverage that is attractive and effective to those at risk. More often than not, lowering the physical risk of the infrastructure to be insured is not a mandatory part of accessing insurance products. The more accurate the HEVRL, particularly the hazard and exposure information, the better a profitable insurance product can be calculated and placed in the marketplace.

Insurance is an example of interdependency in most development processes, including globalization. When related to large-scale international development projects, insurance is customarily acquired primarily to reduce the risk of non-repayment of borrowing countries' loans. Most lending entities consider the primary risk to be avoided is public and private sector financial insolvency, not physical loss. Secondary and indirect economic losses are not normally addressed by governments through insurance. As exposure grows and private insurance becomes more expensive, insurance coverage retreats. The result is that transfer of financial risk to public institutions and local populations is taking place at a growing pace. Consequently government entities and private citizens and businesses are far less able to finance post-disaster relief and recovery than their central government (Messervy, McHale, and Spivey 2014). If and when insurance coverage by national government is not taken, then payment to recover from losses often falls to local governments and individuals.

Yet when disasters occur, local governments are likely less able to finance recovery. Community resiliency declines and vulnerability can escalate. Greater losses from climate change will tend to increase the need for insurers and regulators to promote actual risk-based pricing. However, this will also place affordable insurance coverage out of reach for many more households and private and public entities alike.

At national and local levels, parametric insurance is the fastest-expanding insurance strategy addressing natural hazard event issues. It is touted for improved access to capital for disaster recovery, beginning with much-needed capital for government operations.

Financial risk transfer tied to development is most exemplified by MDB sponsorship and sovereign state use of parametric insurance and catastrophic bonds (CAT bonds), rather than traditional insurance covering actual losses, and insurance pools to control costs in the sovereign states. Parametric insurance focuses not on the risk of physical loss to a specific natural hazard event, but on the probability of occurrence of the actual natural hazard event—an index based on event type, location, and severity.

Sovereign states (such as a Small Island Developing State—SIDS) use these instruments to improve their quick access to capital if a qualifying natural hazard event occurs. Risk reduction of possible loss of capital stock (economic and social infrastructure) is not a qualifying condition for accessing this coverage. CAT bonds are financial instruments sold to investors whose relationship to the insurer or sponsor is through purchase of bonds with a return on investment if the insured, usually a sovereign state, does not meet the triggering parameters for payment. Those parameters may be based on actual losses or, more commonly, indexes of weather events or formal declaration of a disaster. Proceeds from the CAT bond sale provide the insured with funds if the triggering parameters are met. Again, most often no physical loss mitigation actions on the part of the insured are required to access coverage financed through the sale of the bonds.

With parametric insurance, the primary data input to define the loss payout is the location and severity of the qualifying natural hazard event in the insured geographic area (such as a Caribbean island) regardless of the financial, economic, and physical losses suffered by the insured. The actual physical damage and destruction may be minimal or catastrophic.

## Cost-Benefit Analysis

In evaluating economic development actions, cost-benefit analysis of economic and social infrastructure may include investment (expressed in monetary terms) in natural hazard risk reduction to the physical component(s). Generally the development project budget is considered to include the design, construction, and sometimes the maintenance of infrastructure components. DRR actions may be optional or are included through application of relevant codes and regulations. The costs of the action may or may not be identified in design and construction costs. As Roberto Barrios points out, cost-benefit analysis is the "recognition of a cultural trend where policymakers, political leaders, and the public at large propose the subjection of all facets of human life to capitalist cost-benefit analysis as a mechanism for creating social well-being. Related to this particular kind of political imagination is the idea that market liberalization (e.g., the deregulation of labor, environmental policy, and financial markets) will lead to optimal social ends" (Barrios 2017: 8).

Whatever the project cost, private or public, it is usually amortized over the financing period of the infrastructure component. The project usually is not amortized over the design life of the component or the return period (frequency) and severity of a specific event estimated to surpass the actual level of resistance to catastrophic damage of the infrastructure component. The financial benefit of not amortizing the cost of potential damage or destruction over the service or loan life of the component lessens the cost of the project in the budget, in construction and maintenance costs, and on the balance sheet. In other words, the cost of the vulnerable bridge is added to the GDP as a short-term economic expenditure (gain) with no deduction from a cost-benefit analysis for the potential loss in the future. The vulnerable bridge is as valuable to the society just before it collapses as whatever the loan amortization or depreciation sheet states, and the GDP records no loss due to damage or destruction when the bridge can no longer provide service because of damage or destruction.

## Development Trickle-Down

The definition of trickle-down economic effects includes trickle-down development growth that may stimulate expansion of economic and social infrastructure. Effects include the ongoing impact of the development-driven expansion of the built environment, both planned and unplanned. Trickle-down effects are to promote deliberate growth of wealth and expansion of economic infrastructure as the preferred means to stimulate business investment in the short term and are described as the means to benefit society at large in the long term. This economic development theory underlines approaches to recovery following a disaster as directly supporting reconstruction of the built environment (see chapter 5).

But as development moves forward, vulnerability of the built environment is also part of the trickle-down. Thus vulnerability of the components of economic and social infrastructure accumulates year after year, generation to generation. Rarely is an accounting for the accumulated risk of economic and social infrastructure prepared—except, of course, when a natural hazard event occurs. If DRM and traditional development sectors are at odds because of acquiring resources for their respective goals and objectives, what then of globalization and other dominant economic paradigms further strengthening development's role in creating vulnerability while assuming little or no responsibility for risk, loss, and recovery? What of the intended trickle-down effect of raising all boats, i.e., populations? With the lack of affordable risk reduction measures in the face of rising water—figuratively and literally—the proverbial sinking of populations and their infrastructure takes place.

MERRE processes, particularly in reconstruction, are one of the leading institutional means to observe and measure institutional capacity for carrying out DRR. Yet in financing new development, and again in reconstruction activities, there is little interest from those funding economic and social infrastructure to measure risk. Regulation and enforcement are often equated with left-leaning, if not socialist, policies. They are often avoided when dealing with land use planning, zoning, and permitting and not sought as part of construction and reconstruction, particularly turnkey operations. This is a growing topic of research as the social sciences begin to explain MERRE in terms of beliefs, values, and behaviors. Risk avoidance, risk transfer, and risk as a subsidy, intended or not, certainly have the countenance of reward when left to roam freely in the economic marketplace.

## Trade Corridors

There are two particular areas where some measure of DRR is taking place for protection of economic development. These are terrestrial trade corridors and international port facilities—for both continental riverine and maritime transportation trade. Sovereign states for some decades now have organized to protect sea lanes, harbors, and port facilities from the impact of whatever might impede commercial and tourism transport. International waterborne transport corridors maintain interdependency, considering the multinational nature of the commercial vessels. Recognizing vulnerability to natural hazard events of harbors and ports as well as vessels has led to financial risk transfer as well as strengthening the physical transportation infrastructure through international infrastructure design and construction norms and standards.

Formal recognition and management of the physical territory and administrative space occupied by terrestrial trade corridors is far less formal than that of waterway corridors. Each sovereign state sets up and manages its segments of terrestrial corridors (road and rail) in what it deems both advantageous and compliant with its internal and international participants (Gray de Cerdán 2003). International standards and norms for DRM are not corridor specific. Generally accepted international standards and norms for telecommunication, energy, road, and railroad linkages are created through voluntary public and private codes and certifications.

Risk from natural hazard events to coastal, riverine, and terrestrial transportation corridors created and utilized by global partners has increased as needed infrastructure has been built. The global economy has increased the dependency and interdependency of sovereign states on these corridors and the populations and national resources associated with them. Trade corridors spread over the globe as food and manufactured products, resource extraction including oil and gas, and energy transmission evolve in traditional trade corridor routes. The need for access, security, and profitable use of all corridors demands collaborative efforts in DRR, CCA, and water resource management. Such actions are considered by some globalization participants as a priority, necessary, and an integral part of economic development in physical, financial, and economic risk management terms. Moreover, no-regrets strategies are increasingly preferred over considering loss of corridor functionality as an unavoidable disaster event. Short- and long-term risk reduction of corridors presents a competitive advantage option for growth and stability in the future (Bender and Ricciarini 2001).

## In Sum

Globalization and other economic development forces built around multinational strategies, economic justifications, national programs, trickle-down economic policy impacts, and post-disaster recovery have all impacted risk creation in the built environment. The risk comes from processes that promote natural hazard risk management using avoidance, transfer, and/or assumption of risk through a series of sequential actions.

The focus on national, local, and community disaster response has sustained public and private sector support for emergency management, but it masks development as a driver of risk. Processes used to protect investments in economic and social infrastructure routinely do not address physical and economic risk reduction as a priority, with one exception: the emerging example of trade corridors. Environmental management, CCA, resilience, and sustainable development goals do address risk to natural hazard events. They are managed, however, by the development sector through engagement subordinate to priority development goals and objectives, often in terms of return on investment. Nonetheless, efforts to deal with DRR issues through environmental management in its various endeavors, particularly climate change adaptation and sea level rise, are worthy of note and discussion.

# Part III
# DISASTER RISK REDUCTION WILL BE WHAT IT IS CONCEIVED TO BE

CHAPTER 10

# Sustaining Nature of Disaster-Development Linkage

This chapter considers the proposition that the programmed life span of economic and social infrastructure created by development is often not sustainable in conditions of risk to natural hazard events. Natural forces—which occur as part of atmospheric, hydraulic, and geologic systems and the terrestrial ecosystems of the planet—amplify recognition and focus on the sustaining nature of exposure to natural hazard events. This list also identifies the role natural systems play in thwarting and abetting both undesirable and unintended consequences of natural forces on development actions.

The always changing natural phenomena of planet Earth's evolution through time constitutes the sustaining nature of risk in the disaster-development linkage. How humans abet, mitigate, and thwart the undesirable impact of those forces is the subject at hand.

## Sustainability in Conditions of Risk

Given these underlying causes and outcomes of natural hazard events, unsustainability is conditioned by development and vulnerability. Sustainable development objectives focus on broad-brush efforts accompanied (or not) by mandatory (or not) statements that address threats from natural hazard events and other environmental processes. Vulnerability leads to examination of three indispensable views from the environmental perspective. The first is process, structure, and function of ecosystems. Second is natural phenomena presenting hazards impacting development efforts. Third is temporal dimension of development efforts as represented by the intergenerational implications of sustainable development (Bender 1994).

Notwithstanding the quip by Will Durant that our civilization exists by geologic consent, subject to change without notice, current dominant definitions of the terms "disaster," "natural disasters," "development," and "sustainable development" do little to describe the risk linkage between disasters and development in the context of environmental management. Use of these terms is not changing quickly or easily; therefore, discussion of this linkage must continue.

In some quarters the linkage was recognized prior to use of the term "sustainable development." In the 1970s recognition included modest integrated approaches to analysis of the linkage of natural hazard events in the context of development by identification and discussion of hazardous natural events in environmental impact assessments (EIAs) and environmental impact statements (EISs). Such recognition occurred before disaster assistance needs—later detailed as response (relief and humanitarian assistance), recovery, rehabilitation, reconstruction, and resettlement—became individual silos in their own right and sometimes dominant competitors for traditional international financial and technical resource assistance. Stakeholders were asked to fund EIAs and EISs as part of emerging environmental management actions. Stakeholders were also asked to fund disaster assistance as well as development actions. They were not asked to fund DRR, but they were challenged to consider the implications of sustainable development presented by the Brundtland Report in 1987: "Sustainable development is development that meets the needs of the present without compromising the ability of future generations to meet their own needs" (Brundtland 1987: 37).

Vulnerability of the built environment to natural hazard events most often includes the result of choices made by societies. In a similar manner, the naturally occurring vulnerability of ecosystems to natural hazard events is increasingly augmented by societal choices. Vulnerability to natural hazard events rather than the actual declared disaster from those events is emerging as the more important factor in understanding, first, the environmental implications of economic development policies and practices and, second, sustainable development goals of some countries no matter their economic development classification. Non-industrialized, emerging industrialized, middle-income, and developed countries alike find their situations summarized in the following: (1) economic development is not sustainable in conditions of vulnerability to natural hazard events, including climate change and sea level rise; (2) development objectives must focus more on the absolute conditions of vulnerability and less on the relative conditions of wealth; (3) natural hazard management cannot be separated from environmental management; and (4) development planning and practice must contain, and be responsible and accountable for, disaster risk management and environmental management (Bender 1994).

## Sustainability and Vulnerability

Sustainability includes continuing access to food, fuel, building materials, and safe building sites for housing, educational, and health-care facilities and water and sanitation. How natural hazard events affect a community's surroundings is part of an integrated approach to environmental management. If resilience is not part of design, construction, and operation of the economic and social infrastructure, the associated population is often more exposed than it otherwise would be. The structure and function of ecosystems can and will contribute to protection of populations and their related infrastructure as well as provide water, building materials, and building sites, among other resources.

Barbara Carby (2018), researcher and head of national and regional DRR initiatives, notes that each society must create its own vision of resiliency and must map pathways to that vision. Achieving resiliency is a complex undertaking. Susan Cutter (2014b) points out that in resilient systems, the various components including infrastructure—social, institutional, and environmental—are inter-related and interdependent. GAR19 notes the challenge of building resilience across the range of hazards, settings, and populations (UNDRR 2019). Although climate-related events have triggered much of the resilience discourse, that discourse now includes impacting events of both anthropogenic and natural origin.

In light of these proposed resilience programmatic approaches and structures for DRR, some participants consider them too upstream (too early in the planning cycle) and too "in the weeds" (too local and minute) for effective international, regional, and national risk reduction decision-making. In the face of a plethora of pending decisions, which decisions come first? Barbara Carby states, "Though highly desirable, essential even, and the subject of general agreement, building national and regional resilience to hazards will be fraught with challenges. The process will require making difficult choices" (Carby 2018: 8). The identified issues include critical adaptation, resource allocation that challenges existing paradigms and power structures that empower citizens for decision-making, and competing priorities at all levels in terms of policy and practice. Other choices focus on the actual need for additional, more direct investment—often foreign—for capital improvements as opposed to actually enforcing known effective land use planning and design regulation approaches. "Speaking the language of building a resilient future is not enough. The region must critically and carefully reflect on the challenges likely to be encountered on this journey and the commitment which will be required to achieve that future" (Carby 2018: 8).

Modern development models have long since threatened the carrying capacity of ecosystems, particularly in coastal areas, to provide sufficient goods and services for economic and social (including housing) infrastructure. Increasingly, people and the corporations that hire them must purchase these goods (building materials) and services (land for a building site) that require DRR improvements. Similarly, creating building sites that are safe from catastrophic natural hazard impact are increasingly costly, particularly in land markets where the highest and best (economic) use is the driving force. People—especially the poor, disposed, unsettled, and resettled—seek food, fuel, building materials, and building sites where they are safe from natural hazard exposure. Limited by lack of transportation, the poor use up whatever goods and services are available close by, often at the fringes of urban areas where those goods and services are of lesser quality and insufficient quantity to sustain them. Thus, necessity pushes them to migrate to another fringe area. How the poor acquire food, fuel, building materials, and building sites—often not for cash—is at odds with best sustainable management practices for natural resources and in conflict with urban, social, legal, and economic policies.

Land use planning can be used to structure occupation of more or less vulnerable areas using economic purchasing power and to segregate economic classes, sometimes employing natural hazard risk reduction policies as the tool. As Cassidy Johnson points out in *GAR 2011*:

> The case study from Argentina makes the point that the planning regulations and laws, which try to regulate the land market in Argentina, "have had a central impact in determining land values, and in population distribution in cities. These planning regulations are essential in determining the process of spatial segregation, by setting standards for building unattainable by the poorest sectors of the population and by keeping the area's best located and better served with infrastructure for residence and activities of the privileged sectors. . . . People need land to settle on that is safe from disasters, otherwise the land market and city economy are working at odds. Land policies favour rich, which is putting poor more at risk of hazards, thus the land policies need to be addressed before hazards can be really be addressed." (Johnson 2011: 21)

Above and beyond dealing with DRR issues related to settlements housing the poor, nations are experiencing disastrous losses of economic and social infrastructure while having little or no knowledge of present or future exposure. Some vulnerability reduction issues can be addressed case by case, such as the resiliency of individual structures to earthquakes, landslides, lahars, volcanic eruptions, and wind. The origin of hazard exposure counts. But in most cases, vulnerability reduction is beyond the issue of individual structures, particularly for housing of the poor. Actions are best taken collectively and most effectively through community actions supported by public policy and practice, beginning with land use master planning, zoning, building regulations, and enforcement. Most mitigation of risk will be undertaken at the local level, despite national, regional, and even global calls for action on "disaster" and environmental management issues. Lessening loss of life and reduction of the economic impact of natural hazard events begins with public sector policy and private sector willingness, including by individuals, to manage risk to protect economic and social infrastructure and ecosystems.

## Cross-Border Effects

The challenge of addressing disaster-development linkage includes dealing with varying geographic areas and their particular combinations of atmospheric, hydrologic, and geologic events in eco-regions, particularly river basins, aquifers, and other subsurface formations, and networks of components of economic and social infrastructure. The role of sovereign territory and broader multinational and ecosystem-based regions has evolved over time into contemporary arrangements built around trade agreements, calls for environmental management, and international development assistance as seen in use of surface and ground water and mineral rights, as well as the establishment of trade corridors.

More recently cross-border themes have grown to include management of climate change, pollution, and security, each based on political, legal, economic, social, civil, and religious issues, declarations, agreements, and treaties. In these cases, the driving forces of economic development often create or amplify vulnerability of economic and social infrastructure and associated populations and ecosystems.

In the particular case of water, globalization has increased pressure on the earth's water resources and has exposed the trade-offs and choices inherent in development. Sovereign states have chosen to make water-related natural hazard risk management part of integrated water resource management (IWRM) practices in integrated river basin management (OAS-DSD 2014; IEG–World Bank 2009). There are themes about water as a finite and valuable resource, but the emphasis is on the economic value of water. There are calls for civil society participation, particularly at the local level in already identified conflicts over water rights at all administrative levels. But the most stringent calls for risk reduction from natural hazard events to access water as a basic human right have come from UN declarations embedded in forums whose principal subject matter is not water.

## Intergenerational Implications of Sustainable Development

Naming future generations as beneficiaries of present development actions is not specific enough to identify which resources will benefit whom, when and where, and at what cost (Bender 1999). As discussed by Renaud, Sudmeier-Rieux, and Estrella (2013), making choices between structural and ecosystem-based mitigation of natural hazard impact is difficult, but taking action is a more important, arduous, and slow process. This is due, not in the least, to the lack of consultation, collaboration, and cooperation between the sectors of ecosystem management, climate-change adaptation, disaster risk management, and development, each in its own silo. Labeling occurs in conservation and development communities alike: ecosystem-based hazard management approaches can be labeled win-win and no-regrets by proponents. But there are competing ideas for use of ecosystem goods and services based on conservation, preservation, recreation, income streams, user fees, concessions, tax revenues, resource extraction and processing, and profits.

DRR is carried out to avoid direct damage and destruction of ecosystem structure and function. Such actions also help avoid loss of imputed secondary and indirect income from ecosystems now and in the future. The increasing number of disasters worldwide demands new approaches to exposure, vulnerability, and risk reduction, which in development terms means choosing specific beneficiaries. Given the broad transboundary character of ecosystems and natural hazard events, addressing natural hazard vulnerability reduction can build additional ties beyond economic interdependency. Such ties can also bring about mutual support and assistance inside and outside the framework of market economies and political positions attempting decision-making dominance.

## Absolute Vulnerability and Relative Wealth

Focusing on absolute vulnerability refers to the existence of risk to natural hazard events now and in the future. Being specific about identifying vulnerable economic and social infrastructure helps to select the target population for whom development actions are undertaken. Actions such as environmental management, which encompasses land use and natural hazard vulnerability, can address the presence of risk. Development projects, which constitute assignment of resources (physical sites, time, knowledge, funding, natural resources, etc.) for betterment, can lessen vulnerability of a segment of the population. Vulnerability reduction is therefore an increasingly important measure of "for whom" environmental management and development projects are intended, and at what level of physical, economic, or financial risk.

As noted in Chapter 3, in the broadest terms, wealth distribution as the preoccupation of societies has been replaced by management of risk, including the risk of loss of wealth. This coupled with dominance of the trickle-down theory of wealth distribution, puts into focus the relative nature of wealth accumulation, which includes the proportional cost of vulnerability reduction relative to resource availability. Vulnerability reduction focuses on assignment of development resources by necessity and moral standards to certain populations who want or need to control risk over their built environment, sometimes to achieve life safety. Relative wealth is not juxtaposed with numerically equal distribution of wealth but does include socially desirable and mandated community access to resources for risk management.

## Natural Hazard Events and Environmental Degradation

Degradation of ecosystems, often a result of choices made by societies, affects their naturally occurring ability to protect populations from natural hazard events. It must be identified as part of the environmental and natural hazard risk management challenge. Natural processes punctuated by dramatic natural events shape landscapes, flush reefs and estuaries, and form soils. Natural hazard events impact the provision of goods and services: potable water, habitat, food, and building materials. These events can also damage or alter marsh, meadow, swamp, dune, and coral reef structure and function, as well as access to ground water and minerals. And ecosystems provide protection from sea level rise, wind, rain, tides, flooding, storms, and drought.

If sustainability includes provision of food, fuel, building materials, and building sites, then how natural hazard events affect a community's built environment is part of an integrated approach to environmental management. Yet natural hazards other than climate change are often not given attention in environmental management discussions. Of all the environmental issues, atmospheric, hydrologic and some geological natural events are the most readily predicted in terms of place, time, severity, and probability of occurrence. And their impact is the most susceptible to mitigation—particularly non-structural mitigation, beginning with avoidance. Moreover, of all hedges against risk, DRR depends most on changing the way development takes place (Bender 1991).

## Environmental Management Perspective and DRR

The environmental management movement, born of the sustainable development community's desire to influence development decisions, at first did not want to focus on the impact of naturally occurring events on development. But when traditional development sectors were identified as modifying natural events, the sustainable development sector called for change in development processes, goals, and beneficiaries. The call was not through discussion of disaster events and recovery processes or of existing vulnerability of economic and social infrastructure, but it was an opening to address mitigation and adaptation.

If development processes do not highlight potential or existing vulnerability of economic and social infrastructure to natural hazard events, how can environmental management reveal that same vulnerability? Such manifestations call for cooperation and collaboration of the sustainable development, disaster, and climate change communities with the environment community.

Environmentalists continue to use EIAs and EISs as assessment tools. The departure point for assessments is to identify the harm done to ecosystem structure and function and natural resources by development. Such assessments do not customarily examine harm done by natural phenomena to the built environment or ecosystems. Comparisons of introducing EIAs and EISs into development planning and projects in the 1960s forward and using natural hazard risk assessments in the same processes today are a woeful and enduring lesson. In the 1970s, there were concerted efforts to include natural hazard risk assessment information in EIAs and EISs. Development planners could find a natural and workable place to gather and use such information in shaping development projects. But the environmental community's approach focused on how development impacts the environment(s) through the built environment and populations. Natural hazard risk assessments and other impacts of natural processes on development were not to be considered in EIAs and EISs.

In a related matter concerning development actions, EIAs and EISs have traditionally identified the goods and services provided by ecosystems to mitigate the impact of natural hazard events but have not identified the possible impacts caused by natural hazard forces (tides, wind, and rain, as well as landslides, earthquakes, tsunamis, and volcanic eruptions) on those same ecosystems. Environmental management has evolved into assessments aimed at managing development projects to lessen their impact on ecosystems.

DRR has not typically been associated with EIAs and EISs and by extension to environmental management. As a point of reference in the IDNDR mid-decade report on progress in 1994, a recommended action at the community and national level stated, "Consider the possibility of incorporating in their developmental plans the conducting of Environmental Impact Assessments with a view to disaster reduction" (UN-WCNDR 1994). This effort represents one of the last formal efforts to place DRM as an integral part of environmental management.

Complementing EIAs and EISs is the sustainability impact assessment (SIA) tool for supporting major trade negotiations and other endeavors. SIAs provide in-depth analysis of the potential economic, social, human rights, and environmental impacts related to policy, often in the context of negotiations, such as the Green Growth Knowledge Platform. The platform is used to identify combined economic, environmental, and social impacts of proposed development policies and action plans. Environmental impacts are approached in the traditional way: how development goes about its business impacts natural resources. Groups of countries can select the SIA approach when collective review is needed for political and financial support and require evaluation of policy proposals or options, including the economy, society, and environment. But treatment of natural hazard events is not part of the assessment.

Complementary to SIAs is the social impact assessment (SocIA), a methodology to review social effects of infrastructure projects and other development interventions. Although SIAs are usually applied to planned interventions, the same techniques can be used to evaluate the social impact of unplanned events such as natural hazards. SocIAs have been incorporated into formal planning and approval to categorize how major developments may affect individuals, groups, and settlements. But they do not address the likelihood of such an event occurring (exposure) or the level of loss (vulnerability and risk). Like the SIA tool, the SocIA does not add directly to the HEVRL assessment but can help inform MERRE processes for DRR implementation in the corresponding societal unit. There are also assessments related to environmental management concerns. While these assessments were not created or often used to view natural hazard events and economic and social infrastructure, they do relate risk to people and varying environmental settings.

## Adding Value to Landscapes—or Not

Development activities have created vulnerability where none existed before. Where the supply of naturally occurring less-vulnerable land and water resources is becoming depleted, increasing investment must be made to reduce risk through draining wetlands, diking rivers, and stabilizing slopes, for example. A level of risk to a natural event occurrence, severity, and frequency may meet someone's acceptance in order to spawn investment for development. But the actual level of event impact may be far more than anticipated. Investing in lessening the risk presented by an event adds to the country's GDP growth, but the action may be too little. Repairing the damage created by the event's impact adds to the GDP again. But what has occurred is using risk as a subsidy, that is, borrowing from the future. The GDP effectively hides the risk and manifests the damage repair.

## Genuine Progress Indicator

Alternatives to GDP have been proposed, but much is at stake in presenting and explaining development if the measure is the net betterment of the population rather than the accounting for the total monetary value of final goods and services. The genuine progress indicator (GPI) and other economic-social measurements illuminate sustainable economic welfare, rather than solely economic growth. It focuses on three underlying subjects: income inequality, non-market benefits, and negative impacts including environmental degradation and infrastructure loss. Presented in monetary units, it calculates gains and losses caused by natural hazard events while also including investment in DRR and post-disaster reconstruction. GPI calculations give a clearer picture of the short- and long-term impact of natural hazard events, including those modified by anthropogenic actions on both economic and social infrastructure as well as natural resources.

## Enterprise Risk Management

Another assessment built in part on the environment is enterprise risk management (ERM). This approach includes the two dimensions of risk type and risk management. Examples of risk types include (natural) hazard risk identified in liability torts, property damage, and natural catastrophes. Risk management processes document the current conditions in which the organization operates in an internal, external, and risk management context. It also identifies material threats to achievement of the organization's objectives and areas the organization might exploit for competitive advantage.

## Broader Development Planning Perspectives and DRR

Vulnerability reduction is a continuum: the micro aspects are often addressed within macro issues. Selecting the type of risk—physical, financial, economic—bears heavily on how the risk is perceived, who pays, and who benefits. In the case of drinking water resource networks, for example, agriculture, power generation, and transportation assessments may point to the micro as well as the macro aspects of vulnerability impact to the system. Decisions on the applicability of existing environmental management planning, as in the case of global warming and climate change, are necessarily made outside the realm of previous experience and sometimes have never before been addressed in environmental impact modeling.

Land use planning, a critical component of environmental management for resource and space allocation, has been lauded as an important DRR action by international, regional, and national proclamations. However, land use planning decisions are ultimately shaped in large part by development interests and political mandates, but not always with consent or input from local public and private entities. Economic sector entities at the local level may not have or may not choose to dedicate funds for addressing infrastructure vulnerability issues. HEVRL assessments are sensitive to changes in location, severity, and frequency of natural hazard events. Thus, their undertaking may depend on national or international, not local, support. This is particularly true for changes brought on by economic development.

At the geographic scales of national and international river basins, measurements of environmental impact and degradation by development become associated with complex development planning processes. Assessment of natural hazard impact is usually brought to development processes as part of financial risk management but does not necessarily include economic and physical risk management. Environmental impact assessments related to these river basin scenarios, while focusing on how development will impact ecosystem structure and function, may not address how environmental processes will impact development save the ever-growing assessment of climate change impact on specific development sectors and populations. At a regional scale, economic development planning experiences have been noted for their environmental impact analysis but not for their recognition of vulnerability to natural hazard events. The sectors are discussed often by noneconomic sector organizations as to decision-making to reduce vulnerability to natural hazard events. Such analyses will sometimes focus on specifics of vulnerability to natural hazard events and the purpose of vulnerability reduction in terms of how, type of natural hazard, at what cost, and for whose benefit (Bender 2013c).

## Temporal and Spatial Dimensions of Natural Hazards and Development

Traditional measurements of development have looked at economic gains (GDP) and social gains translated into quantitative terms (value of years of completed education and expected life span, income growth, and disposable income) at a fixed point in time conditioned by the past. Sustainable development models demand an examination of desirable future conditions toward which present development must contribute to betterment of future generations. And the concept of tragedy of the commons is bound by a temporal dimension of existing generations at a point in time when successive actions lead to demise of the structure and function of ecosystems and to depletion or lack of access to natural resources.

Some development activities—particularly those sensitive to drought, earthquake, volcanic eruption, sea level rise, flooding, and major storms—become stranded assets. Whether assessments of exposure and vulnerability (if not risk assessments) point out their peril, the assets are stranded in the sense that they lose their market value, perhaps very rapidly, and have little market attraction. Their vulnerability is beyond control by any feasible action or further investment. These assets will require sustained subsidies for the foreseeable future, an admittedly temporal dimension. These can be both physical and financial assets examined as ERM in relation to climate change and CCA.

Subsidies may have been part of creating the development activity in the first place or become necessary as the condition of a stranded asset becomes known. The subsidies, existing or called for, include tax abatements of all kinds, below-market cost access to water and energy, and transportation access paid for by others. When vulnerability becomes evident without an acceptable market-driven solution, subsidies or closure for stranded assets are in the offing. Subsidies can impact taxpayers and investors; closure can impact these two groups and employees, as well as access near and far for the goods or services provided by the asset, whether housing, medical facilities, or manufacturing plants.

Assessed vulnerability of stranded assets large and small says more about financial risk in terms of which sector or where the development activity takes place than it does about calendar time length. Development participants are becoming acutely aware of changing time frames of climate risk as it affects natural resources. Natural resources, beginning with land (which for a long time was considered free or, at the least, inexhaustible), plus labor and capital, are the basis for economic development. And this triad has been the subject of long-standing discussions about risk and development.

On the international stage NGOs are among those noting that no precedents exist for dealing with climate variability or sea level rise. These conditions are currently occurring in many countries where NGOs are actively involved with development and disaster assistance programs for the poor. At the international and regional levels, NGOs may be further along than MDBs in holding discussions on disaster-development linkages. But NGOs are just as constrained as MDBs, both internally and externally, by the previously discussed need to manage risk and "mainstream" disaster risk management into development. There are divisions and turf areas in both NGOs and MDB institutions, built around funded and highly visible yet dual development and disaster management approaches. When risk management of economic and social infrastructure to natural hazards has been identified or addressed in a manner sufficient to rethink development programs, the cause is usually related at present to climate change adaptation. Most often, targeted infrastructure components are the agriculture, education, health, potable water and sanitation, rural transportation, and energy sectors. As such, CCA interventions are not necessarily identified as development actions or DRR initiatives.

## In Sum

Sustainability includes continuing provision of building materials, safe building sites, and acceptable level of vulnerability of components of the built environment to natural hazard events. Acceptable levels of vulnerability mean that loss from a natural hazard event does not constitute a disaster for the impacted societal group and its surroundings. Nor should the loss create dependency that forfeits meeting present needs or needs in the future. DRR is an integral part of environmental management, which is part of sustainable development. Such an approach makes DRR the embodiment of sustainable development. Resilience constitutes the effort at effective disaster risk reduction as part of sustainable development.

Many development actions have visible as well as occult goals of economic growth for immediate gain and intergenerational prosperity. Such actions are coupled to the disaster-development linkage of risk and to the explicit and implicit competition for various types of resources for economic development. These actions range from environmental management as part of sustainable development to natural resource consumption and to pollution as part of economic development. Much in development must change to reduce the risk of loss, increase the resilience of communities, and enhance the structure and function of ecosystems.

The response of environmental management, as with the development process itself, lies in the methods and behaviors employed. Environmental management has tools at its disposal to assess vulnerability of the built environment to naturally occurring events. It also uses many of the same behaviors as development processes to apply those tools. Environmental management experience and tools to identify natural hazard risks and options are clearly needed to achieve successful disaster risk reduction.

The challenge of climate change adaptation in the face of climate hazards is an exceptional case of environmental management, disaster risk management, and the disaster-development linkage. It illuminates present and pending efforts to work with the differences between development actions shaping climate impacts and climate impacts that have and will shape development.

CHAPTER 11

# Climate Change Adaptation and Disaster Risk Reduction in Development

Borrowing countries have signed on to frameworks for integrating climate change adaptation and disaster risk management into development policy and planning at the national and subnational levels. Economic and social infrastructure and ecosystems are to be addressed through implementation by entities, public and private, that are responsible for the built environment. Both CCA and DRR actions seek to lessen vulnerability to acceptable levels that facilitate reaching development goals. This is as true for reducing possible loss of ecosystem structure and function as it is for avoiding damage and destruction of the built environment, including human settlements and their critical and social infrastructure.

Climate change to a verifiable extent is in large part the result of development choices impacting atmospheric and hydrologic events. These lead to changes in the type, location, magnitude, and frequency of climate conditions in both negative and sometimes positive ways. The CCA community was first in the broader disaster risk reduction spectrum to name the specific sectors implicated in causing the alteration of climate hazard events. Governments and civil society are called to resolve vulnerability issues related to climate hazards. This call, however, does not necessarily come directly from owners and operators of economic and social infrastructure. Instead it comes from outside the planning and practices of the development sector, even if some stakeholders and other participants issue the call. The development sector often frames CCA as competing for resources destined for traditional economic development. Yet as the GAR19 document states, "Climate change is a major driver of disaster losses and failed development. It amplifies risk" (UNDRR 2019: x).

From the outset as part of environmental management, climate change and climate change adaptation discussions have called out specific development sectors for their role in global warming and changing weather patterns. Heretofore, the sustainable development community was reluctant to name specific development participants for cause and effect.

It preferred to refer to development needs for expanded economic and social infrastructure and called for sustainability. Climate and other natural hazards, altered by development actions or not, were not specifically identified.

The emergence of CCA as a sector has in some ways made its integration into development processes more difficult. Climate change was initially presented as an environmental management issue that became a development issue linked, initially, to three specific sectors: energy, agriculture, and transportation. Only later would the climate change adaptation community bring global warming to core environmental concerns to more adeptly address development processes and outcomes.

Presently climate change and climate change adaptation are a siloed sector that encompasses a comprehensive approach to environmental management issues in development. It addresses human suffering and proposes alternatives to existing development models and current economic investment objectives and strategies, as well as addressing economic and social justice issues. Calls for DRR in development are now made to avoid creating or exacerbating climate hazard impacts. In contrast, DRR often focuses on creating a more resilient built environment after vulnerable components of economic and social infrastructure are identified from declared disasters or HEVRL assessments.

## Climate Hazards and the Broader DRR Context

Three points regarding climate change, environmental management, and development are relevant. First, as the least vulnerable (and thus more valuable) landscapes and ecosystem goods and services become depleted, value must be added to reduce risk to an acceptable level. This occurs in the face of climate change. Second, natural disasters are no more "natural" than ecosystem degradation. Both result from choices made by societies. And third, natural processes, punctuated by dramatic events, shape landscapes, flush marches, reefs, and estuaries, and form soils (Bender 1994).

We understand the causes, relationships, and risks from climate hazards to development actions. Natural hazard risk reduction and adaptation actions presently take place under the banners of DRR and CCA rather than a development banner. The actions undertaken by entities in the development community often reflect attempts at protection of development processes from being identified with risk creation of the built environment.

Globalization is now recognized for its role in introducing changes to the built environment and creating challenges for DRR. The climate change adaptation community and others have shown how globalization has contributed to greenhouse gas emissions. Varying positions taken by stakeholders and other development participants inform development decisions made by, among others, climate change disbelievers, doubters, and believers, as well as those who are certain. It has been said that when it comes to anthropogenic climate change, it becomes an epistemology, so that conclusions are no longer based on scientific fact but on beliefs and values. The goal is to build resilience and reduce vulnerability regardless of what we call the physical drivers.

Nonetheless, development is carried out with risk to perpetrators and those impacted by climate events alike. *GAR19* states, "Non-linear change in hazard intensity and frequency is already a reality. Affecting the intensive and extensive nature of risk, climate change can contribute to more powerful storms, exacerbate coastal flooding, and bring higher temperatures and longer droughts. Emergent climate-related risks will alter most of our current risk metrics. Growth in death, loss and damage will surpass already inadequate risk mitigation, response, and transfer mechanisms" (UNDRR 2019: x). Dealing with CCA continues to involve development policy and actions as a cause-and-effect relationship. This relationship is formed through successive recognized phases of GHG emissions, perpetrator identification, and assignment of blame; calls for cessation; and demands for compensation, adjustment, and adjudication.

As noted in *GAR19* in its discussion of risk indexing (UNDRR 2019), measuring risk provokes robust debate, particularly when the discussion includes risk related to climate change events. Contributing to this debate is the impact of climate change and climate variability on (1) the risk posed by natural hazard events leading to catastrophic events and (2) risk management policy and planning. In the former, atmospheric and hydrologic events are dramatically changing the risk faced by populations and their economic and social infrastructure and by ecosystems in all types of landscapes. There can be some benefits from climate change and climate variability in some circumstances, usually related to temperature and rainfall. The impact on risk management policy and planning is becoming a policy issue, but risk management is not always an accepted determinant of development policy and planning.

Policy and planning processes belonging to CCA and DRR and those processes identified with development are impacted by natural hazard risk management approaches. An example is the United Nations Framework Convention on Climate Change (UNFCCC) and discussions by less-developed countries on their national adaptation program of action (NAPA). The aim is to foster feasible adaptation actions. In the case of DRR, SFDRR builds on HFA in an approach adopted by UN member countries that lays out strategic goals and action priorities. Expected outcomes are less loss of life, fewer economic losses, and less exposure of populations and natural resources to loss from natural hazard impact (UNISDR 2015b). Sovereign states are to define their own targets for reduction. Approaches to integrating CCA and DRR into national development policy and planning are not specifically mandated for the development sector. There is no mandate for the development sector to take ownership of climate change risk reduction policy formation and implementation, make public chosen risk levels available from its decision-making, or voluntarily use development actions to reduce risk. Indeed, the development community often frames CCA and DRR actions as optional, often costly add-ons to development actions. Yet CCA and DRR implementation depends not only on understanding changes or variability of events that lie ahead, but also willingness to use all societal resources, including those created and managed by the development sector.

International guidance through public and private channels presented to the development community by sovereign states is not a single-focused or consensus approach for successfully integrating CCA and DRR into development policy, planning, and practice. CCA and DRR suggest roles for individuals and communities. Discussion on the inclusion of CCA and DRR actions include whether disaster losses or demands for subsidies by the development community are sufficient to change development choices. In all cases, to be successful, sovereign state guidance is best judged on issues of coordination, responsibility, and accountability, as well as governance, visibility, transparency, and participation. The challenge to governments, the private sector, and civil society alike is to be present through the entire spectrum of development processes.

Through its seven-step approach (Carter et al. 1994; Parry and Carter 1998) and derived methodologies, the IPCC encourages national HEVRL assessments as well as recommendations of adaptation policies, strategies, and measures (Sem and Lu 2007). One of the UNISDR twin policies to reduce risk presented by extreme climate events is to reduce the vulnerability of societies to inevitable climate change impacts. One of the derived methodologies for use by the UNFCCC least developed countries is the UNDP Adaptation Policy Framework (APF). It provides a structured approach to creating and implementing adaptation measures to ensure human development in the face of climate variability and change. Its stages include scoping and designing an adaptation project, assessing current vulnerability of development objectives to climate, assessing future climate change risks to development objectives, formulating an adaptation strategy, and continuing adaptation through monitoring and evaluation (UNDP 2004). From an international finance perspective, climate change epitomizes the complexity of the development challenge in a globalizing, but still highly unequal world. The complexity is not only population access to basic goods and services, but also impact related to exposure, vulnerability, and risk to expected loss due to natural hazard events to all forms of economic and social infrastructure in all types of socioeconomic settings.

Addressing climate change impacts is critical to sustainable development, green, and poverty reduction agendas. These have differing interpretations as to how poverty formation and alleviation is related to and will be resolved by CCA approaches. Climate change increases the initial cost of development if adaption measures are fully accounted for rather than carrying risk as an unfunded subsidy. The development community is challenged to accelerate or maintain robust economic growth in poorer countries even in the face of climate change. The challenge to the CCA community is sustainability if not survival of people and their communities. Climate change adaptation calls for reinvigorating the financial architecture of development at a scale not seen before (World Bank Group 2008). But hard-earned development gains to a great extent have created the underlying conditions of climate change. Losses to climate-hazard-related impacts are already at a scale not seen before, depending on the country and the climate hazard issue. Whatever the financial architecture that is envisioned, stakeholders will be called upon to make climate change adaptation a principal purpose of development through integrated climate change adaptation and resilience efforts, not as an add-on to development. The aforementioned reinvigoration, profit driven or not, will certainly be in the interest of community and sustainability.

Institutional strengthening and linking science to development, mitigation, and adaptation—a first priority for responding to climate change—have long since been identified and continue to be necessary. In light of significant and sometimes irreversible anticipated changes, strategic regional priorities must be focused primarily on forming and implementing specific adaptation measures that illustrate practical options for adapting to climate change effects and help document the costs and benefits of alternative adaptation approaches (Vergara 2007).

As in the case of observing the role of societal values, the role of economic costs and benefits is also dominant. Given the uncertainty of loss, at issue is the cost of risk reduction to climate impacts compared to having greater risk with the benefit of less initial development cost. Sharing or avoiding the cost of risk reduction altogether is often judged preferable to identifying costs linked to actions that are creating the risk. The private sector, including investors, economic sector owners, and insurance firms, avoid accepting or carrying responsibility for risk of loss, not only financial, but also economic and physical loss when possible. They attempt to transfer risk to public institutions, the local community, and risk management schemes focusing on hazard event occurrence, not the resulting damage. Public institutions as owners and/or operators of public service infrastructure are often defined as self-insured. Citizens and homeowners, who constitute the investors in public infrastructure through taxes, fees, and licenses, are left facing financial, economic, and physical consequences of climate event impacts whether reaching declared disaster levels or not.

## DRR, CCA, and Development in Practice

When considered in their entirety, current DRR, CCA, and development policy and planning approaches reveal gaps, obstacles, and challenges. CCA and DRM processes, while having compatible aims and benefits, evolved separately in form and substance. They now coexist as part of an even larger collection of issues promulgated by self-declared communities dealing with risk reduction tasks of global magnitude but with local ramifications. The development community seeks economic growth and population prosperity.

Along with DRR and CCA, environmental management, poverty alleviation, and other crosscutting issues mirror the challenges in working with economic development policy and planning initiatives. In most countries at the policy level there is a lack of national consensus and a common, unified voice on CCA and DRR. This reflects lack of a long-term strategy, legislation, leadership, and effectiveness by named focal point institutions.

Another facet of policy is the residual influence of the "disaster cycle," particularly at the national and local levels in DRR and CCA policy and practice. The cycle often avoids any reference to development and by extension climate change impacts, while recognizing the relationship of the impact of natural hazard events (disaster impacts) on development's reported gains. Laying aside the imagery of the vicious cycle, pairing proposed climate change actions with the development agenda has made visible development-created risk due to natural hazard events in a way that DRR never has. In the end, CCA policy and actions have made more evident the differences between addressing risk reduction as central to new and different development goals and DRR as a follow-up to development actions. This holds also for development actions, whether new components of the built environment, reconstruction after disasters, or most importantly, addressing existing infrastructure vulnerability. CCA has engaged the economic and social old-line sectors to force an understanding of their role in risk creation to natural hazard events. The development sector does not push for a broad, public discussion with the old-line sectors on risk management, be it financial, economic, or physical.

The issue is not whether climate change, climate variability, and CCA are examples of DRR, nor whether DRR is an instructive approach in dealing with climate hazard events. The issue is that natural hazard events, particularly climate-related events, have posed and will continue to pose risks to development initiatives as currently framed.

Lessening loss due to climate impact is essential for meeting international UN-sponsored development goals. All development actions need to be considered in light of CCA and DRR initiatives and evaluated. But in a more direct, practical vein, the CCA community has learned from the HFA experience the need for working with local populations to understand the challenges of implementing CCA. CCA emphasizes populations at risk who are vulnerable or who own and operate vulnerable social and economic infrastructure to identify risk-specific outcomes of event impacts.

The CCA community has examined what happens when every event is labeled a disaster. At the most far-reaching edge of CCA policy proposals is a call for cessation of all funding for development in order to support CCA. Such a position casts development not as a process, but as a set of known outcomes in contradiction with (and perhaps incapable of) addressing climate hazard management. On the other hand, there has been no "either-or" call for an absolute implementation of DRR in place of development. The SFDRR, however, can learn from the CCA experience of associating risk with specific sectors, using identification of causal factors—the drivers of risk—as a policy and political force, and noting that risk reduction must be owned by development.

Traditional economic and social sectors have not been approached by DRM in a systematic way for a variety of reasons. Not least of the reasons is that for development-related sectors, risk management has been presented as a disaster management issue (where every event is named a disaster) for which there is usually a specialized, government-supported (meaning government-funded) disaster management agency at the national, regional, and international level.

Specific sectors, such as agriculture, education, energy, health, housing, mining, transportation, tourism, and water and sanitation may not recognize themselves as most vulnerable to climate hazard events, most impacted by previous events, and most susceptible to future climate variability. These sectors proclaim a historic risk-adverse approach in development project design and execution. Yet post-event analysis shows these sectors made conscious decisions to accept risk at demonstrably high levels. They paid little attention to risk reduction in their work and preferred risk transfer (often with financial gain) or requesting compensation from government for uninsured losses or restoration of essentially services to the public. Moreover, calls for integrating CCA and DRR into recovery have resulted in some instances of projects proceeding through design and funding phases. But descriptions of steps to risk reduction processes are sometimes deliberately or inadvertently turned into merely descriptive information for content in the final report on project completion. Thus, given the pressures of post-disaster reporting, actions of policy and planning become, in part, a surrogate for monitoring, evaluation, reporting, regulation, and enforcement of risk reduction.

Despite calls for decentralization and increased planning for CCA and DRR, governments are confronting bureaucracy, lack of information technology, emphasis to focus on life safety, and administrative and economic inefficiency. The new role for public sector planners and the implications for planning in CCA and DRR comes at a time when public sector planning continues to be out of fashion, if not out of resources, experience, and sometimes expertise. Other issues include clarifying roles, overlapping assignments and responsibilities, lack of research, enabling legislation, risk communication, and access to international cooperation.

The IPCC notes constraints to stakeholder capabilities related to CCA and DRR as limited availability of access to credit and technical assistance, low public investment in infrastructure in rural areas, inadequate education and public health services, poor appreciation of risk, lack of technical knowledge, scarce or incomplete climate databases and other information (including forecasts), and lack of warning systems. Additional constraints include conflicting environmental policies, laws, and regulations related to hazard assessment, land use planning, and building codes (Carter et al. 1994). GAR19 notes, "The development of DRR plans at the local, national and regional levels, and the assessments that underpin them, must integrate near-term climate change scenarios, and elaborate the enabling conditions for transformative adaptation presented by IPCC" (UNDRR 2019: x).

## Community Participation in Risk Reduction Approaches

Community involvement in DRR decision-making and implementation is about participation that includes individuals and groups who are directly, indirectly, and secondarily impacted by loss of economic and social infrastructure. The question of what actually constitutes community participation is relevant. Also relevant is recognition of the extent that community involvement can be the decisive influence on the vulnerability level of their immediate built environment, particularly in post-disaster reconstruction. Whatever the resulting level of risk of the associated economic and social infrastructure through development processes (including self-directed housing construction), the community may or may not lay claim to having played a decision-making role. But who is the community? Often the composition of the community is not identified, nor is their specific role in DRR decision-making. Is "community participation" a surrogate or substitute for making decisions as to acceptable levels of risk of physical infrastructure vulnerability reduction?

Stakeholders in national risk reduction venues need more discussion of strategies for achieving desired outcomes as well as for identifying needs. There is no one model for involvement of stakeholders in this discussion. Moreover, there is no one model for broader stakeholder involvement, particularly that deemed to be community participation. Alexandra Titz, Terry Cannon, and Fred Kruger (2018) identify six issues for comment: (1) "Community participation" is often the default term used uncritically for the participation at the local level, but without specificity to anything other than geographic place. (2) As related to the discussion of CCA and DRR, community participation does not automatically ensure that risk to a component of settlement infrastructure—housing, schools, health facilities, water systems—will not cause disastrous damage and the need for outside assistance. Indeed the level of community "acceptable risk" may be quite high, for example, siting or rebuilding a damaged school in a flood-prone area because it is available and close to the population. Community participation may or may not hold to lower levels of "acceptable risk" than those proposed by authorities or brought about through traditional design and construction practices. (3) Distribution of benefits from community participation-sponsored decision-making is often in favor of the already better-off. (4) In most parts of the global South, significant oppression and exploitation are integral to the systems of power within the so-called "community." (5) Strong self-interest by outside (not local) stakeholders is seen as being largely uncritical of participatory and community approaches. (6) Neoliberal states have also been pushing decentralization (and its latest manifestation, "community resilience") in order to divest, as it would seem, their responsibility regardless of their role in DRR. Participation and community development are earmarked to be part of the mainstreaming of DRR and CCA into development processes at the local level.

In a study of urban poverty and vulnerability to climate change in Latin America, Cassidy Johnson, citing a passage from Hardoy and Pandiella (2009), noted that disaster risk is shaped by "the long-evident incapacity of governments to address risk and to integrate development with the reduction of vulnerability. Meanwhile, within local governments, there is generally an institutional incapacity to address this issue or to control pollution and protect natural resources; and also a lack of accountability to citizens in their jurisdiction and little or no scope for citizen participation" (Johnson 2011: 15).

Generally, there are actions involving the private sector that highlight local stakeholder involvement in CCA and DRR national actions: (1) sector investment where often the first and most ambitious actions are for housing and settlement infrastructure; (2) mandated advice and consent regarding private sector investment most often associated with urban expansion or sprawl, depending on the stakeholder's point of view; and (3) enabling private sector actions beginning with monitoring, reporting, regulations, and enforcement. These actions are often most visible in recov-

---

### Community-Based DRR

A few years before Hurricane Mitch (1998), the Municipality of La Masica on the north coast of Honduras, a rural agricultural area, formed a community early warning system (SAT) for its river valley. It was cochaired by a seventy-plus-year-old teacher and the former head of the local agricultural co-op. The committee received national and international support to undertake a community-based flood early-warning project along the length (one hundred kilometers) of its valley.

Village committees were set up to construct and install simple flood hazard monitoring devices (rudimentary river-level markers and staffs) based on admittedly rough flood-event elevation maps. The people obtained and installed radios for communication and used previously acquired knowledge of evacuation techniques.

During Hurricane Mitch, alarms sounded, evacuations took place, and not a single life was lost. In torrential rains the following December, not only were no lives lost, but all livestock was safely evacuated.

Later the central government with different international support equipped the valley with electronic river flood-stage sensors that remotely transmitted the data directly to the national capitol for monitoring, alerting the countryside, and directing action. Thus local community residents were moved from being the first-to know to the last-to-know about a possible flood event.

But by 2001, a newly organized Community of Municipalities of the Central Atlantic (coast) of Honduras (MAMUCA), which includes the La Masica watershed, set about revitalizing and setting up SATs in the municipalities through direct community direction and participation with national and international support. By 2016, an action plan was adopted to promote SAT operations, and training, field exercises, and maintenance were begun or strengthened throughout MAMUCA.

ery operations of stakeholders but are present also in new development and retrofitting of economic and social infrastructure. The stakeholders undertake the first action in self-interest, recognition, demonstrable need, and positive feedback. The other two actions are more likely than not imposed on the private sector but not necessarily the nonprofit segment.

## Hazard-Resilient Structures and Building More Committees

One of the most notable differences between CCA and DRR stakeholder involvement is the how to address the built environment, particularly economic infrastructure. In general, CCA proponents have established their case around engaging particularly the economic sectors directly involved in global warming, beginning with the energy sector, but now engaging the agriculture, transportation, and urban sectors. DRR proponents, in contrast, often have created their initiatives from a disaster management perspective and associated specialized agencies focusing on social infrastructure component-related DM initiatives such as critical and lifeline infrastructure. Since the 1990s, DRR proponents have also built their initiatives on sector involvement in education, health, and water and sanitation sector facility vulnerability reduction programs.

During economic development planning, together or separately, CCA and DRR proponents may seek direct involvement of international and national level sectors at the ministerial level for political commitment to infrastructure risk reduction for retrofitting and inclusion of infrastructure risk reduction in national plans by the national planning authority. Specialized sector committees (such as in the energy sector) may also be created to deal with climate change at the national level. Coordinating with the cli-

---

**DRR in Two Verses**

Following Hurricane Mitch's severe impact in 1998 of Honduras, the government supported by a MDB undertook the planning for reconstruction of the severely damaged portion of the Pan American Highway on the Caribbean coast. In consultation with an MDB on the highway's reconstruction, the MDB was forthcoming with mandated maps of the proposed roadway work and its relationship to previously mapped habitat areas of endangered bird species. When the MDB was asked about flood hazard maps covering the same area for road reconstruction, the response was that there was no requirement to prepare or use such information.

mate change lead entity, sector-based committees can include specialized functions that cover generation, transmission and distribution of energy, and supply-and-demand institutions such as water and sanitation, health, and agriculture.

Governments may create CCA agencies to deal with specific production and service issues, with agriculture as a priority. These initiatives typically have targeted subnational geographic areas (seacoasts, river basins, high mountain areas), and/or population segments (the poor, indigenous, rural, migrant labor, immigrants). Specifically for the agriculture sector, both CCA and DRM initiatives are most often built around food security, water accessibility, and livelihood issues.

## Ecosystem Protection and Restoration

From early on, proponents of CCA initiatives have consistently explained the impact of climate change on the structure and function of ecosystems, beginning with changes in life zones, water scarcity, habitat destruction, and species survival. Public and private groups concerned about goods and services provided by ecosystems and, more directly, those concerned about natural resource management have become partners in ecosystem protection and restoration. These partners include some who refute the breadth and depth of global warming and climate change assessments. But they have vested interest in sustainable ecosystem management and come from many economic and social sectors, whether or not they also consider themselves environmentalists.

HFA in 2005 and SFDRR in 2015 have clearly noted that expected outcomes of DRR include a reduction of impact on environmental assets. There is still much discussion about collaborative implementation of CCA and DRR actions to address this issue. CCA actions are based on changing development's impact on ecosystems; DRR actions have focused on lessening the vulnerability of the built environment without necessarily naming specific development processes causal or root factors.

But it is clear that changing atmospheric and hydrologic conditions are negatively impacting ecosystems and the built environment. Modifying the events themselves in the short term is probably not possible. But there are opportunities, particularly in the land use development planning and water resource management, to modify the impact of events and to modify exposure of populations, wildlife habitats, and biological production and diversity to negative impact from events.

CAA and DRR initiatives include focusing on priority watersheds and river basins with associated social groups and sustainable use of natural resources. The focus includes agriculture, forestry and soils, vulnerability assessments, and risk reduction of agro-ecosystems including irrigated agriculture. Other priorities include geographic area focus on coastal zones, irrigated plains, biodiversity in the humid tropics, and high mountain valleys. Although dealing with carbon sequestration is a CCA mitigation issue, sustainable management of wetlands is also an area of government initiatives. Nathaniel Forbes notes, "Treat water scarcity as a disaster no less than an earthquake, a tsunami. Unless we converge our professions to address water scarcity, we will not be prepared for the water disasters of the future. We will not be able to protect our companies, we will not be able to protect our communities, and unless we start soon, we may not even be able to protect ourselves" (Forbes 2014).

## Continuing Exposure

Addressing risk to climate hazard events most often provokes a robust debate that includes development-related climate hazards in general and climate change, climate variability, decadal variances, and atmospheric and hydrologic events in particular. The exposure of populations is prompting calls for increased planning and expenditures to save lives. Action areas, such as land use planning and other regulatory measures, no-regret approaches to structural mitigation, transparency and accountability in public administration, and lessening of greenhouse gas emissions, are increasingly cited as necessary to address atmospheric and hydrologic climate-related hazard risks. This is particularly the case in urban and coastal areas.

Climate change discussion is increasingly focused in both the public and private sectors on where and how economic development takes place. Such considerations are within local, provincial, national, and regional political groupings that often depend on (or leave it to) legislation to define acceptable risk and judicial proceedings. Judicial proceedings are often used to ensure enforcement of mandated risk reduction measures or protection from eminent domain procedures, as well as prohibition of certain land use, landscape alteration such as deforestation, and aquifer drawdown.

## Political Will

The price associated with political will—in reality, the willingness to be politically vulnerable—often means having faith in what knowledge, including scientific knowledge, can bring to policy formation, even while acknowledging doubt. Just as in physical science research, political leadership to create policy need not be, and often is not, free of doubt. At present, doubt exists among scientists regarding the origins of current climate hazard conditions. Scientists may doubt—but not disbelieve—that creating policy to address climate hazards is possible, even for events beyond those shown by present, observable cause and effect. This approach to dealing with climate change and climate change adaptation is made more difficult by the situation in areas both urban and rural that are experiencing land use change and natural resource exploitation practices far more rapid and intrusive than they have experienced before.

The opposite of belief is not doubt, but certainty. Some people are certain that climate change does not exist because they find no acceptable proof of it, particularly regarding future events. Such certainty invariably places managing climate event risk reduction itself at risk by avoiding, obfuscating, or casting doubt on an identified causal factor, whether natural or anthropogenic. Through avoidance, transfer, or acceptance of climate risk, individuals, groups, or society must manage physical, economic, and financial risk as best they can. Even when the causal factor is clear, strategies for lessening risk are more evident, but not necessarily easier to implement. The greatest uncertainty having the greatest impact on risk management may come not from science at all, but from human behavior.

## In Sum

Climate hazards, including those classified as climate change and those spawned by development, are part of natural hazard events. They are increasingly part of discussions on environmental management. This is recognized whether the subject of environmental management is sustainable use of the goods and services of ecosystems or the impact of development activities on those systems. There are both opportunities and challenges for development policy and practice to include an effective approach to climate hazard risk reduction.

Certainly, calls for including climate change adaptation on its own or integrated with DRR continue to be sounded. Discussions of how to reflect climate change and climate change adaptation in development decision-making is being addressed very slowly by those sectors identified as impacted by such changes. Yet anticipation of that discussion calls to mind two considerations.

First is using climate change information in HEVRL assessments for DRR. Just as important is using climate change adaptation information in MERRE processes. These topics are quite relevant to upcoming discussions of HEVRL and MERRE in chapters 12 and 13.

Second is including calls for a systemic approach to risk assessment in GAR19. "Given the very threat to humanity posed by the effects of climate change, a more integrated approach is required to adapt to and reduce risk from climate change, as well as from shorter-term risks from natural and man-made hazards, and related biological, technological and environmental hazards and risks, when seeking to prevent the creation of new risk through development. Failure to include climate change scenarios in assessment and risk reduction planning will build inherent redundancy in all we do" (UNDRR: ix). This guidance asks for more than an increased integrated approach to assessment. Called for is including all types of risk and assessing their relationship, interaction, and resulting impact, depending on causal factors. Assessment leads to, but is not, risk reduction. Mitigation action is necessary now and in the foreseeable future based on what is known and what can be anticipated. This will be discussed in chapter 14.

# Part IV
# THEY WHO CALL THE TUNE

# CHAPTER 12

# Built Environment Vulnerability and Development Processes

This chapter looks at the use of risk assessment information in development processes to support DRR. These assessments address hazard, exposure, vulnerability, and risk posed by the physical impact of natural hazard events on the built environment as well as loss following actual events. The expected or actual physical damage or destruction can be expressed not only in physical terms, but also in financial, economic, and social terms in some instances. Loss data of economic and social infrastructure related from events related to populations can be expressed in these as well as social terms.

For most housing and for a large number of other social and economic infrastructure components around the world, there is little or no government control over construction. Stakeholders may simply accept the inevitability of natural hazard event occurrence and loss. Further, the cost of carrying out assessments, particularly in the public sector, falls on institutions that often cannot directly recapture the benefits of lessening risk of loss.

HEVRL assessments used during design and construction of physical components in normal "new development" processes are often not visible to persons outside the actual development project. Sometimes use of assessment data and information may be part of and defined by applicable building regulations. HEVRL assessments and building regulations may lead to discussions of CCA and sea level rise. A less addressed aspect of DRR for the built environment is retrofitting existing economic and social infrastructure to reduce vulnerability and reconstruction of infrastructure in recovery following a disaster.

Stakeholders do not often invite outsiders to comment on their development projects. This is particularly true given that DRR, environmental management, and economic development were set up as silos for operations and to garner political and financial support. The stakeholders' role in HEVRL assessments for DRR in development processes for the built environment is to (1) provide sufficient information based on policy, practice, and knowledge to identify natural hazard risk management issues; (2) frame decisions for acceptable levels of risk; and (3) carry out informed decisions for risk reduction. Stakeholders individually or collectively may choose not to carry out one or another of these three steps by disregarding the information available, or by refusing to assign responsibility and accountability for the risk created.

## Acceptable Risk, and Responsibility and Accountability

At the global level, stakeholders' participation is usually through technical assistance, funding, program support, and/or staffing that involves project site selection, design, and construction and can be decisive. At the local level, stakeholder participation may be similar, but at a much different scale. In both cases, the stakeholders may accept, transfer, or otherwise avoid decision-making regarding acceptable risk and responsibility and accountability for the resulting risk. Risk analysis (sometimes consisting of only vulnerability analysis of the likelihood of damage to infrastructure components) may be part of project analysis.

Use of DRR through HEVRL assessments mirrors other situations, such as use of environmental impact assessments and social-economic analysis. Nominally part of the development process, HEVRL assessments support risk avoidance or transfer, as well as monitoring, reporting, and evaluation, and certainly have role to play in regulation and enforcement. Funds needed for HEVRL assessments actually may come from development resources, but as with most things in development processes, if funding for HEVRL information can come from sources external to development actions, all the better.

Significant in development literature, but less often addressed, is how the physical risk of what is to be built relates to the goals of a project as a whole. In part, such a relationship is incorporated into normal professional practice. For instance, engineers design a dam to sustain an earthquake or a bridge to survive a flood that meets the criteria of a certain hazardous event return period. But designing projects to be resilient in the face of natural hazards is evidently less routinely taken into account by agronomists, lifeline infrastructure at the settlement level, education and health facilities, and water and sanitation installations. Nor is resilience often addressed in economic analysis where expected probable losses from floods, earthquakes, cyclones, or landslides would be compared with the costs of protecting against a certain level of probable of damage and destruction of infrastructure should a hazardous event occur.

> **National Vulnerability Indexes**
>
> Vulnerability indexes at the national, subnational, or urban level usually present the likely occurrence of one or more types of hazardous events without explaining the actual vulnerability of any particular type of infrastructure components. Examples include the CPI—City Prosperity Index, EM-DAT, ESI—Environmental Sustainability Index, GLIDEnumber—Global Unique Identifier Number, GRAVITY—Global Risk and Vulnerability Index Trends per Year, GRID—Global Risk Data Platform, GRIP—Global Risk Identification Programme, GRR—Global Risk Reports, EMI—Earthquake Megacity Index, Natural Disaster Hotspots—World Bank, Risk Reduction Initiative—DARA, VCA—Vulnerability and Capacity Assessment, WRI—World Risk Index.
>
> These indexes most often focus on exposure by including a hazard type and a particular population or infrastructure characteristics. Depending on their units of measure, they can help identify where project benefits probability can be tested in relation to cost-benefit calculations with certain parameters such as land costs, interest rates, or adjusted value of project benefits. For risk analysis these indexes may contribute to estimating probability distribution of the rate of return on investment. In theory, this allows a funding agency to choose between project options or design decisions to maximize probability that project benefits are achieved despite residual risk.
>
> Significant in development literature, but less often addressed, is how the physical risk of what is to be built relates to the goals of a project as a whole. In part, such a relationship is incorporated into normal professional practice. For instance, engineers design a dam to sustain an earthquake or a bridge to survive a flood that meets the criteria of a certain hazardous event return period. But designing projects to be resilient in the face of natural hazards is evidently less routinely taken into account by agronomists, lifeline infrastructure at the settlement level, education and health facilities, and water and sanitation installations. Nor is resilience often addressed in economic analysis where expected probable losses from floods, earthquakes, cyclones, or landslides would be compared with the costs of protecting against a certain level of probable of damage and destruction of infrastructure should a hazardous event occur.

## More on Acceptable Risk

Policies, programs, and practices to create economic and social infrastructure are continually changing. The changes are shaped not only by science, engineering, architecture, and urban design, but also by forces of supply and demand, political support, and profit and loss. Dealing with risk of loss of infrastructure has evolved from informal to increasingly sophisticated building-structure analytical tools. How these tools are chosen, when, by whom, why, and how they are actually used by those involved in MERRE are not always known. Moreover, risk assessments are often not visible or transparent until decisions on vulnerability have been made.

But choosing inadequate HEVRL assessment tools can lead to constructing economic and social infrastructure with considerable residual physical risk. As Susan Cutter has stated, "Each society must create its own vision of what its resilient version will look like, and must map the pathways to achieve resilience. It must be recognised, however, that achieving resilience is a complex undertaking" (Cutter 2014b).

If the level of risk of loss does not exceed acceptable levels, then development participants might call it self-selected, tradition-bound, community-regulated, or properly administratively managed. But if the level of acceptable risk of loss is high and catastrophic damage is likely to occur due to a natural hazard event, the level of risk might be called self-inflicted, absent tradition, lacking community input, or administratively induced. Ultimately, choosing an acceptable level of risk builds on HEVRL assessments but comes about through social construction embodied in decision-making related to MERRE.

## Special Case of Infrastructure Loss Assessments and Their Use

Physical loss is important to understand, particularly when there is lack of information on losses from prior hazard events. When loss assessments are made, donors and recipients, particularly national participants, may express decidedly different views about the extent of damage and destruction in financial, economic, and social terms. In the final analysis, official disaster loss data may be generated by a group of owners and operators of economic and social infrastructure in both the public and private sectors, together with national administration representatives, international development, financing, and disaster management entities, insurance groups, and NGOs.

Typically, loss is measured in monetary terms, but often unclear is whether the damaged and destroyed infrastructure loss is in terms of net present value, replacement cost, or cost of construction when created and in constant dollars.

Loss information is used by stakeholders, particularly for raising awareness and funds for DRR in their projects. Given the link between disaster loss and post-disaster support, "disaster" loss estimates play a key role in stakeholder ability to respond to requests for assistance. In general, loss data are first addressed for humanitarian assistance operations. Loss estimates of economic and social infrastructure may be general and not include impacts on groups (or communities or private businesses and industries) identified by physical location, ethnicity, economic status, religious affiliation, or legal status. Infrastructure loss may also be selectively identified by sector type of damaged projects (education and health facilities, bridges and port facilities, housing) that are part of prior stakeholder initiatives supported by the stakeholders. But disaggregated loss databases (including those of the UN and regional political bodies) are scarce. They can reveal ownership/operator and responsibility/accountability issues in far more detail than stakeholders want to explore. Given the link between disaster loss and post-disaster support, these figures—and how they are calculated—play a key role in stakeholder negotiating positions, sometimes to competing or contradictory ends in the immediate post-disaster aftermath.

Clearly, loss assessments condition to a great extent the qualitative and quantitative form and content of assistance following a disaster. Official loss estimates are often negotiated between and among stakeholder groups and the impacted country. The participants to the negotiations may have alternative ideas and sometimes competing or conflicting views of public understanding of the losses, depending on individual stakeholder image, claims, and forward-looking wants and needs. Post-event fundraising is conducted in response to the most recent disaster declaration. Funds collected often constitute the financial basis for initial response to the next declared disaster.

## HEVRL Assessments in Defining Economic and Social Vulnerabilities

Economic and social infrastructure HEVRL assessments are prepared in recognition of the varying definitions of population vulnerability, which are constructed around three components: life safety, livelihoods, and social cohesion. Beyond identifying the related infrastructure component serving the population, the vulnerability of associated population is presented in terms of population characteristics such as age, gender, income, employment, immigrant status, education level, health, and so on.

If the life safety standard of infrastructure components is referenced, then often considered is the component's relationship to human occupation. If continuity of service is the design and construction standard, then the inhabitants served and the geographic service area are often identified.

This opens the door to preparing population vulnerability assessments of social, economic, and other themes and their relation to specific physical infrastructure components, such as educational and medical facilities, potable water and sanitary sewer systems, food markets, and the like.

In addition to identifying related physical infrastructure data, population vulnerability assessment indexes may include specific natural hazard event information. Examples are population vulnerability (or exposure) indexes to flood, wind, and rising coastal water events related to climate change and sea level rise. The vulnerability levels of the local infrastructure related to that population should not be assumed as similar to that of the population.

When selecting a physical infrastructure site, economic, environmental, and social analysis may have a larger influence on the project than the probability of natural hazard event impact. HEVRL data and analysis can be prepared regarding characteristics of associated population groups. This assists in relating the existence of the hazard threat, degree of exposure, identification of vulnerability, and extent of risk because of the infrastructure component to the various conditions of population vulnerability.

Components of social infrastructure, such as schools, health facilities, and housing, and economic infrastructure, such as bridges, power plants, and transportation/service corridors, are often sited in known vulnerable areas due to economic and social factors—including land costs, physical access, and proximity to commerce, employment opportunities, and settlement housing. Factors such as population density, gender, income, and other units of measure are cited to explain actual or anticipated benefits of using the site. Site analysis does not often include direct, secondary, and indirect costs to the population, government, and private economic endeavors should infrastructure loss occur.

Vulnerability analysis goes beyond technical, engineering, architectural, and physical science contributions. Reducing physical vulnerability of the built environment contributes to but does not necessarily determine the vulnerability of populations. Similarly, identifying socioeconomic, political, and other components of population vulnerability may contribute to but does not constitute the level of vulnerability of an infrastructure component. Yet decisions on acceptable levels of vulnerability of economic and social infrastructure components and DRR implementation have to be based on something. Avoiding discussion of that something—who is vulnerable and why, and who benefits and who pays—facilitates avoiding or masking a decision about the accepted level of vulnerability of the components.

Social protection and livelihoods are part of vulnerability analysis. But given the magnitude of the exposure of people around the globe to natural hazard, climate change, and sea level rise events, simply identifying the inter-relatedness of these hazard phenomena as events may only obscure, delay, or postpone at varying scales meaningful DRR actions that can be taken. These actions are, of course, dependent on the values, judgment, and willingness to act of the involved society.

Vulnerability assessments may now include previously separate discourses on disasters and development around vulnerability, social protection, and livelihoods. This convergence has evolved in no small measure through (1) creation of the recovery sector, (2) specialization of the humanitarian assistance sector pulling away from the disaster management sector, and (3) increasing interest of some stakeholders to address post-disaster recovery as part of development. Merely calling for increased DRR action is insufficient to stimulate on the part of crosscutting-issue participants greater consideration of natural hazards and related vulnerability during development project design and evaluation.

Using vulnerability assessment tools focused on populations by stakeholders already takes several forms. To begin, tools can focus on traditional economic and social issues whose units of measure are monetary or simply quantify the individuals in particular situations. Some tools use as a point of reference a specific environmental issue: global warming and climate change, sea level rise, habitat survival, and species extinction. The root causes and predicted outcomes are also expressed in monetary and (usually) gross population numbers. Other tools focus on the environmental and socioeconomic impact of specific natural hazard and human-induced events on specific population groups. Given the subject matter, each tool can be used in development decisions concerning DRR.

Consider the vulnerability of a school as physical infrastructure in juxtaposition to the vulnerability of the associated population. A school is in a "poor area" with a population characterized by high unemployment, malnutrition, illiteracy, undocumented households, and so forth. However, the associated population may not have all their vulnerabilities rooted in the possible loss of that school. Not all schools in poor areas are physically vulnerable to natural hazard events, but populations associated with vulnerable schools do have aspects of their vulnerability directly, indirectly, and secondarily related to the school's vulnerability.

## Human Vulnerability in Determining DRR of Economic and Social Infrastructure

Economic, social, and environmental vulnerability assessments of populations are increasingly important measurements to determine implementation of DRR to the built environment. They could be in reference to development or adjunct or parallel to development processes. International and regional exposure indexing initiatives use mapping, geographic information system (GIS) analytical tools, and national population data that link place, type of hazard, and population. A few also qualitatively define exposure of particular infrastructure components in relation to the type, severity, and location of the anticipated natural hazard event.

When and how is inhabitant vulnerability noted when deciding on the need for DRR? The acceptable level of risk of an infrastructure component is ultimately based on how society wants to deal with vulnerability of the population. Beyond life safety, an alternative approach choosing an acceptable level of risk of loss so that physical damage or destruction will not occur is the consequence of the loss of the infrastructure component impacted on the population. For example, in the past, government authorities have declared that schools should be at low risk to damage to natural hazard event events so that those structures might serve as provisional shelters for homeless disaster survivors until suitable housing can be found.

Suppose 100 two-story reinforced masonry schools in one country's prosperous rural agricultural region are found subject to collapse from a magnitude 5.7 or greater earthquake. The HEVRL assessments conclude that collapse of these schools is the probable outcome of such an earthquake event. Now suppose that in the capital city of the same country, a similar set of 100 two-story schools are found subject to collapse from the same earthquake scenario. Is there sufficient information to decide which set of schools should be the priority for DRR action?

In reality, which vulnerabilities determine what set of schools receives attention? If one set of schools is in an economically impoverished area and the other is in a high-income residential community, how would a DRR implementation decision be approached?

At a local scale, E. E. Koks et al. (2015) note that social vulnerabilities explain to a great extent the ability of populations to deal with exposure, vulnerability, risk, and loss. Examining HEVRL assessments with social vulnerabilities allows for deciding individual DRR approaches rather than assuming homogeneity of risk. Based on their social vulnerability, heterogeneous population groups faced with the same natural hazard vulnerability (flooding) in the same geographic area are not necessarily able to take the same mitigation actions.

Whether or not HEVRL assessments of the built environment related to natural hazard events occur, additional types of vulnerability analysis now play an increasingly important role in considering DRR implementation (UNDRR 2019). They constitute policy and practice issues for disaster risk reduction of the built environment in terms of their origin, construct, and application. Some twenty-five years ago, Benson and Twigg (1994) identified three challenges to using tools in the assessment of vulnerability, which have been echoed in *GAR19* (UNDRR 2019). In addition to broadening the tools to consider risks from natural hazards and the related measure of appropriate costs and benefits in reducing risk, there are vulnerability assessments related to (1) identifying the specific objective of cost-benefit analysis, whatever the parameters; (2) using environmental impact assessments and related methodologies and evaluation tools; and (3) ensuring there are appropriate tools to analyze and measure both the costs of mitigation and the nature of benefits of DRR actions.

For example, financial cost-benefit assessments often dwell on aspects of vulnerability as "with and without" DRR, but do not specify a desirable level of risk for different levels of natural hazard events. Financial cost-benefit analysis is now more commonly used to identify the cost of DRR as an add-on expense or a parallel consideration during the infrastructure (including housing) project cycle. But associated populations' vulnerability, expressed as the value of human life, or loss of employment, schooling, or health care is increasingly employed to determine the acceptable level of risk of physical loss of a school or health facility.

## Good-Enough Risk Science

Individuals, communities, sovereign states, and international organizations determine acceptable risk based on values and judgments of the social sciences and findings of the physical sciences. What is the "good-

---

**Disaster Risk Reduction Choices in Perspective**

Choices to address exposure and vulnerability can be replete with HEVRL information challenging MERRE decision-making criteria. In 1993 an agriculture sector vulnerability assessment carried out by the Ministry of Agriculture and the OAS-DSD in Ecuador—the first such study in Latin America—identified a major bridge as susceptible to significant damage should an earthquake occur. This bridge facilitated transport of more than 40 percent of Ecuador's leading export crop, bananas. Of all identified vulnerable agriculture sector infrastructure components, the bridge became the priority for retrofitting.

But the bridge was not ranked high on probability (risk) of damage or destruction. It was rated high on the extent of economic impact and social vulnerability of the associated population related to crop production and commerce (e.g., banana producers, workers, financial institutions, shipping concerns) if the bridge should be unusable for any appreciable length of time.

enough" risk assessment, and what is its HEVRL content? The answer depends on the stakeholder and the decisions to be made. But decisions to be made are influenced by the level of risk that stakeholders could, should, or must recognize or for which they will accept responsibility and accountability.

## Public Policy, Right to Know, Rule of Law

HEVRL is the content that right-to-know laws would make available if such laws commonly included issues of risk to the built environment to damage and loss from natural hazard events. But environmental management legislation does not always mandate legal access to information related to public health and safety.

Public policy can involve HEVRL in assessing and acting on risk to the built environment from natural hazard events. It can exercise the precautionary principle, take actions on issues considered uncertain regarding natural hazard risk management, and err on the side of caution. The principle is used by policy makers to justify discretionary decisions when those decisions create possible harm. The principle implies a social responsibility to protect the public from harm when scientific investigation has found a plausible risk, which can be rescinded should further scientific findings provide sound evidence that no harm will result. This approach is much discussed around the globe, particularly at the local level, even if overridden in political, administrative, and marketplace decisions.

## In Sum

Development is full of risk decision points shaping the built environment when considering possible outcomes for what exists and what is to be built. HEVRL assessments can give facts and context to risk in development, notwithstanding development's vast array of goals and objectives.

HEVRL assessments are essentially objective. What, then, are the best arguments for DRR of the built environment? Whose risk and whose risk reduction are candidates for DRR decision-making? For whom does loss constitute a disaster? Thus risk assessments provide information needed for making decisions in each phase of the infrastructure development process.

Risk assessment has two related subjects: (1) risk of a component of economic and social infrastructure to a natural hazard event and (2) risk of population to the same event associated with the impact and/or impacted economic and social infrastructure components.

Now discussion will move to MERRE processes and related activities: monitoring, evaluation, reporting, regulation, and enforcement of risk reduction measures to avoid a disaster. It will take incorporating HEVRL assessments into development beyond a reference to mainstreaming. It addresses an existing part of development planning that has always been present but managed in various ways to manipulate decisions about risk to natural hazard events. HEVRL information in DRR has a recognized vocabulary, but to be examined is how it is to become common in development process guidance, writings, practice, and reporting through MERRE.

# CHAPTER 13

# Monitoring, Evaluation, Reporting, Regulation, and Enforcement

*Del dicho al hecho hay un gran trecho.*
*[Between the saying and the doing is a big stretch.]*
—Popular saying in Latin America

## Having It Neither Way

Referring to MERRE as a harbinger of creating risk is a misnomer. MERRE processes identify, propose, and support the implementation of reduction actions. The processes depend on behaviors, mandated or otherwise, and are chosen by participants associated with them. Human behavior is the harbinger of creating risk through societal processes and actions. Monitoring, evaluation, reporting, regulation, and enforcement are not necessarily value laden. They are expressions by society that are part of development shaping the built environment through its goals and objectives.

The discussion now broadens to processes and behaviors that bring about the built environment. For almost ninety years, in many countries the public sector (rather than nongovernmental groups and individuals) has taken on the primary challenge of delivering a safe built environment. In most instances the citizenry, particularly in participatory democracies, tasks its government to create policy and practice for disaster risk management. Increasingly apparent are government's efforts to apply public resources for more effective DRR (UNDRR 2019). For a long time throughout the world, some economic and social infrastructure components have survived natural hazard events without loss of life and significant damage. This has happened without significant government participation and economic resource competition. Design and construction were carried out in the tradition of what was known to be possible and acceptable in the society. The culture produced practitioners of risk-adverse design and construction as they were then understood. Today in most countries, often there is little or no clear cultural mandate for societal control over acceptable risk and natural hazard risk reduction.

What does "having it neither way" mean in dealing with DRR? First imagine "having it both ways." This would mean that sovereign states individually and collectively, with support from their citizenry and other stakeholders, would implement DRR through development. Their actions would continually inform policy revisions and new policy creation through acquired knowledge and experience. DRR would take place as inhabitants, whatever their groupings, adhered to the rule of law and attendant processes and customs, including regulation and enforcement.

"Having it neither way" means that in many instances sovereign states, acting individually and through collective bodies, succeed neither in effective policy nor practice in reducing vulnerability of the built environment. At present, many countries are generally neither prepared nor predisposed to instigate broad, effective DRR policy and practice, regardless of continuing discussions concerning previous disaster declarations, acquired knowledge and experience, and donor fatigue. Mention of monitoring, evaluation, and reporting of vulnerability can and often does move DRR actions to the fore of discussions of the built environment. The discussions are often led by participants outside of government and address vulnerable populations, emergency management, and national security. Note that the SFDRR has broadened the definition and scope of risk reduction to include risk from human-induced events (see UNISDR 2015b). Stakeholders are expressing support for vulnerability reduction of economic and social infrastructure where political support and opportunities for funding are evident or where challenges to development decisions might come about.

Stakeholders may avoid or refuse to use regulations and enforcement or effective monitoring, evaluation, and reporting to bring about DRR. Whether in policy or practice, most stakeholders, particularly sovereign states, collectively and individually have three challenges. The first is stakeholders' limited capacity to implement DRR at the local level without local participation; second is belief that officially stating what is to be at the international level makes it appear so at the national and, even on occasion, local level. And third, stakeholders may avoid using purported durable actions for DRR if they contradict other promulgated policies and practices pertaining to economic development, particularly in land use planning.

MERRE addresses the acceptable level of risk of damage and destruction of the built environment, but that is only one of three facets when dealing with the issue of acceptable risk. Second is ever more available knowledge of expected monetary and other losses. This knowledge is increasing due to more and better HEVRL assessments and the growing focus on specific natural hazard events affecting specific components of the built environment in specific geographic settings and specific population groupings. It informs the interested parties as to potential loss and helps focus discussion of what is the desired level of risk. The third facet is that in review and execution of development decision-making, there is little transparency as to the decision about the acceptable level of risk and how achieving that level will actually take place. The "how" of achieving an acceptable level of risk is tied to the outcome of discussions by whom, where, and why. These facets help focus desired, acceptable, and resulting level of risk created through development. Embedded invariably in these risk levels is discussion of who benefits and who pays by those concerned with who is responsible and accountable.

## Considering DRR through MERRE

Values, norms, and standards are the basis of MERRE processes and behaviors. How do decisions influence use of MERRE processes, and what is their role in creating or abating vulnerability and risk? What happens if behavioral norms do not include or do not highly value DRR and it is not considered or carried out? What of groups (government as well as associations, federations, and other legal entities) that do not consider DRR responsibility and accountability as part of their standards?

When public sector stakeholders create DRR policy, and government action consists of disseminating policy, meaningful implementation may not ensue. Reasons for MERRE processes not using HEVRL information to address DRR include (1) stakeholders can and do leave aside HEVRL information from early decision-making for development project site and initial design proposals; (2) stakeholders withhold HEVRL information that points to disaster causal factors to avoid critical review before making final development decisions; (3) loss information in recovery operations is sometimes set aside because of its impact on making development decisions about the type and siting of economic and social infrastructure; and (4) stakeholders dismiss HEVRL information as unnecessary input into response, relief, recovery, rehabilitation, and reconstruction actions if deemed not supportive of preferred solutions.

Upon examination, policies and frameworks adopted by countries for DRR do not always prompt necessary development actions at the national, subnational, and local level. A review of the type and occurrence of infrastructure losses reveals vulnerability that otherwise could have been avoided, usually with minimal investment in construction, or a different decision on siting the infrastructure component. The list of economic and social infrastructure components that suffer repeated damage or destruction begins with housing, schools, health facilities, and water systems. Many participants assume that commitment to processes and actions leading to a less vulnerable built environment abounds. Others observe that processes and actions leading to a more vulnerable built environment also abound. As J. K. Mitchell puts it more politely, "The task of hazard reduction frequently involves surmounting problems of divided responsibilities and differing priorities among public agencies" (Mitchell 1988: 26).

Given the breadth of their policy actions, the majority of sovereign states appear to favor using universal tools for hazard assessment to sup-

---

**The Challenge of Resolving Vulnerability**

Mary Comerio, architect, university professor, and internationally recognized expert on disaster recovery, has spoken of the dramatic issues related to representative democracies and the challenges to each of the three branches of government—legislative, executive, and judicial.

One example is the discussion following the California Loma Prieta earthquake of 1989.

The earthquake provoked dramatic loss of crumbling, condemned, or abandoned housing occupied by low-income people. The losses highlighted the estimated post-earthquake reconstruction cost impact to implement the State of California law of 1985. This law required local jurisdictions to inventory unreinforced masonry buildings (URMs) and develop plans for how to strengthen them.

Many municipal building departments had no experience with retrofitting existing buildings and thus created requirements that opponents described as draconian in terms of cost, time, and needed technical capacity to bring buildings up to new code standards. Cities could use the code to force demolition of URM buildings deemed unsafe. Code enforcement could exacerbate the affordable housing problem by pushing a large number of low-income individuals and families out of these buildings with nowhere else to find rental accommodations at comparable rents. Estimated numbers of people to be evicted from code-enforced loss of URM rental housing units approached the expected death toll in a future earthquake affecting the units if occupied.

Ultimately, some California cities, including those in the Bay Area, enacted local codes that were more cost-effective and policies that helped property owners to finance the retrofits to preserve the housing.
(Personal communication with Mary Comerio, February 2018)

port MERRE for DRR implementation (see UNISDR 2015b). When acting collectively on policy matters, nation-states often avoid disagreeing with each other on how to address risk reduction. The official wording of their adopted policies and frameworks respects individual sovereignty. Examples of not adopting universal standards to address DRR include (1) no guaranteed freedom of citizens from disasters as part of human rights declarations and (2) no universal building code for design and construction of primary and secondary one- and two-story schools.

## Least Common Denominator

Governments and other stakeholders may attempt to build consensus for DRR through political and economic approaches. Often the responsible or interested group puts the DRR policy proposal to a vote after the content of the proposal has approached something akin to a least common denominator—in other words, a proposal whose contents meets with approval, perhaps even a mandated consensus. But acceptance does not necessarily mean that the approved DRR actions are fully what is needed. What the acceptance does represent is the point at which all, or at least the majority, accept the proposal regardless of whether the DRR efforts are effective. Thus, implementing DRR using the least common denominator for policy and action reveals that the need for approval is more important than the need for appropriate action.

Acceptable risk reached through MERRE processes can reflect a least common denominator arrived at by popular consensus, administrative dictum, or a majority of the population through legislative actions at the local or national level. The constituencies of development assistance entities may have both recognized and accepted the emerging role of the public sector and governance for risk management of the built environment, as well as calling for civil society participation (see UNISDR 2015b and UNDRR 2019). However, MDBs, DMDAs, and NGOs can be very reserved in voicing or adopting positions differing from those of sovereign states. These stakeholders recognize that sovereign states are by their own mandate the seat of responsibility and accountability for risk management regardless of DRR implementation.

MERRE processes involve selecting, explicitly or implicitly, HEVRL assessments to shape DRR initiatives. The processes use descriptors such as natural hazard event, geomorphologic and administrative setting, specific components of the built environment including the site description, and often the most important factor, the associated segment of the population. MERRE processes can measure and inform in a comprehensive, transparent, and focused manner development of the built environment consistent with accepted limits to loss.

In reviewing the set of descriptors, sovereign states can avoid or refuse to commit to act on risk management issues if choices appear to hinge too directly on internal national issues or if they might become subject to foreign dictates, interventions, monitoring, reporting, regulations, or enforcement. A universal building code for one- and two-story masonry school construction is an example. Many nations reject an outside overview possibility because of declared national competency, availability of work, and local opposition. Yet having to deal with a set of descriptors is precisely how effective identification of targets for risk reduction policies and practices takes place.

## Role of "Community"

Community involvement in DRR decision-making and implementation is participation that includes individuals and groups who are directly, indirectly, and secondarily impacted by loss of economic and social infrastructure. The question of what or who actually constitutes community participation is relevant. Also relevant is recognition of the extent that community involvement can be the decisive influence on the vulnerability level of their immediate built environment, particularly in the case of post-disaster reconstruction. Whatever the resulting level of risk, the community may or may not claim it played a decision-making role. But who is the community? Often the composition of the community is not identified, nor is their specific role in DRR decision-making. Is "community participation" a substitute for actually undertaking decisions as to acceptable level of risk of physical infrastructure vulnerability reduction?

At the community level, descriptors are most often preordained, locally selected, or self-selected. From these circumstances the statement "all mitigation is local" was coined with good reason. However, "community" might also include or be built around a multi-national manufacturing base, an international seaport or airport, or a global tourism destination. Alternatively, as Alexandra Titz, Terry Cannon, and Fred Kruger have written, "How 'community' has become popular in research and with humanitarian agencies and other organisations is based on what can be considered a 'moral license' that supposedly guarantees that the actions being taken are genuinely people-centred [sic] and ethically justified" (Titz et al. 2018: 1).

## Monitoring, Evaluation, and Reporting

Of the MERRE quintuplet, monitoring, evaluation, and reporting most often have defined the core of stakeholder DRR and international development assistance over the past forty years. Moreover, through the evolution of their form and substance, these three processes have become the standard of due diligence, carried out by the international development community, and for compliance, carried out by the sovereign states. But government reporting can be weak when reporting monitoring and evaluation. This can be from lack of commitment, obfuscation, bias, or lack of enforcement capabilities. In some instances, monitoring, evaluation, and reporting processes have been presented as the outcome or product of MERRE. But this does not necessarily mean that actions to reduce existing vulnerability or define and assign responsibility for chosen levels of risk are occurring. The situation is identical to stakeholders reporting procedural actions related to HEVRL assessments as the substance of those assessments. The processes are presented as the product, not the means, for reporting the data, information, experience, and effective action for DRR.

The international development community has widely adopted use of the logical framework (log frame) method (see DID 2002) for defining the development project goal, purpose, inputs, activities, and outputs (the planning sequence) that lead to quantification. This approach is often associated with a Western style of development involving the "tyranny of the method" (Bell 1994). In international development management, "what gets measured gets managed," which is parallel to "if you can measure it, you can manage it." The former phrase is active; the latter is conditional and passive. In regard to the latter, "if you can measure it" might also read, "if you choose to measure it." Most often the units of measurement are economic and monetary.

However, there are nonmonetary measurements of risk and DRR efforts resulting from stakeholder HEVRL assessments and MERRE processes that do impact the content of monitoring, evaluation, and reporting. The logical framework is a means to specify such measurements, not only to relate components and activities to one another, but also to identify the units of measure by which anticipated project results will be monitored and evaluated.

When in 2005 the IDNDR secretariat proposed and the sovereign states adopted the "expected outcomes" of the HFA, it was and continues to be of great value. The expected outcomes measured the quantitative goals, particularly since loss of life, economic losses, and social impact on populations directly related to the built environment. HFA, in the name of sovereign states, declared that sovereign states would quantitatively reduce risk commensurate with prescribed qualitative goals. However, the underlying issues of (1) identification of data sources on losses, (2) varying and incompatible data generation approaches, and (3) unresolved qualification and quantification of measurement schemes and their units during the life of HFA thwarted reporting about meeting the HFA expected outcomes.

In addition, reporting countries grappled with challenges presented by the varying geopolitical scales and other conditioners included in the data, such as building type, geomorphologic setting, and hazard type. As reporting began, countries and other stakeholders took inputs, particularly process elements such as dates, meeting locations, and participant lists, and used them as output products. Reporting process actions as achievements meant that quantifying the number of meetings, commissions, and training sessions with the number of their participants became the reporting norm. Participating countries did not distinguish between the occurrence of natural hazard events and the declaration of a disaster—declared by whom, at what geopolitical scale, affecting which components of the built infrastructure and segments of the population, or the causal factors for the losses.

Another critical issue of monitoring, evaluating, and reporting was collecting and sharing disaggregated data across gender, age, and income, as well as the growing rate of poverty and other factors. Discussions of the post-2015 Sendai Framework for DRR carried this concern forward. They noted that monitoring and evaluation of DRR efforts are often neglected, especially DRR action impact evaluations (UNDRR 2019). Moreover, without reporting, there is less follow-up and follow-through on policy goals and objectives. NGOs have increasingly challenged how data for monitoring, evaluating, and reporting indicators are defined. In some cases, the national or local government depends on outside reporting sources.

## Regulation and Enforcement

Of the MERRE quintuplet, regulation and enforcement (most commonly referred to as the building regulatory system [BRS]) are quite complex in a societal setting. The two actions are becoming preferred (if not the preferred, then the default) processes for carrying out structural and nonstructural DRR related to established government participation in creating economic and social infrastructure.

Throughout the world the primary purpose of BRS is life safety, beginning with housing and places of public assembly, which reflects this trajectory. The BRS is also used to address the vulnerability of lifeline infrastructure and other social and economic components to promote continuity of service and operation for the poor and marginalized after a natural hazard event.

Over time, focus on risk reduction through regulation and enforcement reflects on societies and the "built" space (or the built environment) as to physical character, natural resources, social and economic relations, and culture—certainly true in the beliefs, art, and customs of a geopolitical place. Contemporary regulation to deal with risk includes societal control in governance, the economy, customs, and traditions.

Regulation includes professional certification in a number of fields, academic accreditation, building codes for a variety of structures and involved trades, land use zoning (including for various hazard types), master planning at various scales, permitting for various stages and types of construction, and inspection, which is the basis for enforcement. Regulating building processes is formal through government or informal through recognized and adopted risk management mechanisms. Enforcement is the application of regulation using formal means through executive, legislative, and judicial branches of government (the primary stakeholder in enforcement). But enforcement is also through tradition, custom, religion, and other cultural norms. Enforcement includes inspections; permits, certifications, and authorizations; and citations, civil and criminal proceedings, findings, sentencing, and punishment. The BRS may cover land use planning, siting, design, and construction of economic and social infrastructure components.

The BRS as part of MERRE processes supporting DRR also impacts the development and emergency management sectors. The development community does not want responsibility for vulnerability reduction, but represents the operable space, if not point of intervention, for regulation and enforcement because of actual building design and construction permitting and inspection. Emergency management, and the now popular use of a public sector risk czar, may seek or be assigned responsibility for, but not control of, risk management in development processes through specific economic and social sectors. The exception may be civil defense, particularly when the military institution controls the emergency management sector. In addition, local governments responsible for regulation and enforcement do not commonly ask for responsibility over natural hazard assessments as part of or separate from evolving environmental management regulatory frameworks.

The BRS goes beyond the cost and execution of DRR. Collection of fees for building permits and licenses is often referred to by the payer as "taxes." In some countries, the government designates one or more professional service entities to be reimbursed by whoever is building the infrastructure. The BRS is considered by some as make-work, managed op-

> **Powers, Super or Not, Using MERRE Structure and Function**
>
> "'Back in the 1940s, when the reservoirs were built, this place [rural open space outside Houston, Texas] was way out of town, and they thought that the cows would just get out of the way if there was some overflow,' said Judge Robert E. Hebert, a top elected official in Fort Bend County, a once sparsely-populated expanse that now has more than 700,000 residents, including those in Canyon Gate [a flooded community during Hurricane Harvey].
>
> But in the late 1990s, bolstered by Houston's rapid expansion and the construction of new roads nearby, a residential development company called Land Tejas unveiled plans for Canyon Gate. County officials insisted that the developer warn prospective buyers that the homes lay in a flood reservoir, and Land Tejas agreed to do so, but only by way of an obscure filing. 'This subdivision is adjacent to the Barker Reservoir and is subject to extended controlled inundation under the management of the U.S. Army Corps of Engineers,' the developer stated in 1997 in the fine print of the plat, the county's document approving the Canyon Gate subdivision. 'This is a man-made disaster we're dealing with, make no mistake,' Judge Hebert said. 'All these houses shouldn't have been built in the first place, and now the speculators are moving in.'"
>
> (Romero 2018)

portunities for graft and corruption, and mandatory oversight payments (de Lint 2015). These attributes of the BRS reveal why stakeholders, particularly national governments, may find carrying out MERRE processes technically challenging if not politically undesirable.

At a macro level and to encapsulate discussion, the development community does not attempt to scale back, but rather seeks use of the BRS as the principal tool for implementing DRR. Through MERRE, the development process continually questions and seeks to modify DRR, particularly through the BRS. At the same time, the DRR process cannot be burdened with a process to reform the BRS. DRR cannot be the mechanism to reform the development community's use of the BRS as an administrative least common denominator, nor can it change the political action of dumbing down the BRS to the least offensive (read: interference) level possible.

## The Enabling Society

GAR19 notes that technical staff in doing their assigned work will rely on the willingness of people to "create the right regulatory environment for new and urgent work to proceed" (UNDRR 2019: xv). Yet the willingness of a society to manage risk and undertake risk reduction with responsibility and accountability remains in question. Societies often leave decisions about acceptable levels of risk at the level of the least common denominator through vague legislation or obscure processes. Often the willingness to address risk is specifically seen only in regulation and enforcement. Societies may see the BRS as optimally capable of bringing about DRR as it demonstrates government policy and practice. Nevertheless, the BRS often becomes embroiled in judicially mandated enforcement because of people unwilling to abide by the law. A nation might build schools only to life safety standards not because of custom, culture, tradition, religious, economic, or social imperatives, but because after the legislative and executive branches of government have gone through their regulation formulation processes, only enforcement of the regulations can bring about a safe school.

Furthermore, in an increasingly litigious society, regulation and enforcement become the ultimate means to carry out executive and legislative decisions. In 1998, Ray Burby wrote, "A few innovate jurisdictions—those with extraordinary local leadership and those who have suffered severe losses in the past—will plan for managing land use in hazardous areas. Most, however, will not, either because they lack the adequate information about hazards and planning, or, more importantly, because there is no local constituency pushing in this direction. Thus, hazard mitigation requires partnership. Impetus for land use planning and management must come from above, but the actual planning and conduct of programs must occur at the local level" (Burby 1998: 21).

In 2004, Robin Spence noted, "It is our nature to speculate that growth from natural disasters results from inadequate control of what is being built, and the answer therefore is more and better regulation. Most writers suggest, either implicitly or explicitly, that there is a need for government action through legislation and its enforcement as vital elements of a long-term plan" (Spence 2004: 392). By definition, formal enforcement mechanisms are through the sovereign state, but they are conditioned by the behaviors of those who carry out the MERRE processes.

GAR19 states the following in relation to sovereign states' implementation of the "HFA Priority for Action 4—Reduce the underlying risk factors," the least implemented action item of HFA: "In general, institutional, legislative and policy frameworks did not sufficiently facilitate the integration of disaster risk considerations into public and private investment, environmental and natural resource management, social and economic development practices in all sectors, land-use planning and territorial development. Weak alignment and coherence in policies, financial instruments and institutions across sectors became a driver of risk. Few countries adopted frameworks of accountability, responsibility and enforcement and also appropriate political, legal and financial incentives to actively pursue risk reduction and prevention" (UNDRR 2019: 27).

## MERRE and Development

"One person's transparency is another person's humiliation" (de Lint 2015). Sovereign states and other stakeholders alike hold that risk of the built environment to natural hazard events is always considered in development through the existence of HEVRL and the presence of entities public and private that carry out MERRE processes. Decisions made concerning levels of acceptable risk and loss are integrally bound to development decisions. Development could have made decisions embracing DRR, but then again, development has its priorities. Responsibility, accountability, transparency, and visibility of risk related to natural hazard events are only a portion of development issues that societies must address.

As presented by CIDIE (1988) and referenced by the UN in regard to the DRM community's efforts at DRR (UNDRR 2019: 27, 56, 71), the priority given to HEVRL and MERRE by sovereign states and development assistance agencies is not very high. Expected losses could have been significantly reduced if development activities had implemented DRR actions. While the DRM community failing was identified thirty-five-plus years ago as an apparent lack of governments' awareness to limit losses, now other factors, including deliberate choices, explain the increasing losses. With reference to MERRE, stakeholder perceptions of the potential savings of mitigation are low, accompanied by acceptance of the inevitability of natural hazard events, lack of knowledge about nonstructural mitigation, and often opposition to hazard zoning and land use planning.

Sector-specific organizations and associations may have aggressive, well-designed DRR initiatives, but ultimately the sovereign states dictate the action. As was noted by PAHO in 2006, "The absence of training in . . . mitigation in health facilities illustrates the absence of support or promotion of the subject at the country level" (PAHO 2006: 14). In 2018, PAHO reported that of a goal of fifteen target member countries to include criteria for disaster mitigation and for adaptation to climate change in the planning, design, construction, and operation of health services developing a disaster mitigation plan, two had completed the task (PAHO 2018).

In addition, the international development assistance agencies may sometimes not address natural hazard vulnerability that affects projects for which they have provided funds or technical assistance. The reasons for such actions include low perception of risk and potential losses; tangible and immediate costs of analysis, mitigation, and implementation compared to expected benefits in probable avoided losses; and the significant institutional effort and resources required, especially in the absence of any concern on the part of the country. In the case of stakeholder support to sovereign states, possible benefits of reduced losses pertain to governments rather than to the development assistance agency that shares only limited, if any, responsibility. Hazard analysis and mitigation responsibilities may reside in DRM or other institutional sectors other than those that will plan and execute the development project.

There are calls for integrated vulnerability analysis where research and analysis of risk of populations take place related to the context of their societies (Oliver-Smith et al. 2016). Built environment risk assessments do not routinely identify specific population groups related to specific components of economic or social infrastructure—such as a particular vulnerable hospital is associated with people with specific health issues addressed by that hospital.

> ### Transferring DRR Approaches
>
> As for transferring approaches from country to country or region to region, Armin Wolski, a fire protection engineer and expert on prescriptive and performance building codes and standards, noted, "Perceptions of risk in society have long played a role in influencing the development of . . . disaster risk management. . . . Understanding the risk perception phenomenon and its impact on codes can potentially provide insight to those managing risk and establishing new safety codes in economically emerging countries. Lessons learned from disasters in industrialized countries, now incorporated into their codes, may serve emerging countries well, but these countries should approach any such importation with caution. Risk perceptions might not be directly transferable; therefore, regulatory measures might not be transferable."
>
> (Personal communication, Armin Wolski, March 2016)

There is a need to consider the historic damage chain and the impact on vulnerable populations of triggering events in the past causing disasters. They are of relevance to future consideration of climate change and climate variations in the short term as a component of predicted financial and other measures of loss. While SFDRR calls for more multifaceted indices of risk (UNISDR 2015b), such indices may capture only proximate conditions of vulnerability while masking specific areas where beneficial DRR of specific infrastructure components might take place. Andrew Rumbach has commented on such indexes as working to obscure or obstruct the understanding of the structural and sociohistorical roots of risk (personal communication, Rumbach, May 2018). These roots include MERRE processes and their accompanying HEVRL assessments.

For example, the siting, design, and construction of any type of economic or social infrastructure component, such as a school, hospital, bridge, or commercial center, may involve a flood hazard zone, a landslide-prone area, or a volcanic lahar zone. Economic, social, and environmental analyses may produce measurements of population-related issues supporting the building of infrastructure components on the proposed site. The assessment of exposure of the site may contradict support for its use because of factors such as poverty, employment, physical proximity and accessibility, gender, race, and religious affiliation. The multifaceted nature of needs of those who use the infrastructure is shown with the site and infrastructure component vulnerability, along with sustainable development and environmental management concerns. Thus, inserting additional facets of vulnerability may contradict the natural hazard risk-adverse development project guidelines.

Nevertheless, the focus is on people and how they relate to the vulnerability of the built environment. Lost access to schools, health-care facilities, and water and sanitation, electric, telecommunications, and transportation networks may all be part of their vulnerability. These losses constitute a large and growing number of economic, social, and other vulnerabilities for people experiencing disasters. Assessments may vary greatly at the national or local level, regardless of DRR frameworks and other stakeholder pronouncements. Emphasis is on the roles people and their communities play in vulnerability reduction in addition to the public and private sectors. As E. E. Koks and colleagues note, added to the physical, financial, and economic assessment of risk of loss related directly to a built environment component are risks that address the estimated direct, indirect, and secondary loss for the population (Koks et al. 2015). Another part of the social vulnerability issue is awareness and capacity of the population to deal with differing outcomes of a hazard event. For example, individual, family, and community management of earthquake or tornado hazard risk (site- and structure-specific) is very different from dealing with flood, volcano, or tsunami hazard risk management, where the areal extent of possible impact almost always calls for extensive coordinated action between population groups.

## Why Stakeholders Act, Why They Don't

Discussion now turns to how stakeholders address DRR in development. ISDR stated in 2009, "Almost without exception, no sector has carried out mandated vulnerability and risk assessments of economic and social infrastructure and their related populations sufficient to define vulnerability and risk in order to guide development actions. This includes making the risk management information and choices transparent to those who not only benefit from such actions, but who also depend on the provision of the related goods and services. Presently international vulnerability indexing initiatives using GIS and available national data help shape risk management decisions. They also make visible if not facilitate manipulation of the indexing context and content" (ISDR 2009: 18). Cassidy Johnson notes, "Even though legal frameworks and plans that provide an enabling environment for risk reduction may be in place, it becomes the responsibility of the local/municipal government to implement the measures" (Johnson 2011: 14).

Sovereign states have a checkered history of using self-appointed powers to address natural hazard risk reduction beyond financial risk. At the community level their policy and practice to address economic and physical risk is complicated. Often, neither policy nor practice specifies the beneficiaries (population or infrastructure type) of DRR. Sector responsibilities for MERRE assessments with conflicting or competitive responsibilities are not clear, nor are mandates clear as to the needed focus on hazard type, built environment component, public administration setting, and location.

Stakeholders can refuse or abstain from carrying out natural hazard risk assessments and MERRE processes even when they are mandated by citing potential national security and credit risks. The international development community may not want to deal with the implications of knowing the assessments. Nor do they want to accept emerging technical findings or take on political entanglements that challenge parochial development interests.

When dealing with other stakeholders, sovereign states may choose to avoid or refuse to execute designated support for MERRE and HEVRL operations. Such operations include DRR as part of environmental safeguards, development cost and competitiveness analysis, and as conditions precedent for loans as well as EIAs and EISs as part of environmental monitoring, evaluation, and reporting. The situation includes the use of green accounting, GPI, and GDP assessments. It also includes insurance coverage and financial risk management, as well as land use planning, climate change data and scenarios, and other hazard information to shape public sector decision-making.

## Moral Climate

Ulrich Beck has stated, "In risk societies, the consequences and successes of modernization become an issue with the speed and radicality of processes of modernization. A new dimension of risk emerges because the conditions for calculating and institutionally processing it breaks down. Under such conditions a new moral climate of politics develops in which cultural, and hence nationally varying, evaluations place a central role and arguments for and against real or possible consequences of technological and economic decisions are publicly conducted" (Beck 2009: 6).

The shaping forces that affect the moral climate of development politics and decision-making come from several areas relevant to stakeholder actions. Following their discussions in the recent past on humanitarian crises, UNESCO and COMEST have stated in their definition of the precautionary principle, "Actions are interventions that are undertaken before harm occurs that seek to avoid or diminish the harm. Actions should be chosen that are proportional to the seriousness of the potential harm, with consideration of their positive and negative consequences, and with the assessment of their moral implications of both action and inaction. The choice of action should be the result of a participatory process" (COMEST 2005: 14).

Traditional participatory processes have often gone wanting when the issue is risk to natural hazard events and when MERRE and HEVRL actions are inaccessible by the citizenry even though democratic processes are in place. Enforcement is not always undertaken or constructive even through participatory intervention. Tony Gibbs, a civil engineer with natural hazard impact experience in the Caribbean, wrote in *The Gleaner* (Jamaica), "Of course, no code or regulation will ever serve its purpose well if it is not backed by robust enforcement, but there is enough anecdotal evidence to confirm that enforcement is usually the weakest link in the accountability chain. So even though the code is considered very necessary to minimise loss of life and property, it has to be accompanied by a strong inspection mechanism that will readily apprehend and ensure punishment of those who breach the regulations" (Gibbs 2014).

## In Sum

This discussion of natural hazard risk management goes beyond incorporating exposure, vulnerability, risk, and loss assessments in development planning. It is more than mainstreaming. But it is a part of existing development processes—and has been all along. It is not a question of data, information, and assessments; it is the willingness and ability to manage risk in a visible and transparent manner. It is not a question of mainstreaming DRR or of a multi-hazard approach; it is accountability and responsibility. It is not so much a question of knowing, but of acting through a participatory process to determine and apply acceptable levels of risk through policy and practice.

Enforcement is an increasingly present and necessary player in MERRE than was previously anticipated, expected, or even desirable in some cases. By necessity, and sometimes by preference, societies are addressing the shortcomings of monitoring, evaluation, reporting, and regulation by focusing on a strong enforcement component. As it happens in many democracies, after legislative and executive actions run their course, judicial action inevitably follows.

The point is not that development processes ought to have a DRR phase, but that development processes must be decision-based actions using HEVRL assessments and implementing MERRE processes in recognition of natural hazard impacts on populations. Guidance is not only proposed, but already at hand.

# CHAPTER 14

# Policy Guidance on Disaster Risk Reduction Taken to Development

Vulnerability to natural hazard events including climate hazards is part of development's challenges. Sovereign states are the most dominant force that give physical shape to their respective nations' development. To do so, they use political, economic, and social policies and practices. Development processes in the public and private arenas are challenged with how risk reduction to natural hazard events should be addressed in the face of other risks and priorities. Vulnerability reduction of the built environment to natural hazards may be the responsibility of each nation, but it is not yet the accepted financial responsibility of each government, economic and social sector, owner, or operator of economic and social infrastructure, or even specialized DRM agencies. And policy frameworks used by sovereign states and other stakeholders to implement MERRE processes in a straightforward, quantifiable fashion may focus on vulnerability assessment, but actual reduction of losses may go wanting in the face of development pressures.

*GAR19* states, "To allow humankind to embark on a *development* trajectory that is at least manageable, and at best sustainable and regenerative [consistent with the aspirations for 2030], a fundamental re-examination and redesign of how to deal with risk is essential" (UNDRR 2019: iv; italics added for emphasis).

While certain development actions are already identified as drivers of risk that produce major threats to human population, development is also positioned to be the principal actor for DRR of the built environment. While the *GAR19* recommends a re-diagnosis of the risk assessment approach and risk reduction management, sovereign states and other stakeholders have opted for the most part to focus on what they ask of themselves: monitor and report the presence of risk.

Previous chapters have discussed DRR in relation to the built environment and the disaster-development linkage revealed in policy, practice, and knowledge. They also have explored what stakeholders should know and when, what matters, whose disaster it is, and why. This chapter will explore the guidance at hand for DRR action prepared by and for sovereign states and, by extension, for other stakeholders.

DRR decisions often reflect power, prestige, funding, dependence, and interdependence, resulting in discontinuity of knowledge, policy, and practice in universal and local views. These themes will now be explored as to the manner in which the stakeholders are to proceed. Exploration will involve the juxtaposition of public policy guidance and actual development practice, while both supposedly avoid participating in the construction of risk.

As discussed previously (chapters 6, 7, and 13), early on CIDIE published a strategy to promote natural hazards assessment and mitigation by inducing cooperation from the participating development agencies, both public and private, that actually fund and carry out development investment projects. CIDIE's contribution included identifying natural hazard risk and development issues related to environmental management that are now found in SFDRR and GAR19. In the late 1980s, the development community's interest in DRR, at least for vulnerability reduction of economic and social infrastructure, was related to environmental management in two ways. First, environmental management issues presented early on in EIA and EIS formats included the impact of natural forces on development efforts, a concern paralleling that of development impact on ecosystem structure and function. Second, in planning and practice, development would be a principal participant in environmental management.

Confronted with requests for stakeholder-led actions through UNEP and the IPCC and IDNDR, CIDIE's call for incorporating natural hazard information in development investment project formulation processes was lost. Individual CIDIE members turned their attention to the environment, climate change, and disaster management sector, the last of which clearly described the issue facing nations and populations as a disaster cycle that is void of development as a causal factor.

International discussion of DRR in development has helped give structure and content to major disaster management policy guidance documents, beginning with creation of the IDNDR in 1990 and DRR frameworks that followed. These documents defined and established international and national focus on DRR. They identified the sovereign state as the basic unit of disaster risk reduction action and monitoring; they also identified the role of the military and other security forces in disaster risk management, including issues of national security and terrorism response initiatives.

As the IDNDR got under way, the disaster cycle image was used to explain needed actions. The term "disaster" became the name in everyday

> **Issues Impacting United Nations
> Disaster Guidance Implementation**
>
> Five issues continue to impact implementation of guidance documents through the decades:
>
> - National and subnational government administrations' confrontation with internal political opposition;
> - In many cases dependency of national governments on international financial assistance that limits national and regional options for DRR;
> - Formulation of national budgets and development plans, given national competition for internal and external financial support;
> - International designation of target countries;
> - National constitutional reform and other legislative initiatives that assign or reassign accountability and responsibility for DRR.
>
> In some cases, passing financial resources to a disaster sector focal point in response to natural hazard events further complicates the strategy for development processes to lead DRR policy and practice. Such is the case in creating a national risk, risk reduction, or disaster risk reduction czar to oversee overall economic and social sector DRR activities.

parlance for all natural hazard events. It came about by taking a least common denominator for action by stakeholders participating in the emerging disaster-related sectors. The development sector welcomed separation from disaster-related risk reduction (as well as the emergency management, humanitarian assistance, and the disaster management sector).

The HFA (2005–2015) set as a goal reducing losses of population and physical assets from natural hazard impact in the context of disaster risk reduction and resilience and even cited quantitative goals. SFDRR (2015–2030) includes in its framework emphasis on understanding risk from natural hazards and on "promoting mechanisms for disaster risk transfer and insurance, risk-sharing and retention and financial protection, as appropriate, for both public and private investment in order to reduce the financial impact of disasters" (UNISDR 2015b: 19).

This is followed by SFDRR stating its goal as "to guide the multihazard management of disaster risk in *development* at all levels as well as within and across all sectors" (UNISDR 2015b: 11; italics added for emphasis).

The SFDRR mentions resilience in reference to varying sectors and their physical infrastructure, as well populations and business activities. The Sendai Framework Monitor (SFM) depicts resilience as seen to bundle actions called for in systemic multi-risk assessments (UNDRR 2019: v–xvi).

As Judith Rodin (2014) points out, resilience encompasses preparation, recovery, and adaptation to multiple hazard threats through actions of awareness, integration, diversification, and self-regulation. Embodiment of such DRR actions calls for a both-and approach. Neither the discussion of resilience in general nor in the SFM specifically gives guidance on how to mitigate damage and destruction through development of economic and social infrastructure serving the poor, for all existing vulnerable infrastructure, or on the role of responsibility, accountability, visibility, and transparency.

The SFDRR acknowledges guiding principles, for example: "Managing the risk of disasters is aimed at protecting persons and their property, health, livelihoods and productive assets, as well as cultural and environmental assets, while promoting and protecting all human rights, including the right to development." This is to occur while "taking into account national circumstances, and consistent with domestic laws as well as international obligations and commitments" (UNISDR 2015b: 13).

Ultimately global DRR frameworks with assessment of risk and risk reduction may have become bound up in the disaster community nationally and worldwide, but not necessarily bound in each country's view of its development processes and domestic laws.

## Aspects of the Guidance in Hand

There are thirteen guiding principles, seven targets, and four priorities for action in the SFDRR. These are drawn from the principles contained in the Yokohama Strategy for a Safer World: Guidelines for Natural Disaster Prevention, Preparedness and Mitigation and Its Plan of Action and in the Hyogo Framework for Action. The principles contain notable clarity and equally notable avoidance of troublesome statements related to development.

Five comments concerning the principles, targets, and priorities and their implications are in order.

SFDRR states in the first principle, "Each State has the primary responsibility to prevent and reduce disaster risk" (UNISDR 2015b). In a straightforward observation, regardless of what has or does happen in practice, as policy each sovereign state—the public sector—has anointed itself as the basic DRR unit. In a broad view, there are continuing differing opinions as to the level of natural hazard risk responsibility, accountability, and ownership held by each level of government, mirroring the differing views regarding national, international, and intergovernmental disaster preparedness, response, and mitigation policies and mechanisms. These differences contrast with the international community's promotion of thematic risk integration. But this principle also makes glaringly obvious that governments and the development community are two separate entities and that government here or elsewhere in the SFDRR cannot or will not press, at least for now, the development community about risk creation or for changing development goals and objectives, even though most of the built environment is created by the private sector.

Absent are any mandated, quantitative targets for country-specific aid or other assistance or creation of new obligations to support climate adaptation finance or for any other purpose. By and large, also absent are any absolute quantitative targets for DRR actions. Where targets are stated, they refer to unspecified reductions or increases related to nominally quantified subject issues existing in 2015.

The fourth comment is that the evolution of the identification of primary efforts vis-à-vis the SFDRR consists of sovereign states offering themselves guidance and assistance in identifying in qualitative terms individual country and international community efforts. This contrasts with the IDNDR and HFA, which emphasized using quantitative measures in reporting sovereign state actions.

As a result, monitoring their own HEVRL actions is by design what has been approved by the sovereign states. This constitutes (1) the major focus of their efforts and (2) the focus of support by the UN and the international community to the countries and their populations (UNISDR 2015b: 13).

SFDRR notes the end of a hazard-by-hazard risk reduction approach (UNDRR 2019: iv). Present and future approaches to managing risk emerge by understanding the systemic nature of risk from multiple hazards to the built environment, populations, and other items. Managing risk to the built environment entails not only examining more complex population vulnerabilities. It also demands a more thorough examination of acceptable levels of risk of economic and social infrastructure components. Applicable risk assessments will demand additional knowledge and sensitivities (UNDRR 2019: v). Critical is a less departmentalized approach to discussing DRR strategies. This is related to the Global Risk Assessment Framework (GRAF) and facilitates generating information and insights to sustain and guide public entities in use of tools and funded strategies at all scales (UNDRR 2019: 5). Traditional to these initiatives is a call for enhanced cooperation at all levels, economic and social sectors, and technology and research investment to strengthen disaster risk coordination of stakeholders, to focus on monitoring, assessing, and understanding disaster risk (UNDRR 2019: 11).

## Risk Assessment

Presenting risk assessment as the information centerpiece for monitoring, GAR19 points out that "major renovations of current approaches to risk assessments are therefore needed to be able to realize the outcomes and goals of the post 2015 agreements" (UNDRR 2019: iv). It later adds, "Risk information must be integrated into development indicators, and inform the sequencing of planning, budgeting and action" (UNDRR 2019: viii).

The word "integrated" remains in discussions of DRR and development. To "integrate" can imply that development policy and processes do not consider risk, and that DRR must be added. Not recognized is that risk to natural hazard events is presently considered along with other issues, but development policies, priorities, and actions continue to place risk reduction as relative to cost and perceived benefit. If risk information related to natural hazard events is presently "integrated into development indicators, and informs the sequencing of planning, budgeting and action," then one assumes that risk of loss of economic and social infrastructure is considered, that it is not an overriding objective, and that DRR as a priority will continue to be relative to other priorities not up for discussion. Or, at the least, designating DRR of the built environment as a development priority is beyond the reach of the SFDRR and, by extension, beyond that of the disaster management community. Decisions on acceptable levels of risk remain the domain of the development community.

To state there is need for mainstreaming DRR in development has been a noncombative way to discuss with the development community the issue of DRR. It is a misnomer. Management of risk of loss to natural hazard events is part of development processes. The point is whether responsibility and accountability for DRR takes place—that is, through visible and transparent risk management practices, who pays and who benefits are clear before acceptable levels of risk are determined and appropriate DRR actions are implemented.

GAR19 states, "Major renovations of current approaches to risk assessments are therefore needed to be able to realize the outcomes and goals of the post 2015 agreements: Sendai Framework for Disaster Risk Reduction 2015–2030 (Sendai Framework) itself as well as Transforming our World: the 2030 Agenda for Sustainable Development (2030 Agenda), Paris Agreement, Addis Ababa Action Agenda (AAAA) and New Urban Agenda (NUA)" (UNDRR 2019: iv).

Establishing goals and outcomes demands attention, not only to identify what or whose risk has been reduced and how, but also to show who is at risk and why, to indicate who assumes responsibility and accountability, and to measure acceptable risk in terms of loss.

The specificity of such an approach requires that development processes themselves be named instruments of DRR, with vulnerability reduction of the built environment as a principal goal of development. When the goal is vulnerability reduction of economic and social infrastructure in a durable development framework, integrating risk information into development is not an issue; it is a given. Considering the acceptable level of risk and taking responsibility for the decision are needed.

This is the case whether or not the term "sustainable" is used in conjunction with "development." In practice, a DRR-laden development framework will necessarily focus on creating a less vulnerable built environment as part of (1) new development initiatives, (2) reconstruction of damaged and destroyed infrastructure as part of recovery following a disaster, and (3) the most pressing issue in terms of areal extent and cost of mitigation, which is retrofitting existing vulnerable infrastructure, including housing.

At the same time, lack of natural hazard information as a freely accessible public good thwarts access to HEVRL assessments. Lack of clarity for demanding DRR in development while adopting an all-hazards approach (rather than single hazard/single sector/specific geographic location) may produce avoidance of actions that would otherwise challenge economic development preferences when moving from policy to practice. Finally, making risk reduction of populations to disasters a part of enforceable human rights policy, as some disaster management participants suggest, complicates political and policy discussions about the challenges of vulnerability reduction of populations and the need for vulnerability reduction of the built environment.

## Moving toward More DRR

The Linked Open Data for Global Disaster Risk Research (LODGD) task group of the Committee on Data for Science and Technology (CODATA) is an increasingly important activity connecting DRR to the four priorities mentioned above. The Sendai Framework recognizes the need for connectivity between data generation, distribution, and use among entities in the public and private sectors. In its guiding principles, the SFDRR states, "Disaster risk reduction requires a multi-hazard approach and inclusive risk-informed decision-making based on the open exchange and dissemination of disaggregated data, including by sex, age and disability, as well as on easily accessible, up-to-date, comprehensible, science-based, non-sensitive risk information" (UNISDR 2015b: 13). Assessment processes are challenging, however, because they require collaboration with multiple sectors, data integration and interpretation, as well as an operable mechanism to share data among UN member states, the UN system, and other stakeholders. As GAR19 states, "Open data . . . are the technical enablers of improved data science, risk assessment, risk modelling, reporting, and ultimately evidence-based policies" (UNDRR 2019: vi).

## Monitoring

With multiple stakeholders offering guidance on social, economic, and environmental vulnerabilities, it is not surprising that monitoring is now a dominant (if not the dominant) concern of SFDRR in addressing disaster risk reduction. In MERRE processes, while regulation and enforcement are nominally under the auspices of the public sector, monitoring can and does take place through both public and private sector actions. Monitoring assists in examining the actual levels and bounds for vulnerability, risk, and loss in contrast to officially accepted limits and bounds. But perhaps more important, monitoring provides the baseline data and information for regulation and enforcement. The SFDRR monitoring approach anticipates progress in substantive, multi-hazard HERVL assessments. The monitoring approach also identifies an important role for local participation in crosscutting issues. These crosscutting issues include climate change and CCA, environmental management, the green agenda and green accounting, gender, and minorities, migrants, and multinational-sponsored economic globalization. For example, some thirty years after the formation of the IDNDR, the GAR19 makes note of (1) broadened scope for hazard and risk monitoring under the SFDRR, (2) use of national social and economic development plans, and (3) integration between DRR and CCA plans, including formal reporting to the United Nations Framework Convention on Climate Change and the Paris Agreement, and internationally financed CCA projects (UNDRR 2019).

Having embraced a multi-risk approach beyond naturally occurring hazard events, SFDRR manifests its expectation that more UN member states will experience multiple, sometimes chronic crises. This reformulation of DRR focus supports the possibility of continuing international support by bringing the risk factors in each of the crosscutting issues together for a newly minted, systemic overview of risk. Monitoring is the overlord, the envelopment meant to redefine DRR as the predominant challenge to development to better DRR and the path to sustainable development. SFDRR calls for DRR to be in concert with development goals to present a plausible strategy for collaboration among all nations, regions, and geopolitical settings.

> **Disaster Risk Reduction and Unsustainable Development**
>
> "The clear relationship between risk from natural and man-made hazards and risks to and from development is the core rationale for integrating DRR into development planning and budgeting. Unless nations accelerate their efforts to curb the development-based drivers of risk, sustainable development may not be possible, and certainly not achievable by 2030. Recognition, however, of the need to address these development-based risk drivers, and to accept that disaster impacts are an indicator of unsustainable development, have yet to permeate conventional DRR and development policy and practice. As described previously in this GAR, especially in Chapter 2, recognition of [the] development role as a driver of risk requires a new understanding of risk in the interactions between the environment and human-made systems, and a shift towards systems-based thinking in risk reduction within mainstream policymaking at practice. . . . There has been some progress in DRR mainstreaming through a range of entry points such as policy, organizations, knowledge, stakeholder engagement and finance." (UNDRR 2019: 354)

Through negotiating guidance documents since 2014, sovereign states have voiced opinions both for and against certain facets of risk monitoring. The facets include tracking implementation, developing common monitoring standards and sharing monitoring activities, ensuring compliance with national and local plans, free data open to all or only nonsensitive data access, voluntary peer reviews or review by the HFA monitor, and coherence in monitoring progress. Actually, components for shared targets and accompanying indicator sets can and should be expressed numerically. The objective is to track globally changing disaster risk (risk to having to declare a disaster) and event losses (whether accompanied by a disaster declaration or not) with indicators that are comparable among nations, components of the built environment, and population groups. There is no specific language in SFDRR for tracking DRR implementation outcomes—whether successes or failures.

*GAR19* continues, "National planning bodies with representation from all sectors must develop risk reduction strategies that assume an all-of-State institutions approach to risk reduction, to be able to adequately address the expanded scope of hazards and risks represented in the Sendai Framework. A process to develop a Global Risk Assessment Framework (GRAF) has been established to facilitate the generation of information and insights that would sustain and guide the incorporation of systemic risk and opportunity into policies and investments. Sustained, multi-year and creative funding and collaboration must support State and non-State participants so that they have the tools they need to better recognize and address systemic risks and apply sustainable risk management strategies at all scales" (UNDRR 2019: v).

Assuming that an all-of-state approach to risk reduction is a must strategy is certainly understandable. But creating sustained, multi-year funding and collaboration to support state and non-state participants points directly to impediments in carrying out HEVRL assessments in both the public and private sectors, as well as MERRE processes to ensure implementation of acceptable levels of risk.

## In Sum

Generating multi-risk assessments that cover natural hazards and other events capable of catastrophic loss is the measurable outcome to which sovereign states have committed themselves through the SFDRR. It also has the potential to generate quantitative as well as qualitative analysis of hazard, exposure, vulnerability, risk, and loss among nations using comparable instruments for measurement and reporting.

But multi-risk assessments are not meant to establish a principal role for development to carry out actions for survival of the world's populations in the face of risk from catastrophe, whether from natural hazard or other events. Nor is SFDRR meant to challenge development's role to pick and choose DRR actions within its actions for economic growth and prosperity. This is particularly the case where disasters are a problem for development, but the underlying causes of disasters are not reason for development to change course or change its presently defined role.

SFDRR is the framework sovereign states have created to go forward. MDBs, DMDAs, and NGOs are asked to support and contribute to the national efforts. The guidance countries have ordained for themselves gives the same latitude to other stakeholders, but the guidance can potentially complicate not only conducting the assessments, but also acting on the information provided by them.

There are seven points of note concerning stakeholder guidance, taking into account sovereign state adoption of frameworks up through and including the Sendai Framework:

1. SFDRR guidance stems in great part from the stakeholders, notwithstanding the myriad of cultures and societies impacted by their actions. The guidance is a recognizable version of HEVRL and MERRE when

viewed in relation to DRR implementation of the built environment. The guidance is primarily for the DRM sector; HEVRL assessments and MERRE processes are to be carried out by DRM and development participants.
2. The focus of the assessments is a systemic approach to defining risk from all types of causal factors. This is quite broad, especially in considering risk definitions to guide DRR actions at the local level for specific components of the built environment for threats from specific natural hazards.
3. Absent is a direct call for free and open access to hazard, exposure, vulnerability, risk, and loss information, which promotes limiting the use of each in a for-profit, risk management environment; fees to access HERLV information will affect literally hundreds of millions of people.
4. Absent is a call to present vulnerability levels of economic and social infrastructure components to natural hazard events to the public in a transparent and visible manner, which pairs with the lack of free access to risk assessment information.
5. There is a call for direct community cooperation at all levels of risk reduction. This call will permit, but not necessarily facilitate, cooperation needed for so much of the MERRE processes. In the past, the countries have set quantified action goals (outputs) for UN decades, but those goals were not met. Now the call is for qualitative risk assessments needed to identify and carry out specific (by hazard/economic/physical infrastructure type) risk reduction actions. However, countries may choose to have risk assessments serve as outputs of SFDRR endeavors, rather than identify the assessments as inputs needed to act on existing and anticipated vulnerability reduction issues.
6. Absent is a direct call for identifying the entity responsible and accountable for each component of economic and social infrastructure vulnerable to specific types of natural hazard events.
7. Absent is a direct call for identifying the acceptable, desirable, proposed, and actual level of risk of each component of economic and social infrastructure.

Overall are questions as to the extent that the guidance will build opportunities or constraints for incorporating natural hazard assessment and mitigation into development project preparation and implementation by the stakeholders. Recognizing the linkage between DRR and development guidance is key to focusing on policies and procedures that govern use of assessments and processes related to DRR data and information in project cycles and that help identify specific action proposals.

On the other hand, much of existing international, interagency, and third-party support for risk reduction guidance is reflected in SFDRR. Not surprisingly, guidance that existed before creation of SFDRR was shaped by stakeholders and the communities of which they are constituents for development as well as risk reduction actions.

The requisite matter in the Sendai Framework calling for a systemic approach to a multi-hazard assessment across nations is correct and helpful for understanding an emerging, complex global context fraught with peril. Certain DRR actions could be undertaken based on that information. However, as in the previous forty-plus years, for a significant portion of the known and anticipated vulnerability of economic and social infrastructure components during the coming fifteen to twenty years, no further risk assessment information is needed to act. Like the run-up to the UN International Decade for Natural Disaster Reduction (UN IDNDR), the main issue of disaster risk reduction is the willingness to act.

CHAPTER 15

# What Has Been Found about the Future
## Changes That Change Positions

If the future could be revealed as to how DRR issues will be managed, back-casting—in literature parlance—would show changes at varying points in time. Back-casting follows changes made—in reverse chronological order—to achieve progress. Following discussions of alternatives, the willingness to implement DRR reveals changes that change positions.

The generations coming of age after 2020 face challenges to where they live. They can choose to reshape the use of the landscape through their development actions as to where and what risks they will endure as time goes on. But they, and we who are already of age, must undertake these actions now.

Strategies for meeting difficult challenges related to the broadest scope of development goals, from poverty alleviation to climate change adaptation, sea level rise, species survival, sustainable development, and betterment are already present in today's initiatives. Reducing risk of impact from natural hazard events to economic and social development includes the more precise questions of disaster reduction for whom, by whom, and at whose cost. Not every natural hazard impact will be eliminated, but lessening impacts to populations and their economic and social infrastructure can be targeted, as are all development actions.

Avoiding all new or amplified risk is not feasible. But we can attempt to avoid a great part of that risk.

## Four Views from the Future

### 1. Schools: Life Safety at the Local Level

Dateline: Geneva, Switzerland—July 26–29, 2031:

Students attending more than 450,000 existing primary and secondary public and private schools around the globe are now learning in safer, less vulnerable classrooms.

The United Nations Office for Disaster Risk Reduction (UNDRR) has been lauded for progress in facilitating action with the Global Alliance for Disaster Risk Reduction and Resilience in the Education Sector (GAD3RES). Coordinating the Worldwide Initiative for Safe Schools with countries around the globe, UNDRR and its partners have successfully reduced the structural vulnerability of schools to natural hazard events.

Ministers of education, meeting under the auspices of UNESCO, recognized the work of eighty-seven countries, including twenty-seven "Safe School Leaders," formally participating in GAD3RES.

In addition, for the first time since the GAD3RES Program began in 2015, UNDRR noted that more than twenty thousand new schools built in the past fifteen years have received the meritorious "Safe School" plaque for their entrances. The plaques signify each school's voluntary compliance with basic disaster resistance approaches called for in the UN-sponsored Sendai Framework for Disaster Risk Reduction (SFDRR). The goal is to award plaques to one million Safe Schools, including new and retrofitted structures, and schools rebuilt following disasters.

In informal conversations during the meeting, ministers and participating education specialists noted that the Safe School award still represents voluntary compliance with recommended loss reduction siting, design, and construction standards.

Although numerous ministerial-level meetings have occurred since the 1990s, UNESCO countries have never formally adopted a universal set of safe school building standards. In 1997 with support of Universidad Central de Venezuela, the Organization of American States (OAS) organized for educational and national education entities the Hemispheric Action Plan for the Vulnerability Reduction of the Education Sector to Natural Hazards (EDUPLANHemisferico) to be undertaken in Latin America and the Caribbean, focusing on primary and secondary schools through academic aspects, public participation, and physical infrastructure. In succeeding years sub-hemispheric action plans were formulated and put into action, and in 2004 the OAS organized Disaster Reduction of University Campuses of the Americas (DRUCA), which was carried forward along with EDUPLANHemisferico in support of the United Nations International Strategy for Disaster Reduction (UNISDR).

At this most recent meeting of education ministers, there was no attempt to endorse a proposed mandatory international standard for one-, two-, and three-story education structures in natural hazard-prone areas. Such a standard would be limited to seismic, wind, lahar, and flood hazards. Construction following this standard results in a level of risk to damage and destruction that is targeted at life safety—no loss of life from building damage or collapse. The SFDRR has called for multi-hazard risk assessments going far beyond these four natural hazards for each country to set in place.

But as in previous attempts at agreement on standards, groups of countries sharing parochial interests blocked mandatory guidance. The opposing blocks represent, on the one hand, those against any form of outside interference in the project design, engineering, and architectural interests and, on the other, public and private design and construction entities that largely control the public school building process in a country.

Officially, plaques noting the use of hazard-resistant school siting, design, and construction have been available only since 2024. Before then, ministries of education had no authority to state publicly the level of risk to predominant natural hazard threats to the school or to identify the authorities responsible for the design and construction of the structure. Unofficially, plaques had been placed on new, retrofitted, and rebuilt schools in various parts of the world since 2021 to recognize those making DRR efforts through local, national, and sometimes international entities. The majority of plaque-bearing schools are in poor settlements. In all cases the involved stakeholders have created and maintain free access to risk management resources. Often the school plaques identify those entities responsible and accountable for the risk level of the school.

The period 2015–2025 was a long-sought turning point to broaden DRR efforts worldwide in school vulnerability reduction. School by school, country by country, international and national private and public sector entities—nonprofits, NGOs, foundations, and the like—applied expert knowledge and experience along with their already existing support for school construction.

Numerous international and local community development organizations and professional groups (such as the concrete industry and civil engineer associations), together with international, regional, and national private tourism, environmental management, and agricultural co-ops and green farming entities, have taken on school construction projects primarily to address lack of school facilities, often in poor areas urban and rural.

These entities, together with volunteer technical support, use school disaster risk reduction experience to demonstrate capacity building, skill development, and physical infrastructure design and construction at the community level. They are joined by local parents, community groups, and authorities to demonstrate management of natural hazard issues.

During school construction projects, public school officials are sometimes sidelined from discussions because the education sector often only occupies and administers but does not fund or build its physical infrastructure. Local school officials and private sector interests were brought together by parents, local leaders, and national professional and political groups to agree on key aspects of school siting, design, and construction. The aspects included site selection, materials, and construction techniques that permit reaching consensus on level of risk to site-specific dominant natural hazard events.

Meanwhile an informal consortium of NGOs, philanthropic organizations, private donors, and community organizations with local-to-global program presence attended this recent ministers' meeting, invited as observing parties. When called upon, each stated that they would continue to site, design, build, rebuild, and retrofit schools to performance standards that they consider most in keeping with calls for resilience in the face of dominant natural hazard events threatening life safety and loss of use of school buildings.

The meeting observers noted a strong correlation between countries suffering loss of schools—sometimes numbering more than a thousand in a single year—and countries struggling to meet education, employment, and income goals for people moving out of poverty. Loss of school buildings is recognized by governments, the local community, and the development community as a contributor to economic development weakness, as is lack of willingness by the general public and elected officials to face the challenge of not only primary and secondary education goals, but also raising financial resources for improved teacher training and school facilities.

They also noted that where schools are physically vulnerable, the owner is often not financially capable to retrofit existing schools or has no resources directly available for reconstruction following a disaster. The loss of primary and secondary school education opportunities is a harbinger of weak economic development potential in the future.

The observers included representatives of multilateral development banks (MDBs) that have financed school construction in developing countries for most of the past seventy years. Through specially created entities in the banks to deal with disaster risk reduction, efforts such as the Global Program for Safer Schools since 2014 by the World Bank continue to support strengthening school facilities to make them less vulnerable to natural hazard impacts. The MDB counterparts are ministries of finance, education, and public works, which are exploring decisions to accomplish achievable, acceptable levels of risk for schools. But MDBs do not demand life safety standards for schools as part of lending requirements or grant giving. Nor do they seek visible recognition of their loans for school construction.

The ministers of education will meet in another four years. Many believe that may be enough time for governments to propose, with or without a world conference, a common basis for taking ownership of part or all of the responsibility and accountability for each of their country's educational infrastructure.

## 2. Information: Show Me the Fax

Dateline: New York, New York—April 30, 2030:

Disaster information is a global issue concerning free access, appropriate application, and informed disaster risk reduction decision-making. It includes information not only about natural hazards, exposure, vulnerability, risk, and loss due to specific natural hazard events, but also monitoring, evaluation, reporting, regulation, and enforcement of risk reduction approaches.

Now a private web-based, crowd-sourced information agency, Noah's Ark Home Info, has created a free residential property risk information fax sheet. "Show Me the Home Risk Fax" information sheets describing the known natural hazard risk factors for residential properties can be requested online for most properties in the United States, European Union, Japan, and major cities in Southeast Asia. And the list of countries keeps expanding. The initiative comes from a fifteen-year call for free and open access to risk information for those interested in acquiring, renting, and selling residential property.

Taking a page from the used car and real estate industries and their online information sites, "Show Me the Home Risk Fax" includes the natural hazard event impact history hazard zone classification of a residential location, focusing on flood, hurricane, wind, volcano, earthquake, tsunami, and most recently added (2026), sea level rise.

In 2027, Noah's Ark Home Info added a for-fee residential property information sheet with options for (1) the number of natural hazard event-related insurance claims filed since 1980 involving property damage and (2) the identification of the residential building codes and land use zoning maps by enforcement period since 1960. In this way, the owner knowing the year of construction or remodeling can look into the applicable codes, standards, and performance norms when the house was built.

Not surprisingly, the most requested geographic sites to date are in coastal areas and major river basins. The most popular natural hazard risk factor is flooding. Close behind is information about hurricane, typhoon, and tropical storm winds and surge tides in numerous coastal areas. Similar to available social science research, a person's interest in natural hazard information depends upon the frequency, severity and onset characteristics of the hazard event. The more frequent the occurrence, the more such information is requested; for example, after all types of hydrologic events, earthquake occurrence is requested more than other geologic hazards such as tsunami, landslides, and volcanic eruptions.

Offering faxed risk information sheets supports temporal periods and specific hazards and location, which aid decision-making. In decades past, hazard exposure information was not disclosed due to security, cost recovery, profit, and ownership concerns. Groups possessing information—including government agencies, insurance companies, financial lenders, and real estate entities—worked to retain risk data. Now, much of that information has been gathered from records of declared disasters, damage claims, and repair permits, as well as indexes of natural hazard phenomena and disaster researchers reviewing specific events.

Top-down efforts provide information supplied through international, regional, and national hazard mapping and risk indexing programs. The programs are supported by the United Nations Office for Disaster Risk Reduction, the World Bank, regional development banks, NGOs, and varying disciplinary research at universities. In 2011 the World Bank brought about the Open Data for Resilience Initiative in collaboration with the Global Forum for Disaster Reduction and Recovery.

Through policy and practice, this contribution to the open data movement addresses challenges of building resilience—in this specific case, housing—to natural hazard events and climate change. It is a partnership with governments—initiation of the program normally is country by country—international organizations, and civil society groups that reach a wide range of participants.

But information is also gathered from bottom-up efforts. Private and public groups involved in environmental management, particularly river basin conservation and preservation, climate change adaptation, sea level rise response, disaster risk management operations, and resilience action groups have observed and documented local hazard management issues.

The social science and allied disciplines working originally in "disaster research" in the 1980s and '90s are said to have made the most sustained preparation and dissemination of hazard and risk information. They continue their post-disaster work but are broadening its scope. They draw on guidance from Forensic Investigations of Disasters (FORIN) publications and other research on policy and practice to encompass root causes of vulnerability of populations and their economic and social infrastructure and to bridge the gap between policy and natural hazard event research.

Valuable information for "Show Me the Home Risk Fax" comes from surveys and questionnaires about pre-existing conditions before the disastrous event. Whether defined as "systemic" risk assessment as prescribed by UN signatory countries of the Sendai Framework for Disaster Risk Reduction or focusing on disaster relief and response or on recovery and reconstruction, these surveys and questionnaires have consistently drawn attention to the underlying vulnerability of populations and their built environment. That attention covers pre-event, post-event, and new housing development vulnerability, particularly of the poor and those who are least able to manage natural hazard risk on their own.

### 3. Living the Change: Where the River Flows

Dateline: Lincoln, Nebraska—Earth Day, April 22, 2030:

A major meeting of public and private groups gathered in Lincoln, Nebraska to view progress in reducing Mississippi River Basin flood hazard vulnerability and returning the floodplain to as natural a drainage basin as possible. The progress shows changes in rural and urban settings through managing floodplains as naturally occurring, highly productive areas with the potential for value-added products and services based on river flow before extensive structural flood control measures became the norm.

Participants from federal, state, and local agencies; private sector business and industry; national and regional NGOs and nonprofits; university researchers; volunteer conservation organizations; and private sector agriculture, water resource management, tourism, transportation, and rural and urban land use planning and development gathered to celebrate a milestone. Every county and parish in every state of the Lower Mississippi River Basin now has at the least a consortium of private and public sector entities discussing and acting on floodplain renewal.

Currently less than half the consortiums constitute an official government entity. But all are advisers to both public and private entities. All actively work with elected officials in the executive, legislative, and judicial branches of government, private sector, and local citizen groups who are involved in floodplain management issues and options. Similar groups in the Missouri and Ohio River Basins are forming county-level advisory committees to focus on options for a productive future use of their basin.

Efforts focus on using the entire Mississippi River Basin natural resources in a wider variety of economic and social goods and services. Because of extensive periodic flooding, groups are seeking more diverse agriculture that includes native species of plants and animals and more multi-seasonal use of the floodway for recreation, tourism, and environmental research, as well as agriculture and renewable energy production.

Since the 1950s, entrenched interests following the Great Depression–era public works programs in the basin have insisted on continuation of structural means to control floodwaters (or flowing water deemed a flood, as in bad) and subsequent disasters (as in really bad), provoking repeated repair, rehabilitation, and reconstruction of structural flood control works. Yet flooding can be considered a benefit if it is managed—or better stated, allowed—to contribute to goods and services from the ecosystem.

Consortiums of participants at the basin, sub-basin, state, county, and parish levels bring to discussions and decision-making forums experience and knowledge from previously initiated programs.

In the past some of these forums dealt with broad issues such as environmental quality and incentives for capacity building, landscape conservation, and environmental justice that demanded fair treatment and meaningful involvement by the public in discussions and decision- making. Other forums dealt with property rights, water rights, job creation, exposed capital investment, and manpower needs and labor.

Now, addressing specific issues of economic and social challenges often built around recognizable land use components in carrying out flood management approaches includes floodplain easements, wetlands protection (including emergencies) and restoration, flood prevention, watershed rehabilitation, agricultural conservation easements, conservation of grazing land, and agricultural and forest productivity for working lands and wildlife.

Early progress on restoring river systems came through a consortium of county and parish conservation extension offices, which are known to most of the participating groups. Across basins spanning multiple counties and parishes in two or more states, groups using governmental and private sector mechanisms have discussed reshaping floodways and floodplains in rivers large and small in the Mississippi River Basin. Alternative uses are being identified for damaged and dismantled flood control structures. Adjacent farms, small towns, cities, and states are to reform, adjust, innovate, return, improve, and profit from an altered relationship with floodways and floodplains and their goods and services.

At their inception, programs for floodplain management, conservation, and land use of the United States Department of Agriculture under their Natural Resource Conservation Service (NRCS) were administered though county, parish, and sub-state, as well as state and US regional groups and activities. Each program reflects specific issues, but none of them focuses specifically on a change of river basin flood control management to a priority, nonstructural approach with diversification of economic activities built around expanded floodways, restored wetlands, and altered floodplains. In addition to these efforts, other federal agencies with programs that have joined the discussions include Bureau of Land Management, EPA, Fish and Wildlife Service, Forest Service, Geological Survey, and National Park Service. As well, the Association of State Floodplain Management (ASFPM) have lent its support.

Also participating is the US Army Corps of Engineers–Mississippi Valley Division and its Lower Mississippi River Environmental Program, which provides environmental data to support sustainable development through design, construction, and operation of the Mississippi River levees and channel improvement features of the Mississippi River and Tributaries Project.

Costs and benefits of restoring the naturally endowed structure and function of river basin ecosystems are being studied closely. Certain segments of the industrialized agricultural sector will be challenged to diversify production to include crops that will be grown and processed in less resource-depleting ways, and expand and diversify animal production for human consumption. Estimates are that up to 18 percent of intensive cultivated cropland will be taken out of production. On the other hand, already recognized needs and anticipated challenges of reducing the amount of such cropland to facilitate adaptation to climate change necessitate when, where, and how agricultural land in the basin can and will be used in the future.

In undertaking changes to the Mississippi River structural flood control system, the research work of Gilbert White and the flood control efforts of the US Army Corps of Engineers are ever present. It was White who in 1942 described alternative approaches to flood management that he referred to as "human adjustment" rather than the frequently proposed structural adjustment consisting of dams, levees, dikes, and channel changes. White believed that modifying human behavior was the preferable approach to controlling loss due to flood events. Human occupancy of floodplains, when and where properly sited and constructed, can exist in harmony with flood events with acceptable impacts when compared with the continuing benefits.

In the Mississippi River Basin at varying levels, with differing degrees of accommodation and implementation to date, under discussion are management of floodplains in creeks and streams to the largest rivers, including the Missouri, Arkansas, Illinois, Ohio, and Red River Basins and the Mississippi Delta itself.

Alternative actions that would restore and make working the floodplain profitable are also under consideration. Communities and farms through alternative management approaches for millions of acres would continue to occupy what has been traditionally referred to as river bottom. Most progress on defining alternative management approaches is coming from bottom-up discussions at the county, parish, and state level. These approaches identify concrete benefits and costs—and define the changes that have to be made and by whom—rather than reiterating wordy global and national "sustainable environment," "climate change adaptation," "nonintrusive intervention," and "pro-business" slogans and propositions. Participating groups recognize that change is taking place and that there are opportunities to shape those changes to some extent, but change does require making choices and being fair and just.

At the federal, state, county, and parish levels, ongoing cost and benefit analysis of continuing a "structural flood control first" is no longer a viable economic investment in the face of presently reoccurring flood events and post-disaster reconstruction costs for roads, flood control structures, and settlements in their existing locations.

Analysis of alternative economic development approaches to managing river flow using previous floodways shows that different, sometimes new, products and services can be generated. Available funds would otherwise be used to build and rebuild admittedly vulnerable structural flood control measures, roads, bridges, and social infrastructure, along with settlements and private commerce and industry.

Claims that there is no discernable source of funds, now or in the future, to cover the cost of repairing continuing and repetitive damage to economic and social infrastructure from flooding are undocumented. Some participants believe that revenues made available after a damaging flood are much better spent by putting them directly into the hands of the local landowners, private or public, to restructure the natural floodway and floodplain management.

A baseline assumption from politics of yore is that construction of civil works is construction with a profit incentive, whatever the purpose of the civil works. Enormous sums of both public and private capital will be needed to change the flood management plans and programs of the basin. Participants believe that floodplain renewal activities together with economic development investments in the basin will benefit the basin region as well as local communities as the involved ecosystems' structure and function offer more diverse products and services. The basin's economy will be less dominated by intensive, mechanized agriculture production. It will evolve to working with and maximizing what natural systems provide. "Remember that gain can always be made from the products or services provided," one participant said.

The expected increase in benefit comes from use of the floodway and floodplain, benefits that are minimized from attempting to control flooding for a limited set of economic endeavors. Cost and benefit analyses today include flood impacts. Future analyses will look at cumulative costs and benefits of minimizing flood losses and maximizing use of the basin in a wide variety of economic and social undertakings.

Some of the revised flood management approach will maintain components of the structural flood management system. These include hydroelectric power generation installations that impound, retain, and sell water for electric power generation, agriculture, and urban consumption.

Other structured flood control approaches for draining wetlands and for protecting and expanding arable farmland will be modified or removed, replaced by the creation and management of products and services through restoring floodways, floodplains, estuaries, marshes, and riverine wetlands. This use will actually benefit from increasingly seasonal and storm-driven flood events associated with climate change adaptation.

Flood losses around the world have been increasing at rates that skeptics of climate change only a decade ago declared folly, myth, and a hoax. Not only were the rates of rainfall (and sea level rise) questioned as too high, but the rates of land use change—representing investment, growth, accommodation, transformation, and profit—were considered too low to sustain economic growth.

There is no acceptance in 2030 of undertaking a predominant nonstructural approach to flood control, particularly at the scale of the Mississippi River Basin. But there has been progress—in some states more, in others, less—on tributaries of major and minor rivers flowing into the Mighty Mississippi.

Nonetheless, the NRCS format of issues, funded support, and perhaps most importantly a level table for discussion provides a necessary opportunity for the gathering of private and public groups, each with specific agendas.

For some participants, their agenda is a priority nonstructural approach to floodplain management and/or agricultural, food production, tourism, recreation, and urban development for the future, built on the broadening use of river basin ecosystem structure and function. For other participants, the cost and benefit are the decision basis whereby any further feasible investment in structural flood control is evaluated given the growing magnitude and frequency of flood events.

The benefits of a nonstructural approach are investing available funds into local health, education, and job creation using the rivers' and streams' natural resources. This approach is most often seen at the municipal and county levels and focused on creeks, streams, and the upper reaches of river basins away from major cities.

Sponsoring participants in the Lower Mississippi Basin working group include the already mentioned federal, state, county, and local agencies as well as the Lower Mississippi River Conservation Committee, Mississippi Land Trust, Mississippi River Cities and Towns Initiative, Mississippi River Collaborative, and Mississippi River Trust.

Participants in the Missouri River Basin include the Missouri Resource Assessment Partnership, American Bird Conservancy, Curators of the University of Missouri, Izaak Walton League of America, East-West Gateway Council of Governments, World Wildlife Fund, and those involved in discussions built around the study "The Missouri River Ecosystem: Exploring the Prospects for Recovery," prepared by the US National Research Council with contributions from its Division on Earth and Life Studies, Water Science and Technology Board, and Committee on Missouri River Ecosystem Science.

In the emerging Ohio River Basin working group of the James River Basin Partnership, participants include involved federal, state, county, and local agencies as well as the Ohio River Basin Alliance, Ohio River Basin Consortium for Research and Education, Ohio River Corridor, Ohio River Foundation, Ohio Watershed Network, Ohio River Valley Water Sanitation Commission, and ReImagine Appalachia.

In the Arkansas River Basin consortium, participants include Colorado State Parks, AHRA Citizens Task Force, Arkansas Natural Heritage Commission, Chaffee County, Colorado Division of Wildlife, Colorado Mountain College, Colorado Water Conservation Board, Greater Arkansas River Nature Association, Sangre De Cristo Resource Conservation and Development Council, the Nature Conservancy, and Trout Unlimited. In the Illinois River and Red River Basins, consortium groups are in formation, with participation of various public sector agencies mentioned above and private sector conservation groups focusing on wetland restoration and flood control.

At the state level, typically involved in consortium discussions are representatives from departments and agencies representing agriculture, conservation, economic development, environment, natural resources, rural affairs, transportation, tourism, urban affairs, and the state National Guard.

There is progress. Today every state of the Mississippi River Basin has at least one consortium of private and public sector entities, each with its own agenda, discussing, seeking cooperation, and undertaking floodplain reconstruction for flood hazard reduction and other benefits. Acting on belief in the face of some doubt, consortium participants are working through a constructive, broad look at the basin's potential while taking avoidance, transfer, and acceptance of climate and other hydrologic and atmospheric risks straight on. Alternative strategies to current practices for lessening risk while sustaining development in this context are more evident, but not necessarily easier to implement.

This is the flow of change beginning, literally, where a river runs through it.

### 4. Road Transportation: On the Road to DRR

Dateline: Barcelona, Spain—May 1, 2029:

The International Road Foundation (IRF) has decided to include specific information concerning road vulnerability to natural hazards in their publicly assessable documents on national and regional road transportation networks.

The decision was made at the just-concluded annual IRF meeting held in Barcelona. Impetus for the decision followed more than five years of IRF working group discussions on broadening use of available natural hazard risk information and supporting local efforts for disaster risk reduction of roads of all types.

In concert with the United Nations Office for Disaster Risk Reduction (UNDRR) and the Sendai Framework for Disaster Risk Reduction (SFDRR), ministries of transportation, public works, and finance prioritized road retrofitting and reconstruction following damage and destruction from natural hazard events and sea level rise. The hazard risk information comes from national and regional road trade corridor operations, ongoing assessments of road infrastructure physical condition, along with recently available information on vulnerability of bridges to natural hazards, and detailed climate data on rainfall and flooding.

The IRF has for many years supported professional development through research, education, and training in more than thirty subject areas. In a shift from emphasis on new road building and operation, IRF has introduced road vulnerability reduction to natural hazards for subject areas of (1) new road construction—the traditional priority public sector area; (2) reconstruction of roads damaged or destroyed by natural hazard events—an investment by both public and private sectors; and (3) retrofitting existing roads to lessen vulnerability.

This last area is an ever-increasing engineering and financial challenge, and the largest and longest unattended road construction project in any country, considering the growing threat of climate-change-related flooding and sea level rise.

Progress in road vulnerability reduction was made possible by collaboration with national road agencies and professional groups such as societies of civil engineers and the civil works construction industry.

The IRF in 2025 established road corridors as a priority category for research and technical support for DRR. The decision was based on national and regional experiences with road corridors as major elements in integrated regional economic development dating back to the 1990s in Latin America and Eastern Europe, along with road damage and destruction from natural and man-made hazards worldwide.

Research and technical assistance from international development entities collaborating with regional political bodies focuses on two risk factors. The first is physical vulnerability of road infrastructure to the hazardous event, and the second is economic and social vulnerability of the nation and region expressed in population vulnerability characteristics. Damage and destruction of trade corridor roads goes far beyond the physical and financial aspects of repair and reconstruction; it includes economic development aspects often associated with the road network decisions.

Earlier, following the 2021 IRF world meeting, between 2022 and 2025 these national and regional groups began to access and publicize more detailed road condition information not previously released. Assessments specific to the vulnerability of roads to natural hazards began to be highlighted, particularly regarding sea level rise, flooding, and earthquakes. Preparation of this information was prompted in part by the call in 2019 by UNDRR through GAR19 for multi-hazard systemic assessments of risk at the national level. This followed signing of the SFDRR by United Nations member countries in 2015. That was when the IRF decided to support free access to road risk management information.

More than thirty years ago, national infrastructure "report cards" began to identify the specific needed investment for retrofitting vulnerable roads and bridges. There was not, however, any specific mention of road and bridge infrastructure vulnerability to natural hazard events; rather, all necessary upgrading was placed in their respective infrastructure component category. It is only recently that any qualitative and quantitative information as to the cost of repair and replacement of road and bridge infrastructure due to natural hazard vulnerability has been included in road infrastructure report cards, such as the American Society of Civil Engineers' *Report Card for America's Infrastructure*.

The IRF is paying attention to the increasing number of failing bridges. These occurrences have influenced the IRF to support releasing information on road vulnerability to natural hazards, recognizing the extremely disruptive consequences of bridge damage to road transportation.

Information released included hydrologic and geologic hazard events. Analysis of historical design and construction documentation and post-event damage and destruction assessments showed that many failing or failed bridges now have more hazardous exposure than when originally designed and built. This change is caused by denser land use occupation and the impact of climate change, as well as evolving security, safety, and loading concerns. Many bridges were located, designed, and constructed never anticipating such possible changes in exposure.

For the previous twenty-five years, hazard and risk information on road and transportation corridor conditions was not public, for various reasons. Now such information is accessible free of charge, brought about by IRF's continuing role to address DRR in sovereign states, the MDBs, and private development demands for transportation-related information.

Resolving road infrastructure vulnerability goes far beyond the knowledge, expertise, and control of the ordinary citizen. Depending on the country, current national road vulnerability assessments include prioritizing DRR initiatives while (1) pursuing road network expansion, (2) road infrastructure retrofitting of existing roads and bridges, or (3) repairing and reconstruction of the same bridge or road after a natural hazard event, all in the name of development and DRR.

# Conclusion

Reconciling the necessary components for a DRR strategy—socially acceptable, economically viable, and ecologically sustainable—is a challenge, given the unequal cultural power supporting each of these factors. It results from how and why particular choices are made in society to manage risk (Oliver-Smith 2013). The choices relate to the built environment in a parochial manner that does not always address risk reduction for the most vulnerable populations or even the most vulnerable components of the built environment. In the broad sense, emerging views using risk assessments tied to DRR implementation have come to include differing observations about who is vulnerable and why. The assessments help identify through MERRE processes and their accompanying behaviors the underlying causes of the vulnerability that ultimately lead to choices for implementing DRR.

Andrew Maskrey's 2016 summary of disaster impact observations is quite relevant considering that death tolls from natural hazard events are actually declining. It is also relevant considering the need for emphasis on existing vulnerability. He writes, "Emerging empirical evidence on disaster loss patterns and trends, however, unveils a radically different picture. Ballooning investment in the disaster risk management sector at all scales has been accompanied by equally rapidly increasing levels of disaster related loss and damage, in particular associated with frequently occurring, localized extensive risks. Extensive risks are those that are most associated with underlying drivers, such as environmental degradation, social and economic inequality, poorly planned and managed urban development and weak or ineffective governance" (Maskrey 2016: 5).

Considering these perspectives, for more than thirty-five years there have been repeated calls to address risks of economic and social infrastructure vulnerability, particularly among those least able to reduce their own vulnerability as part of development processes. Indeed, before, during, and after natural hazard events, risk reduction should be proclaimed as a principal development goal. Development must be the principal driver of DRR. Stakeholders may not now consider disaster risk reduction the domain of development, but unwittingly, development has become the domain for survival of human beings.

After fifty-plus years of modern international development and forty-five-plus years of disaster management, the key manifestations of increasing vulnerability of the built environment in both lesser and more developed countries are the following:

- Increased damage and destruction of social and economic infrastructure in both the public and private sectors;
- Only relatively minor changes in generation and application of HEVRL and MERRE to development planning and construction to support the basis of DRR of economic and social infrastructure to natural hazard events;
- De facto dependency on catastrophic events to spawn some change in HEVRL and MERRE use, and then often implemented only in the impacted area or in as limited an administrative space as possible;
- Fierce opposition in much of the private arena of all economic sectors to increase requirements for resilience through acknowledgment of existing levels of risk, and acceptance of responsibility, accountability, and risk reduction costs to be borne by the owners and operators of economic and social infrastructure;
- Continued encroachment of the built environment in known hazard-prone areas with well-funded, politically driven support overcoming dedicated, but limited opposition; and
- Failure to adequately deal with informal and illegal "development" expansion of urban settlements and encroachment on protected areas with all manner of social and economic infrastructure.

## Development

The focus of sovereign states' efforts is still pointedly on development goals defined at their core as economic growth and landscape transformation through the built environment. Yet this guise masks nations' increased risk of economic and social infrastructure loss, some with catastrophic consequences to public administration, health, safety, human welfare, and sustainable economic participation for all. Built environment square footage and GDP economic measurement dominate development vocabulary. In a broader context, development can be viewed as growth and change, adaptation, sustainability, and survivability, but also of who, where, when, and how.

Perhaps the dominant goal of development is actually headed toward survival. Development efforts might well evolve into primarily management over risk of annihilation. Emerging adaptation to risk—physical, economic, and financial—could become a leading economic sector, as in the sourcing and distribution of water as a commodity. Whatever the outcome, the goal of wealth creation and accumulation might become nonsensical, if not worthless. Various components of economic and social infrastructure might become stranded assets with no market value. Betterment will be equated with sustaining life.

Currently the development community includes stakeholders pursuing betterment, that is, betterment through economic investment, economic growth, and globalization. Crosscutting issues interacting with the development community include sustainable development (in its many declared forms), species and habitat survival groups, and climate change and sea level rise adaptation groups. Disaster risk management and emergency management sectors interface with the development community and entities that share interest in a common undertaking, although their motives may differ. Commonly recognized communities are profiled by geographic place, political leanings, ethnicity, religion, income, language, and/or customs, among other characteristics.

## Propositions about the Future

In the short- to medium-term (now to 2040), there are four propositions about the outcome of development-generated risk if it continues at its present pace: (1) disaster assistance will constitute most all non-reimbursable international development assistance; (2) sovereign states, even those suffering losses themselves, will be called upon to provide disaster assistance to countries that repeatedly suffer catastrophic losses; (3) disaster assistance will become more complex in addressing public and private sector losses; and (4) disaster assistance in response to various causal factors will evolve into even more complex relationships within and among sovereign states and private sector entities.

## Development, Globalization, and Disasters

Broad swaths of intra- and international territories are targets for development. They include low-lying continental coastal areas, islands, tropical rain forests, volcanic zones, earthquake fault lines, estuaries, river basins, arid plateaus, and the tropics. All are subject to natural hazard events, and exposure crosses all economic and social strata. The extent of impact is rural, urban, provincial, national, regional, and hemispheric in dimension. It includes not only the impoverished, the displaced, and those forced to migrate, but also the well-established and well-heeled. These groups exist in both formal and informal economies but might not yet be formally embroiled in disaster risk reduction. Exposure of these groups to natural hazard events presently dwarfs the applicable vulnerability assessment capacity of the formal economy. But their vulnerability reduction does not come about simply by sharing additional details of risk drivers absent realistic choices undertaken willingly that would actually lessen their exposure, vulnerability, and risk.

There is little questioning about the current marked difference between economic development and survival. GAR19 states, "The ambition, richness and expansive spirit of cooperation required to meet systemic challenges will require levels of selfless humanism that match the scale of the challenge. Humans can (or should) decide on changing deeply embedded values that define higher level rules of operation and interaction. If not, societies may continue to create wealth at the expense of declining ecological life support functions in a positive spiraling feedback loop that creates systemic risks with cascading effects and makes overarching economic, ecological and social systems increasingly susceptible to collapse" (UNDRR 2019: xi).

Superimposing the location of the poor, the displaced, and those forced to migrate and resettle in zones of prevalent atmospheric, hydrologic, and geologic hazards serves to highlight priority areas for sustainable development to promote human betterment. Priorities for these areas include vulnerability reduction of economic and social infrastructure and strengthening health care, education, water and sanitation, and social services. Local groups should demand access to existing knowledge and expertise not only for their safety and welfare, but also to sustain their economic livelihoods, social constructs, and physical infrastructure.

As noted earlier, disaster shocks can open political space to contest or consolidate political power. Currently, speaking truth to power concerning risk assessments informing MERRE processes is a recognized but not much discussed issue. Ultimately, whatever the form of society responding to vulnerability, the shocks natural hazard events can produce should include speaking justice to truth.

To fully address disasters and development within globalization, societies in the quest for sustainability will strive for community through interdependency that includes those who contribute and those in need, along with those whose roles fluctuate or change.

Development planning and practice should use HEVRL assessments and MERRE processes to form decisions on acceptable levels of risk to natural hazard events reflecting existing knowledge and experience. Vulnerability reduction should be accomplished at whatever level through development as a manifestation of responsibility and accountability to do so in accordance with societal values and preferences.

## DRR Context

Convergence, duplication, and divergence surrounding disaster risk reduction policies, programs, and projects undertaken by political and technical entities exist at all levels. All form part of the underlying risk factors. With IDNDR, HFA, and SFDRR frameworks as a backdrop for acquired commitments and implementation, some international, regional, subregional, and national initiatives now discuss vulnerability reduction in terms of risk factors, that is, reducing the underlying causes of disaster.

Overall, there is progress in DRR, but it varies by economic and social sector and geographic location. For the most part, the tendency of formal DRR framework agreements is toward no quantitative goals, qualitative measurable levels of action, or mandated strengthening coordination between development sectors and with CCA and other crosscutting-issue groups. However, sufficient knowledge and experience exist to make meaningful risk reduction in economic and social infrastructure components, particularly related to lifelines, critical infrastructure, housing, education, health facilities, and water and sanitation systems.

## Risk in Perspective

Vulnerability of the majority of economic and social infrastructure components to damage and destruction from natural hazard events is most often known or anticipated. Development actions, including those of sustainable development, are using information about hazard occurrence in terms of place, time, and severity. The importance of understanding the difference between the risk of damage and destruction of infrastructure and the risk of occurrence of a hazardous event is now becoming recognized as critical to choosing acceptable levels of risk, not only for populations but also economic and social infrastructure.

From this follows the important distinction between qualitative and quantitative estimates of risk of damage and destruction of infrastructure when choosing loss reduction alternatives. This highlights the use of systemic risk assessments of vulnerable populations at a broad scale (e.g., country by country). Its application is different from that of risk assessment of damage and destruction of specific economic and social infrastructure components with associated populations at a province, state, and local level. Clarifying the specifics of vulnerability and risk assessments reveals alternative paths of DRR for those facing overwhelming vulnerability from one or more types of hazardous events.

As detailed in FORIN (Oliver-Smith et al. 2016), "Disaster risk management practice is still very much dominated by reaction and response, to the detriment of development-based risk reduction and avoidance interventions. . . . The physical triggering events of a disaster can vary widely, but the existence of similar approaches to development that privilege economic growth over social and environmental values and priorities is a key factor in their occurrence."

FORIN seeks to establish evidence that supports changes in DRM and development practice, noting the apposition of "corrective risk practices" and prospective, risk-avoidance processes. It also questions whether discussion of resilience goes far enough to identify the root causal mechanism of risk. Reflecting on the nature of disaster events, FORIN states, "Disasters are perhaps best understood as the unfolding of systemic pathological changes. They may also be seen as clear and relevant symbols, representations, and indicators of skewed development." Almost without exception, one way or another development creates the built environment by choice. Current development processes can be structural, and others may be changeable or modifiable, but the approaches are for a purpose, and alternatives may or may not be chosen or implemented depending on customs, traditions, culture, and most importantly values (Oliver-Smith et al. 2016: 6–22).

For many, risk of catastrophic impact on economic and social infrastructure is dwarfed by risk of state-sponsored or otherwise civil, military, and religious conflict, pandemics, hunger, water scarcity, nuclear war, and even human species' annihilation through a meteor strike. The impact of global warming and its links to sea level rise, ocean and terrestrial biological habitat loss, and agricultural shifts goes beyond anything yet experienced as a "catastrophic" natural hazard impact on economic and social infrastructure. But global extinction threats put into perspective the large number of natural hazard threats year to year, and decade to decade, on country and local built environment temporal and spatial scales.

## Risk and Assessment in Social Settings

All disciplines involved in development decision-making should lead preparation of needed risk assessments. Risk analysis should entail not only infrastructure components, but also discrete populations, locations, economic systems, and social activities. Nation-based risk and vulnerability indexing may currently be mandated and increasingly available. Risk assessments should go beyond using sovereign states as the default unit of analysis. Whatever the analysis, it should reveal the ability, if any, of sovereign states to prepare assessments, and any dependency on external financial support and implementation. Risk analysis should use information generated by both citizens and specialists as facilitators. In particular cases, risk assessments will reflect a sense of faith, doubt, or uncertainty (such as those related to climate change) as they are used for DRR initiatives.

How can border areas that are part of multi-country ethnic groupings, shared river basins, trade corridors, and economic development zones embroiled in disparate political, economic, and social competition and integration with one another transform themselves into agents for cooperative opportunities? Trusted interdependency brings benefit sharing, particularly around the issue of water management. This is especially needed in dealing with community involvement for natural hazard events. Particularly urgent is the need to cooperate on water resource management, including trans-boundary, ground, and surface water issues relating to agriculture, energy, mining, recreation, transportation, and drinking water consumption.

Addressing risk—whether to existing economic and social infrastructure, or of what is to be built or reconstructed following damage and destruction—may do nothing about risk in another geographic place. Addressing risk may not only be directly related, but also dependent upon other geographic areas that have the capacity to heighten or lessen vulnerability, such as in the case of flooding. As GAR19 comments on areas of water scarcity, "Unable to support current economic activity and human populations, migration on a scale never before seen may be triggered, with people moving from arid and semi-arid regions to low-elevation coastal zones, thus increasing risk" (UNDRR 2019: x). Such instances involve DRR as important not only to broad development decisions, but also decisions that will impact water resources based on ecosystem structure and function to provide goods and services. Understood is the extent of existing risk at multiple geographic scales and threat levels with accompanying social, political, and administrative consequences.

In addition, in the economic marketplace there exists the possibility of or preference for addressing financial risk over economic and physical forms of risk reduction. Yet in existing UN frameworks that deal with disasters and risk reduction, MDBs and the private sector developers have not embraced economic and physical risk reduction in the same way they have taken on financial risk reduction, which is a subject much closer to home, so to speak.

## MERRE as a Vision

In one vision of the future, MERRE comes about not only through mandated local public and strengthened private participation, but also through stakeholders and other development sector participation. Within this vision, needed changes in public and private participation, market forces, risk, safety, and moral responsibility are discussed. As a result, important differences between managing risk through land use planning and zoning (avoidance strategies), as well as through the design, construction, and maintenance (structural resilience) of economic and social infrastructure components become more apparent. Now emerging are numerous questions about who makes rules to balance the safety of individuals and society's responsibilities. The relevant issues involve tradition, expediency, highest and best use of land, government and inhabitants' rights/preferences/veto powers, the tragedy of the commons, and society's most vulnerable and least powerful.

MERRE processes are to make HEVRL assessments visible and transparent to ensure responsibility and accountability in decision-making. MERRE constitutes the "both-and" process of using appropriate, rightful decisions about reducing physical risk while pursuing further definition of systemic risk of the population. These decisions are made in complex societal contexts that consider competing claims for resources and differing values, political positions, and economic interests.

## Reducing Risk

The supposition is that something different should be done. The reality is that something already known can be done.

A more systemic diagnostic approach to risk may often lead to a decision process that produces a least-common-denominator solution that focuses more on political agreement than on effective action. This observation applies most directly to the stakeholder group formed by sovereign states and their regional organizations and agencies. Collectively, sovereign states may avoid or refuse committing to act on risk management issues that might become subject to foreign dictates, interventions, monitoring, reporting, regulations, or enforcement. Yet dealing with HEVRL and MERRE is precisely how effective targets for risk reduction policies and practices are identified.

A more systemic description of risk does not necessarily address the reduction of risk of the built environment. Known vulnerability of education and health facilities, housing, water and sanitation systems, and bridges can be reduced without depending on additional assessments of social, economic, political, administrative, and other forms of vulnerability of the population. Admittedly, some DRR actions will be shrouded and packaged in a do-no-harm, no-regrets approach distilled from "annihilation to survival" discussions. But recognizing that an acceptable level of risk for economic and social infrastructure components includes responsibility and accountability is the foundation of a both-and approach. Both-and DRR actions are needed where the lack of attention to feasible mitigation of critical economic and social infrastructure in the short- to mid-term might lead to loss and destruction in the longer term.

> ### DRR and Day-to-Day Decision-Making
>
> Jane Murphy Thomas, an accomplished international community development consultant in Asia, noted in her book draft, "People are well aware of disaster risks, but they have more immediate potential risks or crises that drive their decision-making day-to-day. . . . 'Yes, this is an avalanche (or flood) prone area, but we are not going to move anywhere else,' or 'Yes, my old house collapsed in the earthquake, but I am rebuilding it the same way it was before.' In other words, to be most beneficial, risk assessment needs to look at the immediate risks as well the big physical risks" (personal correspondence 2019–2020).

## Risk Reduction in Recovery

The issue of risk reduction is growing more visible in economic and social infrastructure reconstruction policies, programs, and projects. It is often instigated or insisted upon by NGOs and international donor, humanitarian assistance, and community development institutions. Their dialogues and shared experiences often take place outside of the development sector-led economic and social infrastructure recovery operations. To their credit, MDBs now report post-disaster reconstruction as a growing part of their portfolios. But there is yet no clear identification of the type or number of supported infrastructure projects with identified levels of acceptable risk.

In reconstruction operations, DRR guidance will benefit from specific hazard risk reduction information while not being held responsible for resolving multiple, complex risk construction issues dating back to before the occasion of the disaster. MDB and NGO donor-driven DRR initiatives may have a demonstrable impact on post-disaster reconstruction and new economic and social infrastructure risk management long before any substantive risk reduction of existing economic and social infrastructure ever takes place.

## Redefining DRR in Development

DRR is now seen as something more than a humanitarian assistance issue. "Managing risks rather than managing disasters—Disaster risk reduction needs to be reinterpreted" (UNISDR 2015a: ix). Thus, the key challenge is to change development approaches. By making DRR visible and transparent, economic and social infrastructure component owners and operators are heading toward responsibility and accountability for decisions concerning physical risk to natural hazard events. In addition, societies, communities, and individuals are more likely to define the level of risk they will accept.

Characterization of vulnerable populations can and should include the type and extent of physical, financial, and economic vulnerability of related economic and social infrastructure. But current calls for more comprehensive risk analysis may reflect a misunderstanding by some stakeholders. Some may have a view that disaster risk reduction means (1) zero physical risk as a goal; or (2) risk is best addressed solely as a technical issue; or (3) knowledge about hazards, exposure, and vulnerability at local levels is insufficient to discuss acceptable levels of risk; or (4) all natural events are disasters, and their impact can and should be addressed by the DRM sector.

## Guidance

As part of a systemic systems-based approach, GAR19 states that the Sendai Framework is to go beyond the risk reference points presented in *GAR 2015*. GAR19 pronounces that "there are profound implications in making the shift from a hazard-by-hazard view of risk, to a holistic understanding of disaster risk as a dynamic three-dimensional topography that changes through time" (UNDRR 2019: xiv). Thus, sovereign states through the UN have set up the framework for and the call to carry out a multi-hazard, multifaceted assessment of the creation, impact, and outcome of multiple risks affecting a specific geographic site.

Understanding the interconnection of risk drivers should lead to better understanding the qualitative and quantitative impact of studied multiple risks worldwide. Preparing and presenting systemic risk assessments may leave aside for now and the proximate future policy and practice that clearly illuminate the disaster risk reduction challenge—reducing vulnerability of economic and social infrastructure, particularly for education and health facilities, water and sanitation systems, and small-scale agriculture.

One outcome of systemic risk assessments, intended or not, is to solidify the political, professional, and operational basis of a DRM sector. At the same time, the climate change sector and other crosscutting issue sectors are beginning to incorporate DRR approaches that are alongside the development sector with its "mainstreaming" as well as the DRM sector.

Preparation of such assessments may become an end in itself, that is, a lauded outcome rather than a tool. Moreover, while DRM specialists work at preparing assessments, the development community is conditioned to accept the status quo of risk creation, disaster impacts, and DRR implementation.

The Sendai Framework Monitor is linked with national statistical offices through the framework to include disaster-related data within official statistics containing economic loss data for all participating countries. One implication is that the data will promote greater efforts at risk assessment in the context of global economic expansion, financial hazard risk management, and placing vulnerability data in the marketplace. Another implication is assumed presence of an entity that through whatever means will make risk assessment information freely available and accessible to all.

The Sendai Framework endorses community participation in implementing DRR. What the endorsement does not explore are the limitations of that participation. It can be limited or thwarted by regimes (democratic or otherwise), by control through voice or vote regarding community preferences, claims, goals, and objectives, or by simply refusing to fund community-preferred actions.

## Future of DRR with Guidance

Current DRR implementation, including vulnerability reduction of existing economic and social infrastructure, does not mirror the stated goals of SFDRR. The situation becomes understandable given that the Sendai Framework emphasizes that government should be the principal participant. SFDRR does not name the development community as principal DRR implementer, with the private sector as its principal participant and economic development as the context for risk reduction.

Yet the vocabulary of SFDRR guidance includes development-based drivers of risk. What happens if economic expansion takes place, but social inequality, built environment exposure, population vulnerability, and ecosystem degradation continue to grow? Such growth might well be due to changing natural hazard events impacting economic and social infrastructure. The GAR19 position identifying natural hazard events as one of multiple risks to human population reflects, then, a complex situation. In a both-and approach to DRR, identification of specific natural hazard risks should be undertaken and include priority for those impacting educational and health facilities, water and sewer systems, housing, and small-scale agriculture infrastructure, particularly for the poor and dispossessed.

## Will and Willingness

Sovereign states may not give up easily their nuanced maneuvers to continue using inputs as outputs, process as product, and policy formulation as manifestations of practice. In the end, political will—which is a social behavior, not a tool—must be practiced in order to implement DRR. Honest and comprehensive discussions depend on leadership that combines political risk-taking and inspiration, along with forward-looking options for making often difficult decisions.

What then is the path by which information about hazards, exposure, vulnerability, risk, and loss becomes part of development planning and implementation? How will societies decide who is responsible and who pays, when, at what cost, and who benefits?

Risk management of built environment vulnerability to natural hazard events is not merely different from other risks; it is intrinsically different. Risk reduction of economic and social infrastructure can occur, literally, structure by structure, classroom by classroom, hospital by hospital, water system by water system, and bridge by bridge, at least for life safety. Such actions can occur even as the more complex natural hazard risk issues of the population are addressed. Whatever the situation, vulnerability reduction to natural hazard events is contingent above all else on the willingness to do so.

The power to will—in the colloquial, willpower—is needed, along with the willingness to take action.

When DRR is willed into action, owners and operators of vulnerable components of economic and social infrastructure demonstrate successful risk reduction. Societies at whatever scale need to understand much more about natural hazard risk of their built environment and social, economic, and political relations.

Those within a representative democracy governed by laws that protect not only individual rights but also the broader population must constantly discuss and decide what to do about risk. Understanding gaps between knowledge, policy, and practice related to risk reduction accompany what is known about who is at risk, why, and what can be done about it, especially for the poor. Those within a free market economy that derives economic power by maximizing gains with minimal risk to personal wealth must constantly discuss and decide who will benefit and who will pay, how, when, and to whom.

## The Willingness to Consider a Beginning

Notwithstanding present stakeholder policy and practice on DRR, the premises on which development actions might be considered sustainable are: first, vulnerability reduction should be an expressed objective of development; second, development should not enhance the risk of disasters; and third, carrying out sustainable development actions should mitigate the impact of natural hazard events.

An argument for DRR, then, is to consider that in order to manage risk of any natural hazard event, the exposed population is told the event location and severity together with the specific components of the economic and social infrastructure that will be damaged or destroyed. In other words, in considering an evacuation for extreme weather events, the evacuation uses information as an opportunity for survival informed by the underlying knowledge of what can happen. What then of hazard, exposure, vulnerability, and risk assessments or other natural hazard events? Can they not be used in the same vein as preparations for evacuations? And what of a society's reasons for and ability to call for an evacuation? Is it not the same as monitoring, evaluation, reporting, regulation, and enforcement? Development must continually bring DRR to its processes as the harbinger of survival, measured and expressed by something other than economic gain and landscape transformation. Disaster risk reduction is a development choice that must include the willingness for implementation.

Populations around the world are no strangers to the threat of catastrophic loss or annihilation. When faced with threat of nuclear war and almost certain annihilation of all societies, the sovereign states were willing to accept a risk management strategy called MAD—mutually assured destruction—as the deterrent to reduce the threat.

Now populations around the globe again face a risk of catastrophic loss generated by human action—put simply, development-induced vulnerability to natural hazard events, including climate change and sea level rise. But this time governments and communities ought to manage the risk with an acceptable, collective strategy. That strategy is MAS—mutually assured survival.

# Glossary

**Acceptable level of risk (*also* acceptable risk):** In discussion of the built environment, the level of damage or destruction considered to be tolerable by a society or authorities in view of social, economic, political, and economic cost-benefit analysis, usually expressed through plans, norms, codes, and regulations. If so stated, it can also relate to loss of life of a population.

**Built environment:** All economic infrastructure (e.g., agriculture, commerce, energy, industry, mining, transportation, telecommunications) and social infrastructure (the arts, education, health, public assembly, religious, public safety, and housing) at whatever scale, wherever placed, and whatever quality. The built environment consists of systems, networks, sets, groupings, and components. It includes all buildings that are part of neighborhoods, settlements, villages, towns, and cities. Examples in no particular order include lifelines, critical facilities, trade corridors, telecommunication networks, potable water networks, agricultural irrigation systems (including water storage); transportation (road, rail, air, and waterways), hydroelectric power generation, transmission, and distribution networks; and tourism facilities. It also includes education and medical facilities, neighborhoods with housing and service infrastructure, commerce and industry (including just-in-time production facility networks for all sorts of goods and services); public facilities corresponding to the legislative, executive, and judicial branches of government and public safety; and places of public assembly, including those for the arts and religious worship.

**Construction:** The physical creation of the built environment, unless identified as the creation of risk through societal forces.

**Deconstruction:** The term will be used in the sense of dissecting and analyzing a social phenomenon, such as risk to natural hazard events, in order to understand its origins.

**Dependency:** Not only a subservient position, as in underdevelopment and dependent on outside assistance for stability, survival, or business, but also a sought-after relationship characterized as voluntary interdependence, as in collaborative economic endeavors.

**Development:** The policy, process, and practice of applying society's resources at whatever scale by whomever to obtain betterment or progress. More broadly, development also means the development community—for example, all participants and actors who focus on economic development and all other human development participants. Development also refers to development sector participants organized into institutions, programs, and silos to bring about economic growth and change if not health, safety, and welfare of a population. The development sector works in tandem with the social sector, the environment sector, etc. It is a process of increasing or causing something to become larger or more complex or more efficient or more advanced as needed or wanted by a societal unit. Development takes place over a period of time.

**Disaster:** As properly understood, and in the context of this book, overwhelming a societal unit (family, village, city, province, country, or global region) by an event to such a degree that assistance is required from outside the impacted societal unit to address the resulting crisis and consequences of the event.

**Disaster declaration:** An appeal through formal political channels (often the United Nations) or other means for assistance from outside the affected societal unit. Most of the discussion will focus on disaster reduction for sovereign states supported by the other three major stakeholders.

**Disaster risk:** The probability by type and degree of expected loss that would prompt the impacted societal unit to declare a disaster. This is in concert with the UNISDR use of the term as "the potential loss of life, injury, or destroyed or damaged assets which could occur to a system, society or a community in a specific period of time, determined probabilistically as a function of hazard, exposure, vulnerability and capacity" (UNDRR n.d.). Disaster risk can be read in "light of the concept of systemic risk" (UNDRR 2019: xiv).

**Disaster risk management (DRM):** "The application of disaster risk reduction policies and strategies to prevent new disaster risk, reduce existing disaster risk and manage residual risk, contributing to the strengthening of resilience and reduction of disaster losses" (UNDRR n.d.). The process may include reducing, as well as retaining and transferring risk, depending on the type of risk; included are financial, economic, and physical risk. It includes not only technical and scientific research, but also economic, social, and political decisions where issues must be weighted and prioritized. Disaster risk management is a crosscutting "sector" such as migration, labor, environment, etc.

**Disaster risk reduction (DRR):** Policy and practice before, during, and after natural hazard events to lessen loss to a level deemed acceptable by the subject societal unit. DRR aims to protect development gains—particularly construction of the built environment—from destruction, damage, and loss of service, to the extent that the affected societal unit—most often a sovereign state—does not have to declare a disaster. This parallels the UNDRR definition, "Disaster risk reduction is aimed at preventing new and reducing existing disaster risk and managing residual risk, all of which contribute to strengthening resilience and therefore to the achievement of sustainable development" (UNDRR n.d.). Because disaster risk reduction is part of DRM, its goals and objectives are defined within DRM risk reduction strategies and plans (UNDRR n.d.); thus, it is not a sector.

**Emergency management (EM):** A sector and discipline with theory and practice related to preparation and response to crisis in a society. Disaster management refers to the emergency management sector, but also to the theory and practice of avoiding natural hazard and other risk of events so as to avoid emergency situations.

**Environment:** Unless otherwise noted, the structure and function of all ecosystems that surround and support human life therein. There is no one environment, but an infinite number of environments, and they are shared. The terms "environment" and "ecology" are not interchangeable. The latter is a science that defines relationships between and among living things and their environments. It does not mean environment, nor is it a synonym for nature or natural resources. Ecology is a body of knowledge and a method to add to that knowledge (Saunier and Bender 1988).

**Environmental risk reduction:** The reduction of loss, damage, and destruction of ecosystems. It is particularly concerned with protecting human populations in all their needs and ecosystem structure and function.

**Exposure:** The situation of people, infrastructure, housing, production capacities, and other tangible human assets located in hazard-prone areas (UNDRR n.d.).

**Globalization, global economy:** A process by which interaction and integration of people, companies, organizations, and governments with social and cultural aspects around the globe develop influence through an increasingly integrated economy marked by trade, flow of capital, and use of raw materials, manufacturing facilities, and labor. "Globalization" and "global economy" will be used interchangeably to include not only economic but also supporting political, cultural, communication, scientific, and technological aspects of sharing that creates greater interdependency and voluntary dependency for economic gain.

**Hazard risk:** The probability of occurrence of a specific natural hazard event with a specified location, severity, and frequency.

**Knowledge:** The fact or condition of knowing familiar information gained through association, which includes policy, practice, and/or experience.

**Least common denominator:** A policy or practice approved and adopted by sovereign states or other organizations or groups formally or informally. The adopted actions represent the the maximum (or minimum) amount of effort the necessary number of agreeing participants will adhere to or support.

**Mainstreaming:** Bringing disaster risk reduction as an operation into the center of development processes. The term implies that risk assessment and risk reduction are not presently included in choices made in defining and carrying out development policy and practice, which is not often the case.

**Natural disaster:** A misnomer in use for more than forty years that contains two misconceptions. First, the "disaster" is the resulting impact of a naturally occurring hazardous event according to the exposure of the population and its built environment. In fact, the disaster is the societal unit's inability to deal with the outcome of the impact of a natural hazard event due to exposure, vulnerability, and risk. Second, much of media and other segments of society, particularly in the political realm, use the term "disaster" to name a specific natural hazardous event and refer to the natural hazard event itself as the disaster: "The disaster struck, leaving people homeless."

**Natural hazard event:** A material force with potential effects that affect populations and their related built and natural ecosystem environments.

**Natural hazard risk reduction:** Reducing the risk of impact of natural hazard events on populations and their built environment.

**Natural hazards:** Natural processes or phenomena that may cause loss of life, injury or other health impacts, property damage, loss of livelihoods and services, social and economic disruption, or environmental damage (UN-SPIDER 2019). The possible losses are related to the degree of exposure of populations to their surroundings in addition to the characteristics of the natural event. The actual natural phenomenon or event can be characterized by its magnitude or intensity, speed of onset, frequency or return period, duration, and geographic area of extent.

**Participant(s):** An organization, institution, agency, or group of whatever formation and individual(s) that takes an active role in some process or is engaged in a process. Identified stakeholders are participants and are considered actors.

**Policy:** Includes all forms of prudence and wisdom, whether codified or not, in social relations and culture that shape planning and guidance. Such forms embrace general goals and acceptable procedures, especially of a governmental body or other structured societal organizations.

**Practice:** Includes direct observation of or participation in events as a basis for acquiring knowledge and formulating policy.

**Recovery:** Restoring or improving livelihoods and health, as well as economic, physical, social, cultural, and environmental assets, systems, and activities, of a disaster-affected community or society, aligning with principles of sustainable development and "build back better," to avoid or reduce future disaster risk (UNDRR n.d.). Unless specified differently, recovery will also include repair, rehabilitation, reconstruction, and resettlement to facilitate discussion of recovery related to the built environment. It will be used to denote post-emergency assistance following a crisis or disaster. When necessary, a specific part of recovery will be noted.

**Resilience:** "The ability of a system, community or society exposed to hazards to resist, absorb, accommodate, adapt to, transform, and recover from the effects of a hazard in a timely and efficient manner." It includes the preservation and restoration of essential basic structures and functions through risk management (UNDRR n.d.). As such, DRR can be considered an element of resilience, although much present work on resilience focuses on absorption, accommodation, and adaptation rather than resistance through reducing risk as development takes place or by retrofitting the built environment at risk.

**Response, relief, and humanitarian assistance:** Actions in immediate response to the crisis. The terms are used interchangeably, or one term is used collectively for most purposes.

**Risk:** The quantification or probability of a specific level of loss, injury, damage, or destruction in a specific place due to a natural hazard event with a specified location, severity, and frequency. Unless otherwise noted, risk refers to a particular component of economic or social infrastructure of the built environment; it is not used to refer to the probability of the occurrence of the natural hazard event itself. Because the subject of this book is the built environment, emphasis is on assessing risk as the quantitative probability of physical damage and destruction, as well as economic and financial loss directly related to underlying causes. This use of the term differs somewhat with that expressed in *GAR19*, which defines risk as something other than quantifying the qualitative description given by vulnerability. (See notes on UNDRR terminology in chapter 14.) The distinction between vulnerability and risk is important when considering the dimensions of the expected impact of a natural hazard event. Also important is distinguishing between vulnerability and risk of a component of the built environment and between vulnerability and risk of an associated population in understanding the underlying causes and the options for risk reduction.

**Sector:** Unless otherwise noted, a part of society that can be separated from other parts because of its own special character such as, but not limited to, one of the areas into which specific economic and social activities are divided. But it can just as well be built around any selected theme, discipline, or activities described as crosscutting issues. Thus a sector is an identifiable group of participants organized to achieve the same or similar goals.

**Silo(s):** An operational structure designated as a sector, program, or area dedicated to a specific set of activities that are different from or contrast and compete with other activities of the organization. Silos can be multi-organizational in participation with entities pursuing the same objectives. Typically they have participants with similar skills and experiences. In some instances organizations have deliberately created or allowed a program or a department to work as a silo in isolation (or independence) from their main activities or other silos.

**Social environment:** The physical setting in which people live or in which something happens or develops, the culture in which the individual lives, and the people and institutions with which they interact.

**Stakeholder:** A sector, organization, group, or person who has an interest in any number of enterprises, such as development, risk management, disaster management, and creation of the built environment at the policy, program, project, and/or practice level, and whose support is required for an enterprise to be successful. In some instances a stakeholder is an independent party not having direct investment, financial or otherwise, in an enterprise, but who holds financial, economic, and/or physical investments in the enterprise of those who do have a direct investment. In social science research, the term may be used interchangeably with "actor."

**Structure:** An element or component of the built environment, unless otherwise noted.

**Vulnerability:** The conditions determined by physical, social, economic, and environmental participants or processes that increase susceptibility of an individual, community, assets, or systems to the impacts of hazards (UNDRR n.d.). The term refers to the type and impact of the hazardous event on a component of the built environment or a population group and can be expressed in qualitative physical as well as financial, economic, and social terms.

# References

ADB-Asian Development Bank. 2004. *Disaster and Emergency Assistance Policy—R Report*. Asian Development Bank, May. https://www.adb.org/sites/default/files/institutional-document/32118/disaster-emergency.pdf.

———. 2008. *Action Plan for Implementing ADB's Disaster and Emergency Assistance Policy*. Asian Development Bank, April. https://www.adb.org/sites/default/files/institutional-document/32116/in103-08.pdf.

Barrios, Roberto. 2017. *Governing Affect: Neoliberalism and Disaster Reconstruction*. Lincoln: University of Nebraska Press.

Beachy, Ben, Michael Shank, and Justin Talbot Zorn. 2013. "How to Build a GDP Measure for the Real Economy." *Atlantic*, 24 October. https://www.theatlantic.com/business/archive/2013/10/how-to-build-a-gdp-measure-for-the-real-economy/280820/.

Beck, Ulrich. 1992a. *Die Risikogesellschaft. Auf dem Weg in eine andere Moderne*. Frankfurt am Main: Suhrkamp. As noted by O. Renn, "Risk Communication: Towards a Rational Discourse with the Public." *Journal of Hazardous Materials* 29, no. 3 (February): 465–519.

———. 1992b. *Risk Society, Towards a New Modernity*. Translated by Mark Ritter. London: Sage Publications. First published 1986.

———, ed. 2009. *World at Risk*. Cambridge: Polity Press.

Bell, Simon. 1994. "Methods and Mindsets: Towards an Understanding of the Tyranny of Methodology." *Public Administration and Development* 14, no. 4: 323–338. https://doi.org/10.1002/pad.4230140401.

Bender, Stephen O. 1989. "Disaster Prevention and Mitigation in Latin America and the Caribbean." In A. Kreimer and M. Zador, eds., *Colloquium on Disasters, Sustainability and Development: A Look to the 1990s*, Environment Working Paper 23: 88–92. Washington, DC: World Bank.

———. 1991. "Managing Natural Disasters." In Alcira Kreimer and Mohan Munasinghe, eds., *Managing Natural Disasters and the Environment: Selected Materials from the Colloquium on the Environment and Natural Disaster Management*, 182–185. Washington, DC: World Bank.

———. 1994. "The Sustaining Nature of the Disaster-Development Linkage." *Ecodecision*, April, 50–52.

———. 1999. "Reducing Vulnerability of Infrastructure." *Natural Disaster Management—IDNDR Commemorative Volume*. London: NDM Press.

———. 2009a. "Hemispheric Study." In UNISDR and OAS, *I Session of the Regional Platform for Disaster Risk Reduction in the Americas [Proceedings]*, First Plenary Session, Part A. City of Panama, March.

———. 2009b. "Reflection and Analysis Surrounding the Commitments and Initiatives to Support the Implementation of the HFA from a Regional Perspective—Full

Draft." In *ISDR and OAS Regional Platform for Disaster Risk Reduction in the Americas*, April. http://www.eird.org/plataforma-regional/estudios-resumenes/hfa-regional-study.pdf.

———. 2011. "The Development of Disasters." World Conference on Humanitarian Studies, "Changing Realities of Conflict and Crisis," Tufts University, Medford, MA, 2–5 June.

———. 2012. "Disasters as Underdevelopment and Vice Versa: How We Have Shaped International Development Policy and Built Environments to Embody Risk and Dependency." Panel presentation, Society for Applied Anthropology (SfAA) 2012 Annual Meeting, "Disasters and Globalization," Baltimore, 27–31 March.

———. 2013a. "Annex C: Participant CVs & 2-page overviews." *The Future of Disaster Risk Management—Draft Synthesis Document, Meeting Notes, Background Papers and Additional Materials*. Scoping Meeting for GAR 2015, FLACSO (Latin American Social Science Faculty) and UNISDR (United Nations Office for Disaster Risk Reduction), San Jose, Costa Rica, 18–19 April. https://www.desenredando.org/public/2013/20130814_UNISDR_FLACSO_GARscoping_Document_LaRed.pdf.

———. 2013b. "The Gap between Knowledge, Policy, and Practice That Results in Natural Hazard Events Becoming Disasters: A View from Looking at Four Groups of Stakeholders." Panel presentation, "The Gap between Knowledge, Policy, and Practice Concerning Disaster, Part I," Society for Applied Anthropology (SfAA) 2013 Annual Meeting, Denver, CO, 20–23 March.

———. 2013c. Presentation notes, *Climate Change and Security in the Andean Region—Regional Dialogue*. Adelphi Research and Universidad de Los Andes.

———. 2014. "Collective Disaster Risk Reduction Regulation Policy and Practice through Sovereign States: Having It Neither Way." Panel presentation, Society for Applied Anthropology (SfAA) Annual Meeting, Albuquerque. Unpublished.

———. 2016. "Appendix 1 Survey Answers to the Question: What in your view are the most important aspects of a successful recovery operation following a natural disaster?" In Ian Davis and David Alexander, *Recovery from Disaster*. London and New York: Routledge.

Bender, Stephen, and Ricciarini, Sylvana. 2001. "General Study on the Vulnerability of Road Segments to Natural Hazards of the Pan American Highway and Its Complementary Corridors in Central America—Working Document." OAS, Unit for Sustainable Development and Environment. Washington, DC: OAS and US Department of Transportation.

Benson, Charlotte, and John Twigg. 2004. *Measuring Mitigation: Methodologies for Assessing Natural Hazard Risks and the Net Benefits of Mitigation—A Scoping Study*. Geneva: ProVention Consortium, December.

Briceño, S. 2015. "Looking Back and Beyond Sendai: 25 Years of International Policy Experience on Disaster Risk Reduction." In *International Journal of Disaster Risk Science* 6: 1–7. https://link.springer.com/article/10.1007/s13753-015-0040-y.

Brundtland, G. H. 1987. *Our Common Future: Report of the World Commission on Environment and Development*. United Nations. http///our_common_futurebrundtlandreport1987.pdf.

Burby, Raymond. 1998. *Cooperating with Nature: Confronting Natural Hazards for Land-Use Planning for Sustainable Communities*. Washington, DC: Joseph Henry Press.

Carby, Barbara. 2018. "Building Resilience: Imperative Questions for Caribbean Policymakers and Disaster Risk Management Practitioners." *Sustainable Futures*

*Policy Brief*, no. 1 (April): 1–9. http://www.uwi.edu/salises/pdf/SALISES-Policy BriefApril2018-Issue1.pdf.
Carter, T. R., M. L. Parry, H. Harasawa, and S. Nishioka. 1994. *IPCC Technical Guidelines for Assessing Climate Change Impacts and Adaptations*. London: Department of Geography, University College.
Cavallo, Eduardo, Sebastián Galiani, Ilan Noy, and Juan Pantano. 2010. *Catastrophic Natural Disasters and Economic Growth*. IDB Working Paper Series IDB-WP-183: 1–30.
Christopolos, Ian. 2006. "The Elusive 'Window of Opportunity' for Risk Reduction in Post-Disaster Recovery." Discussion paper, ProVention Consortium Forum 2006, "Strengthening Global Collaboration in Disaster Risk Reduction," Bangkok. https://www.humanitarianlibrary.org/sites/default/files/2014/02/ProVention_Elu siveWindowOfOpportunity.pdf.
CIDIE. 1988. *Incorporating Natural Hazard Assessment and Mitigation into Project Preparation*. Vol. 2. CIDIE Publication Series. Washington, DC: Organization of American States, Executive Secretariat for Economic and Social Affairs, Department of Regional Development. https://www.oas.org/dsd/publications/Unit/oea77e/ch2.htm.
Comerio, Mary. 2013. "Resilience: An Engineering Challenge." EERI Distinguished Lecture, University of California, Berkeley, 14 October.
COMEST. 2005. *The Precautionary Principle*. UNESCO, March. https://unesdoc.unesco.org/ark:/48223/pf0000139578.
Cutter, Susan. 2014a. "Building Disaster Resilience: Steps Toward Sustainability." *Challenges in Sustainability 2013* 1, no. 2 (January): 72–79. https://pdfs.semanticscholar.org/64d3/f3244aaecf3aa7ef902d2ee03ca4031b0e69.pdf.
———. 2014b. "In Harm's Way–Natural Hazards: Why More Knowledge Is Not Reducing Losses." Gilbert F. White Lecture in the Geographical Sciences, National Academy of Sciences, Washington, DC, 4 December. http://dels.nas.edu/global/best/GW-Lecture.
———. 2016. "The Changing Context of Hazard Extremes: Events, Impacts, and Consequences." *Journal of Extreme Events* 3, no. 2: 1671005. https://doi.org/10.1142/S2345737616710056.
de Lint, Michael. 2015. "The Formal Structure of Building Regulatory Organizations." Panel presentation, "Urban Risk Management for the Informal Sector," SfAA Annual Meeting, Pittsburgh.
DICAN. 2016. "Disaster Capitalism as Creative Destruction." Panel abstract, "EASA Anthropological Legacies and Human Futures." Convenors: Mara Benadusi and A. J. Faas, EASA Disaster and Crisis Anthropology Network (DICAN). https://nomadit.co.uk/conference/easa2016/p/4149.
DID. 2002. *Tools for Development: A Handbook for Those Involved in Development Activity*. Department for International Development of the United Kingdom. www.dfid.gov.uk/pubs/files/toolsfordevelopment.pdf.
DIRDN. 1994. Conferencia Interamericana sobre Reducción de los Desastres Naturales, Foro Preparatorio para la Conferencia Mundial del DIRDN–Colombia. "Declaración de Cartagena, 21–24 de marzo de 1994." *Desastres y Sociedad* 2, no. 2 (July): 3, 5. Red de Estudios Sociales en Prevención de Desastres en América Latina.
Forbes, Nathaniel. 2014. "Water and Emergencies: The Impact of Thirst." Presentation, Integrated Research on Disaster Risk (IRDR) 2014 Conference, "Integrated Disaster Risk Science: A Tool for Sustainability." http://www.irdrinternational.org/2014/06/08/forbes/.

Fraser, Evan D. G. 2009. "Economic Crises, Land Use Vulnerabilities, Climate Variability, Food Security and Population Declines: Will History Repeat Itself or Will Our Society Adapt to Climate Change?" In Centre for Climate Change Economics and Policy Working Paper No. 1, London.

Geleta, Bekele. 2010. *World Disasters Report 2010—Focus on Urban Risk*. Geneva: International Federation of Red Cross and Red Crescent Societies (IFRC).

Gibbs, Tony. 2014. Editorial. *The Gleaner (Jamaica)*. http://mobile.jamaica-gleaner.com/gleaner/20140208/cleisure/cleisure1.php.

Giesecke, Alberto. 1994. Letter, as member of the IDNDR Scientific and Technical Committee. *IDNDR Informs—Latin America and the Caribbean* 4 (January–March). www.nzdl.org/gsdlmod?e=d-00000-00---off-0paho--00-0----0-10-0---0---0direct-10---4-------0-1l--11-mi-50---20-about---10-0-1-00-0--4----0-0-11-10-0utfZz-8-00&cl=CL1.7&d=HASH0188d9d3f4134e77a467c1ca.1&gt=2.

Gray de Cerdán, Nelly. 2003. "Políticas de cooperación internacional para la gestión de riesgos en los Corredores de Comercio de América Latina." *Revista de Cooperación Internacional* 9: 31–36, CETEM-FFyL- UNCuyo.

Guest, Iain. 1999. "From the Editorial Desk: Rebuilding after Mitch—The Role of Civil Society, On the Record; Central American Civil Society after Mitch." *Advocacy Project* 1 (11 May).

Hagman, Gunnar. 1984. *Prevention Better Than Cure: Report on Human and Environmental Disasters in the Third World*. Stockholm: Swedish Red Cross.

HFA. 2009. HFA Regional Platform for Disaster Risk Reduction in the Americas. *Report Surrounding the Commitments and Initiatives to Support the Implementation of the HFA from a Regional Perspective: A Contribution to the Preparatory Process for Carrying Out the 1st Session of the Regional Platform for Disaster Risk Reduction in the Americas*. ISDR, 8 March.

Hinshaw, Robert E. 2006. *Living with Nature's Extremes: The Life of Gilbert Fowler White*. Boulder, CO: Johnson Books.

Hoffman, Susanna. 2015. "Are There Universals in Risk, Disaster, and Policy Issues, or Are All Aspects Local and Specific?" Panel abstract, Society for Applied Anthropology Annual Meeting, Pittsburgh, PA.

IADB. 1999. *Reducing Vulnerability to Natural Hazards: Lessons Learned from Hurricane Mitch; A Strategy Paper on Environmental Management*. Stockholm: Inter-American Development Bank, 25–28 May.

———. 2000a. *Facing the Challenge of Natural Disasters in Latin America and the Caribbean: An IDB Action Plan*. Washington, DC: Inter-American Development Bank, Sustainable Development Department. http://idbdocs.iadb.org/wsdocs/getdocument.aspx?docnum=823495.

———. 2000b. *Natural Disasters: A Challenge for Development of Latin America and Caribbean*. Inter-American Development Bank. http://idbdocs.iadb.org/wsdocs/getdocument.aspx?docnum=823495.

———. 2005. *Preliminary Companion Paper to the Draft Disaster Risk Management Policy*. Inter-American Development Bank, 19 December. http://oas.org/dsd/documents/idb-draftcompanionpaper121905.pdf.

IACNDR. 2003. *Inter-American Strategic Plan for Policy on Vulnerability Reduction, Risk Management and Disaster Response (IASP)*. OAS. http://www.oas.org/en/sedi/dsd/GeneralDocs/IASP_Eng_Original.pdf.

IEG–World Bank. 2009. *Annual Review of Development Effectiveness 2009: Achieving Sustainable Development*. Independent Evaluation Group, World Bank.

ISDR. 2004. *Living with Risk: A Global Review of Disaster Reduction Initiatives*, 2004 version, vol. I. UNISDR. https://www.preventionweb.net/files/657_lwr1.pdf.

———. 2009. *Implementation of the Hyogo Framework for Action in the Americas.* Global Platform for Disaster Risk Reduction, Geneva, 16–19 June. https://www.preventionweb.net/globalplatform/2009/background/documents/IFD-04-ENG-HFA-Americas.pdf.

Jha, Abhas K., and Zuzana Stanton-Geddes, eds. 2013. *Strong, Safe, and Resilient: A Strategic Policy Guide for Disaster Risk Management in East Asia and the Pacific.* Directions in Development. Washington, DC: World Bank. doi:10.1596/978-0-8213-9805-0. License: Creative Commons Attribution CC BY 3.0.

Johnson, Cassidy. 2010. "Urban Disaster Trends." Chapter 2 in *World Disasters Report 2010: Focus on Urban Risk.* Geneva: International Federation of Red Cross and Red Crescent Societies (IFRC).

———. 2011. "Creating an Enabling Environment for Reducing Disaster Risk: Recent Experience of Regulatory Frameworks for Land, Planning and Building in Low and Middle-Income Countries." *Global Assessment Report on Disaster Risk Reduction—GAR 2011.* Geneva: UNISDR, April. https://www.preventionweb.net/english/hyogo/gar/2011/en/bgdocs/Johnson_2011.pdf.

Klein, Naomi. 2007. *The Shock Doctrine: The Rise of Disaster Capitalism.* Toronto: Knopf.

Koks, E. E., B. Jongman, T. G. Husby, and W. J. W. Botzen. 2015. "Combining Hazard, Exposure and Social Vulnerability to Provide Lessons for Flood Risk Management." *Environmental Science & Policy* 47 (March): 42–52.

Krimgold, Frederick. 2008. "Letter to the World Business Council for Sustainable Development." Personal correspondence, October.

Lassa, Jonatan A., Akhilesh Surjan, Mely Caballero-Anthony, and Rohan Fisher. 2018. "Measuring Political Will: An Index of Commitment to Disaster Risk Reduction." *International Journal of Disaster Risk Reduction* 34 (March): 64–74. https://doi.org/10.1016/j.ijdrr.2018.11.006.

Lavell, Allan, and Andrew Maskrey. 2014. "The Future of Disaster Risk Management." *Environmental Hazards* 13, no. 4 (July): 267–280. https://doi.org/10.1080/17477891.2014.935282.

Levy, Brian. 2014. *Working with the Grain: Integrating Governance and Growth in Development Strategies.* Oxford: Oxford University Press.

Malalgoda, C. I., R. D. G. Amaratunga, and C. P. Pathirage. 2010. "Exploring Disaster Risk Reduction in the Built Environment." CIB 2010, University of Salford, Manchester, 10–13 May. http://usir.salford.ac.uk/id/eprint/9769/1/1614.pdf.

Maskrey, Andrew. 2013. "PH to Suffer Biggest Loss in Case of Powerful Quake." *Manila Bulletin*, 4 June. https://ph.news.yahoo.com/ph-suffer-biggest-loss-case-powerful.

———. 2016. Preface to A. Oliver-Smith, I. Alcántara-Ayala, I. Burton, and A. M. Lavell, *Forensic Investigations of Disasters (FORIN 2): A Conceptual Framework and Guide to Research.* Beijing: Integrated Research on Disaster Risk. IRDR FORIN Publication No. 2.

McIlvaine-Newsad, Heather. 2016. "Disasters, Tough Decisions, and the New Normal." Tri-States Radio website, 17 February 2016. http://tspr.org/post/disasters-tough-decisions-and-new-normal#stream/0.

Messervy, Max, Cynthia McHale, and Rowan Spivey. 2014. *Insurer Climate Risk Disclosure Survey Report & Scorecard: 2014 Findings & Recommendations.* Ceres Insurance Program, October.

Mileti, Dennis. 1999. *Disasters by Design: A Reassessment of Natural Hazards in the United States*. Washington, DC: Joseph Henry Press.

Mitchell, J. K. 1988. "Report on Reports—Confronting Natural Disasters: An International Decade for Natural Hazard Reduction." *Environment* 30, no. 2: 25–28.

Mitchell, James K., Karen O'Neill, Melanie McDermott, and Marianna Leckner. 2016. "Towards a Transformative Role of Local Knowledge in Post-Disaster Recovery: Prospects for Co-production in the Wake of Hurricane Sandy." *Journal of Extreme Events* 3, no. 1. https://www.worldscientific.com/doi/abs/10.1142/S2345737616020024.

Natsios, Andrew. 2009. "Public Private Alliances Transform Aid." Stanford Social Innovation Review 7, no. 4 (Fall): 42–47. Stanford Graduate School of Business, Center for Social Innovation.

———. 2010. "Essay: The Clash of the Counter-bureaucracy and Development." Center for Global Development. www.cgdev.org/content/publications/detail/1424271.

OAS. 1984. *Integrated Regional Development Planning: Guidelines and Case Studies from OAS Experience*. Washington, DC: Organization of American States, Department of Regional Development, Secretariat for Economic and Social Affairs. http://www.oas.org/usde/publications/Unit/oea03e/ch12.htm.

OAS-DRD. 1991. *Primer on Natural Hazard Management in Integrated Regional Development Planning*. Washington, DC: Organization of American States, Department of Regional Development and Environment, Secretariat for Economic and Social Affairs. https://www.oas.org/dsd/publications/Unit/oea66e/begin.htm.

OAS-DSD. 2014. *Mainstreaming Disaster Risk Reduction and Adaptation to Climate Change*. Washington, DC: OAS Department of Sustainable Development, Executive Secretariat for Integral Development.

———. 2016. "Asuncion Declaration: Guidelines towards a Regional Action Plan for the Implementation of the Sendai Framework." First Meeting of Ministers and High-Level Authorities on the Implementation of the Sendai Framework for Disaster Risk Reduction 2015–2030 in the Americas, Asunción, Paraguay. http://www.oas.org/en/sedi/dsd/riskmanagement/Events/SendaiAmericas/Documents/Declaration_SendaiAmericas.pdf.

O'Keefe, Phil, Ken Westgate, and Ben Wisner. 1976. "Taking the Naturalness Out of Natural Disasters." *Nature* 260 (April): 566–567. https://www.nature.com/articles/260566a0.

Oliver-Smith, Anthony. 2009. "Understanding Hurricane Mitch: Complexity, Causality, and the Political Ecology of Disaster." In Marisa O. Ensor, ed., *The Legacy of Mitch: Lessons from Post-Disaster Reconstruction in Honduras*, 1–21. Tempe: University of Arizona Press.

———. 2013. "A Matter of Choice." *International Journal of Disaster Risk Reduction* 3: 1–3.

———. 2015. "Conversations in Catastrophe: Neoliberalism and the Cultural Constructions of Disaster Risk." In Fred Kruger, Greg Bankoff, Terry Cannon, Benedikt Orlowski, E. Lisa, and F. Schipper, eds., *Cultures and Disasters: Understanding Cultural Framings in Disaster Risk Reduction*. New York: Routledge.

Oliver-Smith, A., I. Alcantara-Ayala, I. Burton, and A. M. Lavell. 2016. *Forensic Investigations of Disasters (FORIN): A Conceptual Framework and Guide to Research*. IRDR FORIN Publication No. 2. Beijing: Integrated Research on Disaster Risk (IRDR).

PAHO. 2000. *Natural Disasters: Protecting the Public's Health*. Scientific Publication No. 575. Washington, DC: Pan American Health Organization. www.paho.org/hq/dmdocuments/2010/9275115753.pdf.

———. 2004. *Resolution CD45.R8—Disaster Preparedness and Response*. 45th Directing Council, 56th Session of the Regional Committee. Washington, DC: Pan American Health Organization. https://iris.paho.org/bitstream/handle/10665.2/255/CD45.r8-e.pdf?sequence=1&isAllowed=y.

———. 2006. "Progress Report on National and Regional Health Disaster Preparedness and Response, CD47/INF/4." Washington, DC: Pan American Health Organization. http://www.paho.org/english/gov/cd/CD47-inf4-e.pdf.

———. 2018. "I. Plan of Action for Disaster Risk Reduction 2016–2021: Progress Report, CE162/INF/20, Rev. 1." 162nd Session of the Executive Committee. Washington, DC: Pan American Health Organization, 4 June. https://www.paho.org/hq/index.php?option=com_content&view=article&id=14263:162th-session-executive-committee&Itemid=40453&lang=en.

Parry, M., and T. Carter. 1998. *Climate Impact and Adaptation Assessment: A Guide to the IPCC Approach*. London: Earthscan. http://www-cger.nies.go.jp/ or http://www-cger.nies.go.jp/cgere/e_report/r_index-e.html.

Planitz, Angelika. 2013. "Mainstreaming Disaster Risk Reduction into Development in UNDP." Presentation at "Mitigating Disasters, Promoting Development: The Sendai Dialogue and Disaster Risk Management in Asia; Panel 3: Strategies for Mainstreaming Disaster Risk Management in Development." The Brookings Institution, Washington, DC, 10 May. https://www.brookings.edu/wp-content/uploads/2013/04/Presentation-by-Angelika-Planitz.pdf.

Renaud, Fabrice G., Karen Sudmeier-Rieux, and Marisol Estrella. 2013. *The Role of Ecosystems in Disaster Risk Reduction*. Tokyo: United Nations University Press.

Riederer, Rachel. 2015. "How the Rich Profit from Natural Disasters." Review of *Disaster Profiteers: How Natural Disasters Make the Rich Richer and the Poor Even Poorer* by John Mutter. *New Republic*, 5 October.

Rodin, Judith. 2014. *The Resilience Dividend: Being Strong in a World Where Things Go Wrong*. New York: PublicAffairs.

Romero, Simon. 2018. "Houston Speculators Make a Fast Buck from Storm's Misery." *New York Times*, 23 March. https://www.nytimes.com/2018/03/23/us/flooding-canyon-gate-hurricane-harvey.html.

Rumbach, Andrew. 2016. Personal email communication, 18 May.

Sartre, Jean Paul. 1944. *No Exit and Three Other Plays*. https://www.vanderbilt.edu/olli/class-materials/Jean-Paul_Sartre.pdf.

Saunier, Richard, and Stephen Bender. 1988. "The Urban Dimension of Environmental Concern in Latin America and the Caribbean." The World Bank Seminar on Urban Areas and Environmental Issues. Environmental Awareness Seminar, Washington, DC, 26 May.

Sem, Graham, and Xianfu Lu. 2007. "Vulnerability and Adaptation Assessment within the Framework of the Second National Communications (SNC)—Context, Scope, Methodology, Reporting, Good Practices." NCSP Workshop on the Initiation of Preparing Second National Communications for Pacific Island Countries. Apia, Somoa, July.

Spence, Robin. 2004. "Risk and Regulation: Can Improved Government Action Reduce the Impact of Natural Disasters?" *Building Research and Information* 32, no. 5: 391–402.

Svistova, Juliana, and Loretta Pyles. 2018. *Production of Disaster and Recovery in Post-Earthquake Haiti*. New York: Routledge.

Titz, Alexandra, Terry Cannon, and Fred Kruger. 2018. "Uncovering 'Community': Challenging an Elusive Concept in Development and Disaster Related Work." *Societies* 8, no. 3: 71. https://doi.org/10.3390/soc8030071.

UN. 2015. *Paris Agreement*. UNFCCC. https://unfccc.int/files/essential_background/convention/application/pdf/english_paris_agreement.pdf.
UN Stockholm Declaration. 1972. United Nations Conference on the Human Environment. UNEP. https://mwvlw.rlp.de/fileadmin/mwkel/Abteilung_2/8206/06_Nachhaltigkeit_global/1972_Stockholm_Erklaerung_en.pdf.
UNDP. 1990. *Human Development Report 1990*. Oxford: Oxford University Press.
———. 2004. *Adaptation Policy Framework*. UNDP. http://unfccc.int/files/adaptation/methodologies_for/vulnerability_and_adaptation/application/pdf/undp_adaptation_policy_framework__apf_.pdf.
UNDRR. 2019. *Global Assessment Report on Disaster Risk Reduction 2019—GAR19*. United Nations Office for Disaster Risk Reduction. Geneva: UNDRR. https://gar.unisdr.org/sites/default/files/gar19distilled.pdf.
———. n.d. "Terminology." https://www.undrr.org/terminology.
UNISDR. 2015a. *Making Development Sustainable: The Future of Disaster Risk Management; Global Assessment Report on Disaster Risk Reduction—GAR 15*. Geneva: United Nations Office for Disaster Risk Reduction (UNISDR). GAR2015_EN.pdf and www.preventionweb.net/gar.
———. 2015b. *Sendai Framework for Disaster Risk Reduction 2015–2030*. Geneva: UNISDR. https://www.unisdr.org/files/43291_sendaiframeworkfordrren.pdf.
UN-SPIDER. 2019. "Risks and Disasters." Knowledge Portal. United Nations Office for Outer Space Affairs. http://www.un-spider.org/risks-and-disasters.
UN-WCNDR. 1994. "Annex I: Yokohama Strategy for a Safer World," in *Report of the World Conference on Natural Disaster Reduction*. Yokohama, Japan, 23–27 May.
Vergara, Walter, et al. 2007. "The Impacts of Climate Change in Latin America." In *Visualizing Future Climate in Latin America: Results from the Application of the Earth Simulator*, Latin America and Caribbean Region Sustainable Development Working Paper 30. Washington, DC: World Bank, November.
Vernon, Phil, and Deborrah Baksh. 2010. *Working with the Grain to Change the Grain: Moving Beyond the Millennium Development Goals*. London: International Alert. https://www.international-alert.org/sites/default/files/publications/MDG.pdf.
von Oelreich, Eva. 2004. "October 13th International Day for Disaster Reduction—Urgent Action Needed to Reduce Impact of Disasters." *The Island* online edition, 13 October. http://www.island.lk/2004/10/13/news21.html.
WCDRR. 2015. "Ministerial Roundtable: Reconstruction after Disasters; Build Back Better." In *Proceedings: Third United Nations World Conference on Disaster Risk Reduction*. Sendai, 14–18 March. https://reliefweb.int/sites/reliefweb.int/files/resources/45069_proceedingsthirdunitednationsworldc.pdf.
White, Gilbert F., Robert W. Kates, and Ian Burton. 2001. "Knowing Better and Losing Even More: The Use of Knowledge in Hazards Management." *Environmental Hazards* 3, no. 3: 81–92. https://scholar.colorado.edu/geog_facpapers/1.
Wijkman, Anders, and Lloyd Timberlake. 1984. *Natural Disasters: Acts of God, or Acts of Man?* London: Earthscan.
World Bank. 2012. *The Sendai Report: Managing Disaster Risks for a Resilient Future*. Washington, DC: World Bank.
World Bank Group (WBG). 2008. *Development and Climate Change: A Strategic Framework for the World Bank Group—Technical Report*. Washington, DC: World Bank. https://openknowledge.worldbank.org/handle/10986/28201.

# Index

absolute conditions of vulnerability, 136
acceptable risk, 62, 86, 95, 98, 111–12, 115–16, 120, 136, 157, 161, 168–70, 175, 179, 182, 189, 200, 230
African Development Bank (AfDB), 31, 93
agriculture, 31, 33, 38, 41, 47, 82, 125, 145, 147, 150, 155, 159, 160–61, 175, 213–14, 216, 218, 228, 282, 233
all-hazards approach, 28, 49, 66, 201
architecture, 6, 22, 94, 96, 104, 169, 135, 153
Argentina, 138
arms, 40
Asian Development Bank (ADB), 31, 93
asymmetrical knowledge, 115
Austin, 19

back-casting, 7, 207
Beck, Ulrich, 41
  on ownership of wealth, 41
  on risk, 107
belief, 8, 20, 22–23, 26, 76, 86, 109, 129, 151, 162, 179, 186, 216
benefactor-victim relationship, 15, 20, 55, 60, 62, 66, 76
Benson, Charlotte, 44–45, 56, 174
best local practice, 32, 65, 84
betterment (as in the context of development), 1, 3, 17, 64, 84, 100, 117, 119, 140, 144, 146, 207, 224, 225
Boston, 19
both-and, 36, 84, 100, 116, 198, 229, 230, 233
Brazil, 38
BRE (building regulation and enforcement) and BRS (building regulation system), 26, 185–88

Briceño, Sálvano, 43
Brundtland Report, 136
build back better, 65, 72–73, 75, 77, 122
building regulatory system (BRS), 186–8
built environment
  new infrastructure construction, 77, 92, 108
  recovery and reconstruction, 15, 32, 64, 71, 76, 121
  retrofitting existing construction, 56–57, 79, 81, 87, 95–96, 108, 115, 159, 167, 175, 181, 201, 208–10
Burton, Ian, 94

California, 19, 181
Callejon de Huaylas, 27
Cannon, Terry, 157, 183
Carby, Barbara, 137
Caribbean Development Bank (CDB), 31, 93
Carvallo, Edwardo, 70, 123
Central American Bank for Economic Integration (CABEI), 31
certainty, 153, 162, 228
citizen participation, 158
climate change adaptation (CCA), 2, 7, 15–16, 32–33, 35, 40–41, 43, 45, 48, 50, 56, 60, 66, 68, 80–81, 96, 99, 101, 107, 117, 121, 130–31, 140, 146–61, 167, 202, 207, 212, 215, 217
Comerio, Mary, 126, 181
Committee of International Development Institutions on the Environment (CIDIE), 79, 93, 95, 103, 189, 196
community
  development, 21, 66, 83, 157, 209, 230
  participation, 48, 65, 156–57, 183, 232

consensus, 53, 70, 84, 105, 108, 152, 154, 182, 210
constituent(s) (constituencies), 3, 28, 34, 78, 82, 91, 182, 188, 206
cost-benefit analysis (CBA), 53, 111, 128, 175
CPI—City Prosperity Index, 171
cross-cutting issue(s), 14, 41, 43, 48, 68, 78–81, 83, 96, 102, 126, 154, 173, 202, 224, 226, 232
culture, 13, 22, 44–46, 52, 109, 112, 178, 186, 188, 204, 224
Cutter, Susan, 97, 137

decision-making, 137
dependency and interdependency, 2, 8, 20, 130
development
  of disaster(s) and the disaster of development, 27, 85
  measure itself, 123
  planning, 7, 18, 25–26, 67, 108, 111–12, 114–15, 117, 119, 121–22, 136, 142, 145, 159, 160, 177, 193, 203, 223, 226, 233
  as risk reduction, 2, 8, 17, 40, 232
  as unsustainable in conditions of risk, 203
diagnosis, 26, 37, 39, 52, 94–95, 111, 115, 117, 195
disaster
  capitalism, 66, 87, 121
  cycle, 35, 61 (figure 4.1), 35, 61–63, 69, 86, 91, 93, 154, 196
  development continuum, 7, 26, 36, 41, 78
  management, 2, 7, 14–16, 19, 25, 32–33, 47–50, 78, 80, 92, 94, 99, 120–21, 147, 159, 223
  management cycle, 69
  management sector, 32, 104, 173, 196–7
  prone, 104
Disaster and Crisis Anthropology Network (DICAN), 70, 86
disaster by design, 8, 45
doubt, 86, 162, 218, 228

early warning system (SAT—*sistema de alerta temprana*), 158

eco-regions, 139
ecosystem structure and function, 76, 93, 123–24, 140, 142, 145, 149, 160, 196, 217, 228
Ecuador, 175
either-or, 79, 155
El Niño-Southern Oscillation (ENSO), 41
EM—DAT, 171
EMI—Earthquake Megacity Index, 171
enabling effect, 64, 103–4, 109, 115, 119, 169, 172, 209, 219
engineering, 6, 18, 22, 27, 29, 56, 61, 68, 91, 94, 96
enterprise risk management (ERM), 144
environmental impact assessment(s) (EIA), 93, 136, 143, 145–46, 168, 175, 196
environmental impact statement(s) (EIS), 93, 136, 196
ESI—Environmental Sustainability Index, 171

financial risk management, 136
First World, 21
floodplain, 214
Florida, 60
Forensic Investigations of Disasters (FORIN), 85, 104–5, 212, 227
free access, 47, 110, 203, 205, 209, 211, 220
free market economy, 5, 26, 70, 87, 234
fundraising, 62, 80, 171

gap(s), 7, 13–14, 17, 24–29, 30–36, 37, 44, 52–53, 63, 66, 76–77, 154, 104, 212, 233
generation of DRR information and the development planning process for creating the built environment (table 8.1), 111, 115
genuine progress indicator (GPI), 144, 192
geographic information system (GIS), 174, 192
Gibbs, Tony, 193
Giesecke, Alberto, 92
GLIDEnumber—Global Unique Identifier Number, 171

globalization, 7, 20, 34, 50, 55, 59, 62, 66, 85, 103, 117–20, 122, 126, 129–30, 139, 150–51, 202, 224–25
government
    executive branch, 23, 59, 70, 112, 181, 186, 194, 213
    legislative branch, 23, 59, 70, 81, 112, 179, 186, 192, 195, 213
    judicial branch, 23, 59, 70, 81, 112, 181–82, 186, 194, 213
GRAVITY—Global Risk and Vulnerability Index Trends per Year, 171
GRIP—Global Risk Identification Programme, 171
GRR—Global Risk Reports, 171
green accounting, 123–24, 192, 202
gross domestic product (GDP), 34, 48, 67, 70, 123, 128, 144, 146, 192, 223
Guatemala, 21
guidance, 7, 18, 28, 35, 66, 68, 84, 96, 152, 163, 177, 194–99, 201–6, 212, 230–32

Hagman, Gunnar, 13, 20
hazard-prone, 52, 60, 208
health care, 13–14, 42, 86, 118, 137, 175, 191, 225
Hinshaw, Robert E., 98
Hoffman, Susanna, 22
Honduras, 38, 58, 159
Houston, 187
Huaraz, 21
human rights, 14, 58, 83–84, 143, 182, 198
humanitarian assistance, 2, 4, 14–16, 20–21, 29–30, 32, 42, 45, 47, 49, 50, 66, 71, 77, 80, 83–84, 91, 95, 97, 101, 136, 171, 230
Hurricane Andrew, 60
Hurricane Harvey, 87
Hurricane Mitch, 38
Hyogo Framework for Action (HFA), 42, 80, 184–85, 188, 197–99, 203, 226

IEG-World Bank, 139
index
    as in exposure, 173
    as in indexing risk, 151, 212
    as in vulnerability, 169

industrial-disaster complex, 66
inputs as outputs, 30, 44, 182–83, 203, 231
insurance, 23, 42, 48, 67, 99, 116, 121, 125–27, 153, 170, 192, 197, 211–12
integrated regional development, 64, 219
Inter-American Committee on Natural Disaster Reduction (IACNDR), 45
Inter-American Development Bank (IADB), 31, 65, 93
*Inter-American Strategic Plan for Policy on Vulnerability Reduction, Risk Management and Disaster Response (IASP)*, 45
interdependency, 55, 66, 102, 107, 119, 126, 130, 140, 225, 228
International Decade for Natural Disaster Reduction (IDNDR), 45, 61, 93–94, 96, 98, 142, 184, 196, 199, 202, 226

Jeggle, Terry, 97
Johnson, Cassidy, 29, 114, 138, 157, 192
justice to truth, 101, 104, 225

Koks, E. E., 174, 191
Krimgold, Frederick, 113
Kruger, Fred, 157, 183

La Masica, 158
land use planning, 188
land use, 188
Lavell, Allan M., 94
least common denominator, 45, 59, 84, 105, 199–200, 182, 187–88, 197, 229
least developed countries (LDCs), 20, 38, 152
life safety, 99, 110, 112, 141, 156, 171, 174, 185, 188, 207–8, 210, 233
life span, 135, 146
lifelines, 68, 85, 226
link(s), 13, 18, 24, 33, 37, 48, 52, 75–76, 87, 170–71, 174, 193, 227
local knowledge, 66
low value DRR, 86

252 • Index

mainstream (including mainstreaming), 33, 34, 48, 54, 91, 177, 193, 203, 232
   mainstreaming DRR, 54, 80–81, 96, 157, 194, 200
market society, 125
Maskrey, Andrew, 52, 54, 94, 104, 222
McIlvaine-Newsad, Heather, 76
measure it (management), 184
measure of, 70, 97, 129, 141, 175
Mexico City, 20–21
Mileti, Dennis, 8, 45
misdiagnosis, 94–5
Mitchell, James K. (Ken), 67, 98, 181
multi-organizational, 197
multi-risk, 197, 202, 204

nation-states, 57, 184
Natural Disaster Hotspots—World Bank, 171
neither way, 178–9
no regret(s), 86, 130, 140, 161, 228
non-regular, 30, 45
nonstructural, 114, 185, 189, 214, 217
norms, 58–59, 71, 92, 130, 180, 186, 211

Oliver-Smith, Anthony, 1, 26, 67, 71, 105, 190, 222, 227
open access, data, source, 110, 201–2, 205, 211–12
optimal social ends, 128
Organization of American States (OAS), 29–30, 38, 56, 79, 112, 139, 175, 208

Pan American Health Organization (PAHO), 29, 45, 93, 189, 208
parametric insurance, 48, 126–27
Paris Agreement, 105, 200, 202
pathology, 27
Peru, Peruvian, 20, 21, 27
physical risk management, 35, 145
physical sciences, 109, 119, 175
plaque, 31, 123, 208–9
policy makers, 5, 176
political
   space, 5, 64, 89, 159, 223, 231, 231
   will, 161, 233

the poor, 29, 35, 48, 58, 63, 67, 77, 92, 103, 122, 138, 147, 160, 186, 198, 213, 225, 233, 234
postcolonial, 91
precautionary principle, 176, 193
pre-disaster, 18, 69, 72, 77
pre-existing conditions, 117, 212
pre-existing vulnerability, 65, 75
principal driver, 2, 59, 80, 222
private sector, 2, 17, 30, 35, 41, 49, 60, 70–71, 82, 86, 99–100, 107, 112, 116–17, 119, 121–22, 139, 156, 167, 178, 180, 182, 186, 192, 198, 202, 209, 213, 218–19
private volunteer organization (PVO), 21, 42, 82
protect economic growth, 74
public good, 110, 201
public sector, 2, 17, 30, 35, 41, 60, 70–71, 82, 86, 99–100, 112, 116–17, 119, 121–22, 139, 156, 167, 178, 180, 182, 186, 192, 198, 202, 209, 213, 218–19

regulation and enforcement, 6, 23, 25–26, 29, 31, 36, 42, 44, 46–47, 51–52, 58, 72–74, 87, 97, 112–13, 129, 156, 168, 177–79, 185–86, 188, 202, 211, 234
rehabilitation, 16, 49, 62, 73, 101, 136
relative conditions of wealth, 136, 140–41
remittances, 120
repair, 14, 31, 46, 62, 65, 69, 73, 108, 125, 144
responsibility and accountability, 29, 34, 44, 46–47, 50, 54, 57, 62–63, 67–68, 75, 87, 92, 95–96, 100–102, 104, 110, 112, 116, 124–25, 152
retrofit, retrofitting, 56–57, 79, 81, 87, 95–96, 108, 115–16, 159, 167, 175, 181, 201, 208–10, 219–21
right to know, 16, 176
risk
   as in acceptable level of, 34, 81, 98, 108, 111–14, 120, 125, 170, 175, 179–80, 183, 201, 230
   adverse, aversion, 8, 155, 178

construction of, 26, 64, 86, 104, 196
creation, 34, 39, 56, 59, 67, 76, 78, 113, 117, 131, 150, 154, 199, 232
czar, 186
ranking, 101, 213
as in residual, 97, 111, 119, 169
science, as in good enough, 175
as subsidy, 124–25
tolerance, 49, 68, 73
transfer, 8, 48, 87, 99, 103–4, 121, 125–27, 129–30, 155, 197
Risk Reduction Initiative (DARA), 169, 171
risk-neutral, 44
risk-prone, 24, 44, 59, 77, 116
risk-taking, 101, 213
river basin(s), 22, 139, 145, 160, 211, 213, 215, 217–18, 224, 228
river, 134, 145, 212–15, 217–18
rural, 25, 33, 41, 58, 117, 147, 156, 158, 160, 162, 174, 184, 209, 212, 218, 225

Sartre, Jean Paul, 75–6
science, 18, 22, 29, 56, 61, 85, 91, 94, 96, 153, 162, 169, 175, 202, 218
sea level rise, 33, 56, 116, 118, 123, 131, 136, 141, 146–47, 167, 172–73, 207, 211–12, 217, 219–20, 224, 227, 234
self-insured, 60, 154
Sendai Framework for Disaster Risk Reduction (SFDRR), 42, 57, 74, 80, 82, 86, 96, 115, 118, 151, 155, 160, 179, 190, 196–206, 208, 212, 219–20, 226, 232
Sendai Framework Monitor (SFM), 197, 232
Silicon Valley, 19
silo(s), 15–16, 28, 41, 51, 53, 61, 78–80, 83, 119, 136, 140, 167
Slow World, 20
Small Island Developing State (SIDS), 127
social construction of risk, 26, 54, 104, 170
social impact(s), 67, 143, 184
social impact assessment (SocIA), 143
social science(s), 6, 18, 22, 56, 129, 175

sovereign state, 20, 22, 30–32, 43, 46, 115, 119–20, 127, 130, 152, 188, 196, 198–99, 204
stakeholder, 2, 16, 25, 28, 30, 45, 63, 67, 70, 77, 79, 85, 91, 93, 156–59, 168, 171, 176, 184, 186, 189, 190–91, 193, 196, 203–4, 229, 234
stop-work order, 23
stranded assets, 146, 224
subsidy, 124–25, 129, 144, 153
as in development, 104
as in risk as, 124–25, 129
supply chain(s), 43, 125
survival, 40, 76, 79, 102, 117, 153, 160, 173, 204, 207, 223–25, 230, 234
sustainability impact assessment (SIA), 143
Sustainable Development Goals (SDGs)
UN, 48, 91, 116, 131, 136
systemic assessment(s), 40, 80, 220

Tegucigalpa, 38
Texas, 187
Third World, 20, 38
Timberlake, Lloyd, 13, 20
time frame, 124, 146
Titz, Alexandra, 157, 183
tools and processes, 57–8
trade corridors, 85, 121, 129–31, 139, 228
tragedy of the commons, 49, 146, 229
transboundary, 140
transparency, 33, 48, 87, 126, 152, 161, 180, 189, 198
trickle-down development, 128–29, 141
trickle-down economics, 66, 128
trickle-down effect, 129
trump (v.), 60–61, 99–100
truth to power, 101, 104, 225
Twigg, John, 44–45, 56, 174
tyranny of the method, 184

United Nations (UN), 40, 54, 73, 80, 220
United Nations Development Programme (UNDP), 3, 93
United Nations Office for Disaster Risk Reduction (UNDRR), 88, 208, 212
universal and local (or particular), 22, 60, 87, 196

Universal Declaration of Human Rights, 83
universal standards, 58, 182
unreinforced masonry buildings (URMs), 181
urban, 25, 29, 41, 56, 82, 113, 117, 138, 158–59, 161–62, 169, 200, 209, 213, 216–18, 222–23, 225

values, 6, 8, 17, 39, 53, 58, 71, 73, 102, 116, 129, 138, 151, 153, 173, 175, 180, 225–27, 229
VCA—Vulnerability and Capacity Assessment, 171
victims, 20, 66, 76, 78, 84, 106
von Oelreich, Eva, 104
vulnerable
  as in vulnerable built environment, 5, 58, 69, 101, 181, 201
  as in vulnerable infrastructure, 30, 57, 83, 87, 105, 108, 115, 198, 201
  as in vulnerable populations, 30, 32, 40, 48, 63–64, 179, 190, 222, 226

water and sanitation, 41–42, 47, 65, 99, 110, 120, 137, 147, 155, 159–60, 168, 169, 191, 225–26, 229, 232
water resources, 14, 130, 139, 143, 145, 160, 213, 228
wealth, 3, 6, 41, 55, 87, 106, 123, 129, 136, 234
  as in accumulation of, 55, 141, 224
  as in ownership of, 87
  as in relative conditions of, 136
White, Gilbert F., 94, 98, 215
will power, 100
will, as in the willingness to, 8, 24, 26, 29, 34, 39–40, 77, 100, 103, 106, 117, 139, 152, 161, 173, 187–88, 194, 206–7, 210, 233–34
window of opportunity, 35, 75–76, 106
with and without, 14–15, 25, 43, 47, 60, 84, 104, 175
World Bank, 31, 79, 92, 139, 153, 169, 210, 212
WRI—World Risk Index, 171

www.ingramcontent.com/pod-product-compliance
Lightning Source LLC
Chambersburg PA
CBHW051531020426
42333CB00016B/1881